GLOBAL BUSINESS PRACTICES:
Adapting for Success

Camille P. Schuster, Ph.D.
Professor of Marketing
California State University San Marcos

and

Michael J. Copeland
Procter and Gamble International Training and
Development Manager, Retired

Australia • Brazil • Canada • Mexico • Singapore • Spain • United Kingdom • United States

THOMSON

Global Business Practices: Adapting for Success, First Edition
Camille P. Schuster, Michael J. Copeland

Composed by: Interactive Composition Corporation

Printed in the United States of America by West Group

1 2 3 4 5   09 08 07 06
This book is printed on acid-free paper.

ISBN 0-324-23309-4

This publication is designed to provide accurate and authoritative information in regard to the subject matter covered. It is sold with the understanding that the publisher is not engaged in rendering legal, accounting, or other professional services. If expert assistance is required, the services of a competent professional person should be sought.

Library of Congress Cataloging in Publication Number is available. See page 248 for details.

For more information about our products, contact us at:

Thomson Learning
Academic Resource
Center
1-800-423-0563

Thomson Higher Education
5191 Natorp Boulevard
Mason, Ohio 45040
USA

This book is dedicated to those bold and adventurous people who leave the familiarity of hearth and home culture to make their way through the multicultural milieu of the larger global tapestry.

ACKNOWLEDGMENTS

We have built on the ideas of the giants in the field—from Hall to Hofstede to Trompenaars to Chua. Where appropriate, footnotes and primary sources are provided. However, just thinking of the subject brings all of the seminal thinking in this field into mind. It is impossible to write on the subject of cross-cultural interactions without acknowledging these insightful people.

Dr. Michael Tucker, Colorado Springs, U.S.A., and Father Robert J. Ballon, S.J., Sofia University, Tokyo, Japan, were the primary sources and refiners of the original Classification of Cultures Model. Their thinking and analytical approach to culture has been our inspiration and the germ of the concept for our work.

Over the years, we have been helped immensely by the careful thinking, challenging observations, and helpful suggestions of colleagues, friends, and students. None of our work would be ready for publication without this enriching interchange of ideas. For their efforts, we are truly grateful.

We would like to express our appreciation for the support provided for this project by several organizations and individuals. Steve Momper from Thomson South-Western has been an advocate of this project for many years. Without his interest and support, this project may not have seen the light of day. Kim Kusnerak, Elizabeth Lowry and the staff at Thomson provided excellent advice and support.

Our families have been selflessly supportive and encouraging throughout the development of the ideas and many phases of the book's publication. We will always return to them for our home culture.

PREFACE

Over a single lifetime, events are magnified due to the relative brevity of an individual's life. Wars, international realignments, the rise and fall of competing systems, and the compelling urge to survive define an individual's perspective on global activities. The instant exchange of ideas and communications results in adding complexity to the resolution of conflicting issues. In these circumstances, many people approach the differences in cultures somewhat defensively and judgmentally.

Writing this book has been the product of our two lives. We have been able to reach thousands of people through our careers in business and academia, testing our premises, developing our models, and refining our thinking through each interaction and class. Many of our colleagues and students have listened, commented, and critiqued our thinking, which has contributed to this book. Our discussions across the globe in varying venues and formats have enriched every aspect of this work. While presented as our point of view, this book is really much more broadly shared and refined than the mere product of two lives.

Regardless of where the international traveler is, the single most important thing to keep in mind is that what is experienced in the local culture works and that it is believed to be normal by those native to the region. This is also the single most difficult thing to keep in mind, since everyone traveling is absolutely sure that what he or she brings is also normal and correct and universally understood. People of every nationality, ethnicity, or clan assume they are unique from everyone with whom they have contact. The way people are raised and manage their way in their world gives them a sense of self-control and power that a temporary visitor doesn't have. The local person has a feeling of confidence and knowledge of the environment that the visitor will rarely have and often senses the discomfort of the visitor.

We present several models to help in broadly thinking about going to and working with people from different areas of the world. These models may be useful, especially for those unfamiliar with business behavior in a pending location. Models are tools to assist in developing approaches to business and social interchange in unfamiliar environs. In thinking about how international interactions will play out, the models presented in this book serve as a quick reference for determining the difference between the home culture's norms and the visited cultures' anticipated behaviors. Models can help in orienting and in setting expectations, but it must be unequivocally stated that regardless of the likelihood of shared behaviors, beliefs, and values that a cultural group exhibits, every individual within the culture has complexities and variations that can never be adequately demonstrated by models based on the larger group. Therefore, before ascribing behaviors and motivations to individuals, let the local person demonstrate his or her normal behavior to the traveler first. We are always surprised at the range of competencies in any location and never limit what we see to what we expected in the first place.

While there has been an apparent homogenization process taking place in certain aspects of the business world, the truth is that cultures barely change at all on a bedrock basis. On the surface, there are a lot of blue jeans and fried foods, recognizable music and common event sharing, but, underneath, the cultures of the world are often sublimely oblivious of the small changes taking place in the world of fashion, fads, and entertainment. The assimilation and integration of profound culture-changing norms is rare and should not be expected. Assuming common approaches to business and problem solving usually results in mistakes. While universal standards and behaviors such as courtesy, decency, and respect are accepted globally, their definitions and applications vary within different regions and cultures. We are presenting our experience and success models for your application as you go to a new country and culture to conduct your business.

The past decade has brought a new focus to the concepts in this book. Multinationals cope with the differences in business practices globally and the needs of the nations in which they operate. The nations of the world are struggling with the needs of their populations, often contentiously, as they try to articulate and deal with the balance of their national interests and the compelling needs of local populations, many of which are interested in far more mundane issues such as meeting family needs and survival. It is rare to find more than a mere intersection of ideas in this complicated and dynamic world and, rarer still, to discover mutual understanding.

The international businessperson must be realistic, yet optimistic and hopeful in the midst of cultural interaction and complexity. Our intent is to help international businesspeople by providing an awareness of differences and to bridge the gaps to find common ends.

TABLE OF CONTENTS

CHAPTER 1

UNDERSTANDING GLOBAL DYNAMICS

Businesspeople routinely participate in transactions with colleagues and suppliers from diverse regions of the globe. For the most part, they go directly to the task at hand, ignoring cultural differences for expediency. As a short-term approach, this can, and often does, work. Using this task accomplishment approach is deceptively successful. If, however, the objective of conducting business is more than the short-term result, cultures create a distinct challenge to the traveling businessperson.

Whether home is North America, Asia, Australia, Africa, Latin America, or Europe, conducting business successfully requires, at the very least, an awareness of the different ways individuals see the same event. Beyond awareness, astute businesspeople have the flexibility to adjust personal approaches to business dynamics, resulting in their unique ability to meet business objectives and build the kind of sustaining relationships needed to nurture strategic business relationships for long-term success.

Cultures have developed to meet the needs of the local population over hundreds of years. While changes in technology, trends, and fads seem to be unrelenting, with ongoing adaptation in cultures, the truth is that cultures act as the bedrock upon which surface changes come and go. Cultures, like all human products, are not fixed; and true changes to cultures require generations to become instilled with any real sense of the term *culture*.

We work from several models, developed over years of applied learning and work, to give experienced international businesspeople a clear framework and outline for success when traveling to a different area of the world for the first time. These models have stood up well through the scrutiny of experienced travelers, in on-the-ground success in business situations and in the demanding environment of training executives en route to assignments outside their home countries.

Two things need to be foremost in the mind of the traveler. First, by definition, the traveler is the foreigner in the new country. While that fact seems simple and obvious, it is usually forgotten. The local people, conducting business in their own language and idiom, are usually willing to accommodate the visitor in some way or another. Therefore, it is incumbent upon the

1

visiting businessperson to accept the local people and to listen before giving advice or direction. Not only is it courteous and respectful, but it also makes good sense if the visitor expects courtesy and respect in return. A wise foreign language trainer once explained, "I will give you half the vocabulary you need to talk, to ensure you will have to listen, first."

Second, the visitor needs to temper adapting to the local situation with the purpose of the visit. In other words, if the visiting businessperson is traveling to fix a problem, cultural adaptation is less valuable than problem solving. If the visitor is transferring experience and technology to the new location, adaptation is more valuable and desirable. If the visitor is trying to sell a product or service that has a number of other, reasonably acceptable competitors, then adaptation is critical for success. Adaptation is one of the most important skills of the visiting foreigner and must be used effectively wherever appropriate.

In all cases, learning about the new location is desirable. In our experience, most travelers spend very little time doing this and, as a result, are not capable of making needed behavioral changes without professional coaching and training. Often, the resources are available but are not used. The Internet, books, and highly qualified trainers are reasonably available but are simply not considered prior to going abroad. Until this learning is done routinely, using books like this one is the only way to try to sort out the complexities of foreign lands within a short period of time. Even experienced foreign travelers have limited time, and the likelihood of return visits may be low. Therefore, learning only the most important characteristics of the anticipated location is the desired goal. This book provides useful tools for identifying general concepts to be aware of and to apply when conducting business around the world, wherever the opportunities arise.

Even with training, complete understanding of another culture is not a reasonable goal. Cultures are complex, with layers and layers of conflicting needs modified through years of trial and error and revealed in what is accepted as the "local culture." Every nation, and often regions within nations, has ways of getting things accomplished that seem odd or strange at first glance but that make sense once you begin to see why and how specific issues are resolved. Every cultural group has its own accepted set of norms for conducting business and solving problems. Recognize that the new culture you are facing has its own set of accepted behaviors; compound that fact with both a new language and culture shock; and approach business ambiguity with a new level of understanding, recognizing a need for your adaptation.

Since an in-depth understanding of the new culture isn't a likely outcome, we have identified similarities and differences across cultures that can be used as a starting point for conducting business. Since these generalities are by nature broad classifications, it is incumbent upon the traveler to adapt these to the individuals with whom the work is done. To conclude that "all people here do things the same way" is a stereotype that will not be realized.

The cultural characteristics we used in this book are really part of the "code breaking" the businessperson must do on a routine basis. These characteristics are intended to be helpful in determining the likely starting point of working with the local people, and not a determinant of individual behaviors or where the individuals will end up, on any scale. The code-breaking process needs to continue for an understanding of the unique characteristics of the company, the objective of the task, and the values and personality of the individuals involved.

The models presented in this book are intended to be graphic ways of understanding behaviors that will probably be seen. We encourage users to be flexible and adaptive in all locations and to recognize that the purpose of travel is to deal with situations face to face. Personal contact is, after all, a very human need. With it comes trust, understanding, and relationships. In the long term, you will remember the individuals, not the situations, in detail. How **you** are remembered will also be a result of these interactions.

This chapter presents an overview of the process of adaptation proposed in this book and of the models used to illustrate the process.

Thinking Globally

Commercial, political, and economic systems have become increasingly interdependent over the past decades. While it is comforting to think only of the local situation, it is unrealistic to believe that decisions made in the home country are independent of what will happen abroad. Despite the sincere efforts of people opposed to globalization, it has already happened and cannot be undone.

The concern of some, that multinational corporations would supplant international organizations, making national boundaries irrelevant, has not come to pass. Multinationals have adapted to working conditions wherever they do business. Quickly they realize that transformation is not their business. While nations, trading blocs, and world organizations continue to struggle with the realities of history, ethnicity, infrastructure, and national goals, multinationals have taken a very small role in the internal struggles of nations. By hiring the best available talent and developing small and effective businesses within and across countries, multinationals have stayed within the scope of their charters and remained almost totally free of the anticipated need to supplant local governments. Companies continue to conduct business wherever opportunities arise and leave the business of government to governments.

While macro decisions are what move organizations and define strategy, implementation will always be on a person-to-person basis. All parts of an organization now routinely operate across multiple time zones and cultures. Just a few years ago, "cultural pioneers" were the only people responsible for knowing and acting appropriately in another country. With today's communication vehicles, the location of suppliers, account representatives, order processing, contact centers, or purchasing departments may be in another country, so every interaction has cultural connotations. Where at one time only high-level managers were responsible for being culturally aware, today every employee must be culturally adept.

For the businessperson involved in conducting international transactions, technical competence has always been the primary requirement. This is still important, but it is not sufficient by itself for long-term success. The individuals involved are expected to know the situation in the country on the other end of the transaction, as well as the hierarchy in both organizations. For example, Sydney and New Delhi have specific ways of conducting business that the international businessperson needs to be aware of prior to getting into the middle of a situation that can become very complex very quickly. If Madrid, Paris, and Prague were all simply European, life would be much easier. Ask any traveler if that is the case. From a micro view, individuals must develop a cultural knowledge base so they can be culturally competent when performing a technical task.

International success is measured by results, and results come from individual interactions. Products and services are now readily available and easily adapted to local needs. The reason some people and organizations succeed and others do not is that individuals, acting across boundaries and barriers, conduct business successfully in local cultures. Adapting to local situations requires a framework to provide context for individual interactions and circumstances. The purpose of this book is to provide a basis from which the astute businessperson can adapt skills to be more effective in international transactions.

Adaptation encompasses both form and substance. Differences in the use of language, patterns of logic, place and use of hierarchy, fundamental values, and the decision-making process are all part of how business is conducted.

Success depends on being able to modify the home country approach to the international location. Individuals must decide for themselves the degree to which they will adapt to pursue success. Being able to adapt to each business situation and partner is critical to one's success when operating across cultures.

The global environment encompasses constraints that demand adaptation. In response to those constraints, local businesspeople adopt accepted behaviors and practices. The next section describes the constraints that exist in the global marketplace: the role of government and the legal system, location and environment, marketplace conditions, communication, and culture. Chapter 2 presents three models that will be used to discuss characteristics of specific cultural groups.

The Role of Government and the Legal System

Assumptions regarding the relationship between business and government are one of the constraints that create the development of unique business practices. Each culture has a set of assumptions about the role of government, the role of business, and the relationship between the two. In some countries—for example, The People's Republic of China—the government is free to intervene in business activities at any time. Belgium, as another model, requires significant involvement of the government, whose representatives must be party to all transactions. In some parts of the world, governments have developed large and complex bureaucracies that become part of the transaction process. Germany is an example of that type of relationship. In other places, such as the United States, there is a separation between government and business activities. In this situation, the government creates the boundaries and guidelines for conducting business; within these boundaries, businesses are free to conduct transactions without government involvement.

In some instances, business results in conflict between governments or between a specific business and its own government. For example, direct foreign investment is sometimes regarded as a mechanism for creating jobs in one country at the expense of those jobs in another country. Finding the lowest-cost provider of services or production often results in the transfer of technology and jobs from location to location. While this process may be good for the specific business, it results in a loss of jobs from one country to another. Foreign-owned companies are sometimes viewed as threats to the local economy, since profits are taken out of the country and the foreign-owned business represents direct competition to local businesses. Japanese businesses in the United States and U.S. businesses in Indonesia are examples of this kind of issue.

Even in countries fostering separation of business and government, business transactions must adhere to local and national laws. Assumptions regarding individual rights, the roles of government, and the role of society are all part of the legal system. As opposed to doing business within one country that has the same set of laws throughout the country, international business involves more than one jurisdiction and often more than one legal system, which has significant influence on the structure, implementation, and enforcement of business agreements.

Today's business environment must also consider the legal constraints created by regional trading blocs such as the European Union (EU), the Association for Southeast Asian Nations (ASEAN), and the World Trade Organization (WTO). Regulations define in-groups and out-groups of countries sharing legal guidelines. Informed and skilled local legal advice is often essential to conducting business successfully across cultures.

Location and Environment

In international face-to-face business situations, one of the following conditions exists: Party A does business with Party B in B's country, Party B does business with Party A in A's country, or Party A and Party B travel to a third country to do business. Whichever of these conditions exist, at least one party is out of its home culture and environment, having to manage in a different time zone in many cases, perhaps using a different language, eating different food, working within different time schedules, operating in unfamiliar office conditions, lacking easy access to their files and office support, incurring significant business expense, encountering different business practices, experiencing jet lag, and probably dealing with culture shock.

The result is that at least one party in the business process has an additional level of pressures or constraints that may affect performance and outcomes. Those experiencing such conditions must anticipate these circumstances, build them into their work process and expectations, and find ways to manage to a satisfactory outcome within the given situation.

Marketplace Conditions

The on-the-ground reality of the market is always a challenge to the foreign businessperson. Recognizing obvious differences in sound and smell is often overwhelming to first-time visitors. In addition, the norms of business, the willingness of local people to deal candidly and openly, the ability to develop trust and confidence in partners, and the subtleties of business protocols are all variables that require foreigners to rely on trusted and informed local advice when attempting business in another culture.

Compared to working in one country, fundamental issues such as local currency, pricing strategies, exchange rates, hedging methods of payment, barter, payment-in-kind and moving money across borders with or without a viable banking system, and economic policies may involve a more complex system of pricing and negotiation. The price and method of delivery must be determined for the goods or services, as well as the targeted market segment. In addition, the currency of payment, method of transfer of payment, timing of payment, and exchange rate must be clearly understood by all parties prior to concluding an international transaction.

Communication

Communication across cultures is always a challenge. While the speaker or presenter is seemingly confident and comfortable with the subject matter, getting the desired understanding and subsequent response from business partners is problematic. Misunderstanding and misinterpretation occur because people from other cultures have a different worldview, provide and use different context cues, and differ in how they say things or express values.

Language is usually a starting point for misunderstanding. Participants from diverse countries may try to conduct business in a common third or fourth language that is the native language of neither partner. Asking someone to "touch base" with another manager before proceeding to place an order may make no sense to someone whose native language is not English, especially when the major sport in that person's country is field hockey or soccer and not baseball or cricket. Many businesspeople use home idioms so regularly that they assume universal understanding, regardless of their foreign colleagues' linguistic abilities. It is more realistic to expect that misunderstandings will occur and allow time to clarify and ensure common understanding. Successful strategies include selecting a specific language; relying on interpreters when necessary; using charts, graphs, and pictures to express difficult topics; and explaining expectations of both process and outcome whenever possible.

Each businessperson needs to conduct a personal inventory of the skills useful in the international arena. For example, flexibility, the ability to deal with ambiguity, the need for closure, linguistic skills, a willingness to learn, adventurousness in food and living conditions, and the ability to give trust are all skills and behaviors that are usually called upon in international dealings. Since the location and culture shock of international business conditions may stretch the traveling businessperson to the point of fatigue, knowing oneself and being sincere are critical for success. There is no substitute for being genuine and forthright in all dealings, regardless of the location. This is the only true "currency" the international businessperson really has.

Culture

Culture is a total way of life held in common by a group of people. Learned similarities in speech, behavior, ideology, livelihood, technology, value system, and society bind people together in a culture. It involves a communication system of acquired beliefs, perceptions, and attitudes that serves to supplement and channel instinctive or inborn behavior. (Jordan and Rowntree, 1986)

Culture establishes the way people view the world, interact with others, and make decisions while providing assumptions about the actions of the members of the cultures. Each culture has a set of values, beliefs, goals, ideals, priorities, and customs of its own that influence how people react to one another; what they assume to be true; what their expectations are; what their patterns of thought are; what they assume the future will bring; and what they believe is important, degrading, or annoying.

Hofstede (1980), Trompenaars (1991), Hall (1976), and Laurent (1991) have examined cultures around the world; and each has identified a set of concepts that differs across cultures of the world, such as time, individuality, uncertainty, power distance, time spent talking, bureaucracy, high-context versus low-context language, and/or loyalty to people. This book concentrates on examining and understanding the application of these concepts with regard to behavioral business practices. Because businesspeople are members of particular cultural groups, they do not always share the same view of the world, values, goals, assumptions, or perceptions of time and space.

As a result, what is accepted as "normal" effective business behavior is not the same around the world. For instance, "acceptable" business behavior in one country may be more formal; and businesspeople in that country may react negatively to aggressive influence strategies. Compromising to resolve conflict may be viewed positively in one country, while creating new conflicts may be viewed positively in another country. Deciding what items go on an agenda, how the agenda is put together, and how that agenda is used during a sales or negotiation process may differ from one country to another. Once a decision is reached, the perception of the "finality" of the agreement may differ among countries, with some participants believing that it is "normal" to renegotiate a signed contract after a period of time.

Given different opinions as to what is considered "normal," "rational," "appropriate," or "acceptable" behavior, business practices differ among cultural groups. Therefore, learning the style of business practices in another country is essential to understanding the other side, more effectively establishing a relationship with the other side, assessing the other side's expectations, reducing the amount of conflict, and developing more effective strategies. By anticipating different behaviors, participants can view those behaviors as independent of the substance of the discussion. Realizing that the other side may behave differently as a result of cultural differences, participants can make the effort to set the specific behavior aside and deal with the substance of the discussion.

Six areas create an environment for doing business globally that is significantly different from domestic markets. Movement of money, legal systems, national languages, currency, assumptions of acceptable business behavior, and familiarity of location create a sense of stability for doing business within countries. Across countries, each with unique cultural groups, the assumptions vary, resulting in different business practices. Therefore, when conducting business around the world, businesspeople need international experience and cross-cultural skills to prepare and to participate effectively.

Cultural understanding entails more than merely learning how to present a business card, which gestures are unacceptable, or how to greet your host correctly. Surface politeness and appropriate behavior is only an opening demonstration of respect. Participants also need to understand business behaviors, assumptions, values, and attitudes. Ultimately, someone who is culturally sensitive can "swim like a fish" in another culture.

Where to start? How to begin? Learning the language, religion, history, geography, family structure, norms of society, politics, art, dance, music, and folklore of every country around the world is impossible. While it is true that the more of this knowledge that is acquired, the easier it is to understand how to do business in another country, each person cannot acquire all this information for every country. In the next chapter, we present three models to facilitate this process of using such knowledge to understand the other culture's predispositions. A brief introduction is provided here.

The Classification of Cultures Model places major cultural groups on a continuum. This easily recalled model provides a structure for assimilating cultural information and for exploring similarities and differences across groups. The Global Business Practices Model identifies assumptions of each cultural group on elements of culture that directly affect business behavior. This approach provides information that generates an understanding of the reasons behind particular behaviors and provides the foundation for adaptation. The Inner-Outer Circle Model describes the levels of acceptance that structure relationships.

Knowing how cultural groups differ from one another and understanding the rationale behind business behaviors is an invaluable tool. With this framework, businesspeople can classify and categorize an otherwise overwhelming amount of information, anticipate differences in doing business around the world, and adapt their own business behaviors for success.

After presenting each of the models in Chapter 2, Chapters 3-12 will focus on describing business behaviors for each group identified in the Classification of Cultures Model. The final chapter will discuss techniques for adapting your business practices.

Chapter 2

Framework for Adaptation

The foundation for effective adaptation is knowing yourself; your culture; your company; your objectives; **and** the people, culture, company, and objectives of the other side. Learning all of the details of every cultural group around the world is not a realistic goal. Remembering, pulling up, and applying each individual piece of information from every cultural group around the world are not feasible or practical techniques in a dynamic business situation. Models serve the purpose of providing a framework for categorizing, classifying, and organizing many individual pieces of information into a structure that permits comparisons, generates understanding, and creates a foundation from which adaptive behaviors can be created.

This chapter describes three models that are useful tools in global business situations: the Classification of Cultures Model, the Global Business Practices Model, and the Inner-Outer Circle Model. The Classification of Cultures Model identifies major cultural groups around the world. One chapter will be devoted to describing each group. The Global Business Practices Model illustrates the importance of specific cultural elements as they are typically associated with each cultural group. The Inner-Outer Circle Model represents the degree of closeness members of each group have to local businesspeople. Chapters 3–12 will describe the particular combination of elements for each cultural group and its impact on business practices. The last chapter will discuss tools and techniques for adaptation.

Although the Classification of Cultures Model organizes groups across the continuum of three dimensions, you need to keep several caveats in mind. First, cultures are dynamic and in a constant evolutionary state of change. The fundamental culture of a country changes slowly, with behavioral or linguistic changes occurring naturally over generations or in response to specific traumatic national events. Therefore, a static assessment of a culture is never completely accurate.

Second, each country exhibits a range of cultures. Assuming that all members of a country are operating from the same cultural norms is problematic. Each region, major city, and/or ethnic group has its own set of cultural assumptions that are related to the country's overall culture but are not necessarily identical. The foreigner must identify the paradigms of the local culture and be prepared to adapt appropriately.

Third, each person's past socialization and development affects his or her cultural assumptions. Because business activities are conducted on a person-to-person basis, a static set of cultural assumptions might not be appropriate for the individual with whom you meet and do business. Fourth, if a foreigner tries to develop a relationship but is unprepared to deliver on the relationship over time, the trust that is lost will likely never be recovered. Trust in relationships must be delivered unreciprocated, then reinforced before a sound, firm basis for the relationship can be established. If there is no sincere intention to be part of a long-term relationship, it is better, strategically, to remain within one's own cultural norms and work across cultural boundaries within the limitations of common commercial interests and with no inherent long-term expectations.

Classification of Cultures Model

Assumptions regarding the use of time, the approach to the task at hand, and the role of relationships in making business decisions vary throughout the world. Inspired by Tucker's (1982) presentation, adapted by Copeland (1987, 1988, 1993), and modified by Ballon (1994), Schuster and Copeland (1996) created the Culture Classification Model for use in training and develop-ment work with international colleagues. The model is anchored by elements fundamental to business decision making around the world. The elements of task, time, and relationship do not change with the new model. However, the Asian economic crisis, expansion of the European Union, transition of countries that were part of the former Soviet Union, and inclusion of The People's Republic of China as part of the World Trade Organization have significantly altered the original classification of coun-tries. This chapter presents the Classification of Cultures Model (Figure 1).

Time is a constant, with 24 hours in each day the world over, and time is an underlying dimension across all cultures. Depending upon the impor-tance of task and relationship issues in each country, time is used differently. Those cultures on the left-hand side of the continuum generally emphasize the importance of tasks and allocate their time accordingly. Changes in emphasis—with more time being spent building, nurturing, and maintaining relationships—occur as groups are placed closer to the right-hand side of the continuum.

The model presented here typifies cultural groups based upon these three characteristics and is a useful framework for preparing and thinking about how to adapt to the business practices of different cultural groups. While these

Figure 1 Classification of Cultures Model

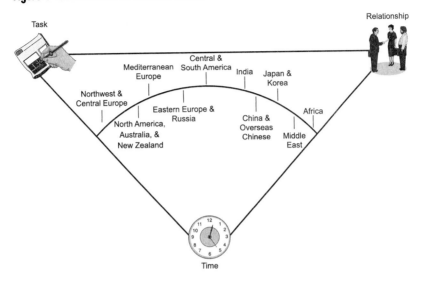

classifications hold in general, they vary among individuals and within cultural groups. Individual interactions do not always follow the model and may, in fact, deviate significantly from the model, depending upon how much an individual adheres to the norms of the major cultural group in that country or the degree of biculturalism an individual exhibits. Although surface behaviors might be recognizable or even similar, fundamental values and beliefs of each culture are distinct, and the foreign businessperson must identify and respect these differences. This model provides a sound classification system for use in comparing and contrasting similarities and differences in business practices around the world, which is a critical element for preparing to adapt your behavior.

The original Culture Classification Model had a section for Traditional Cultures that included major Asian countries, developing countries, and those countries that have, or recently had, a centrally controlled economy. A fundamental similarity in the way of life across these groups created a similar perspective toward the process of doing business. Countries within the Traditional classification have a strong agrarian tradition, whereby the means of making a living and daily activities are inherently part of the fabric of life in the local community. This basic similarity creates a reliance on a network of contacts that dominates the business process across the diverse groups.

As these countries evolve from an agrarian-based economy to an industrial- or information-based economy, their business practices also evolve. Because the countries classified as "Traditional" are at different points in a transition process, have taken different directions as they evolve, and/or have dominant cultures, they need to be addressed as separate groups. Therefore, the Classification of Cultures Model does not have a Traditional Cultures section; instead, it contains separate classifications for Eastern Europe and Russia, India, China and Overseas Chinese, Japan and Korea, and Africa.

Northwest and Central Europe

Opinions vary regarding the classification of European countries, and every system is different and legitimate in its context. We classify Northwestern and Central European countries as Switzerland and the European countries to the north and west, with the exception of France. Paris is included in this discussion, but the prefectures outside greater Paris tend to be more compatible with the orientation of Mediterranean Europe.

Keep in mind that the group of countries in Northwestern and Central Europe are not homogeneous by any means. Differences in culture do exist. Some people say the differences are becoming more pronounced as the EU matures, but the common thread is stronger than the differences. The hegemony of countries including Denmark, France, Germany, England, Norway, Sweden, and Netherlands has passed through the history of the continent and created a way of thinking that is the root of the EU.

Continental nations and cultures with contiguous borders have developed an ability to accommodate stronger and more influential neighbors in a way that is clearly distinctive from their island neighbors. The United Kingdom and Ireland have remained separated, both in fact and in spirit. The ability to accommodate the viewpoint of others is not a notable characteristic of an island nation, safely isolated over the centuries by unpredictable navigation and relatively isolated by primitive technology in past ages. It is much more difficult for the Continentals to penetrate these nations, even today, due to the island's relatively ethnocentric perspective developed over the centuries.

One European tradition to consider is that of conquest and domination, with wars occurring about as frequently from one century to the next and involving some type of collective action by armies, political parties, religious groups, or classes of people. As a result, the world is seen as an unsafe and painful place with war as a normal condition or certainly a good possibility. Therefore, to the European, it is necessary to stay alert. For instance, in Sweden, civil defense plans still make provision for bomb shelters for the entire populace; speed-limit signs on the Autobahn in Germany list two speeds—one for cars and one for tanks; Swiss law requires that people store enough food for 60 days in their homes. The threat of the pain caused by war is never entirely gone. Having seen empires crumble, individuals tend to have relatively modest aspirations, characterized by a certain level of accepting an inevitably less-than-ideal solution. Knowing that the result of all their efforts could finally end in disaster through no fault of their own, people are prepared to risk very little and prefer small but guaranteed gain as opposed to the great risk of knowing it could all be lost. Whatever is agreed upon today can always be improved upon in the future.

Given the uncertainty in the world, the primary focus of business activities in Northwest and Central Europe is on getting to the task at hand and accomplishing it as efficiently and effectively as possible. Typically, the relationship between business representatives engaged in a task is less important than task completion. Time is an important component in these cultures, and using it efficiently is a critical goal and an admired measure of skill.

Time dominates business dynamics. In the United Kingdom, Germany, and Scandinavia, businesspeople tend to regard a meeting's starting and ending times as fixed boundaries that are expected to be honored. Foreigners who do not respect this time orientation are perceived as somewhat less professional or less sophisticated than the local nationals who do. Local nationals expect meetings and meals that are scheduled for a specific time to begin and end on time. If the discussion has not been brought to closure, either subsequent meetings will be scheduled or the business will be concluded by correspondence. Regardless, extending the discussion beyond the scheduled time is usually not allowed.

Business practices in Northwest and Central Europe are typically formal. As a rule, local nationals expect titles to be used. *Mister* or *Ms.* or the local equivalent, for example, *Madame, Frau, Doctor,* or *Professor,* are used throughout the business interaction. The structure of meetings is also formal and expected to be announced ahead of the meeting, with an agenda circulated before the meeting. During the meeting, the agenda serves as a tool for measuring the effectiveness of the meeting and the level of professionalism of the participants.

Assuming that business conduct and behaviors are the same in all circumstances is usually incorrect. However, realizing that value judgments will likely affect the foreigner who does not respect norms and practices and that those judgments will adversely affect the business process, it is incumbent upon the foreigner to behave properly. Assume that, as a foreigner, you must be ready to adapt, to be flexible, and to observe more formal speech patterns; therefore, you will need additional time to analyze and plan appropriate business activities.

North America, Australia, and New Zealand

Developmentally, the United States, Canada, Australia, and New Zealand have similar histories. Native tribes were already established in each country when explorers from Europe arrived, bringing their language, politics, laws, and financial systems with them. In each instance, the newcomers assumed dominance over the indigenous populations and created the systems and structure by which the new country would be governed. Depending on which groups of Europeans settled a region, the traditions and culture of each country evolved in substantially different directions. However, all were essentially British colonies in their early development and, as such, have strong similarities.

However, the founders who ultimately succeeded in creating the structure of government and law in each of these countries came from Northwest and Central Europe. In each of these countries, the newcomers traveled a long distance, had to rely on their own group for survival, and adapted structures and systems to fit their circumstances. As a relatively small group of people occupying relatively large land masses and with time and distance forcing local action with little consultation with the home country, a sense of independence from the colonizing country and camaraderie with members of their own group developed quickly. Given harsh living conditions, the necessity of relying upon one another, the nature of the antagonistic relationship between colonizers and Native tribes, and the relatively small groups of the founding populations, each country developed its distinctive culture.

Distance from England encouraged flexibility when interpreting legal regulations, government structures, and business practices. One fundamental similarity in the organizational structure of Canada, Australia, and New Zealand that is different from that of the United States is the decentralization of government. With a legal system that is primarily under provincial or state jurisdiction, a contract negotiated in one province or state may not necessarily follow the same legal guidelines in other provinces. This is significantly different from the United States, where federal authority supersedes state authority in contract law. Issues affecting the conduct of business in Canada, Australia, and New Zealand are assumed to be more local. Contracts must adhere to the local regulations of the locale in which business will be conducted. The legacy of this system is that businesspeople must find their way through a maze of bureaucracy to obtain permits and to ensure compliance with the laws of the province. A contract that abides by federal regulations is generally accepted throughout the United States.

Another area of difference is that the governments of Canada, Australia, and New Zealand tend to have a stronger social policy orientation than the government of the United States. When developing contracts in Canada, Australia, and New Zealand, regulations such as those governing health coverage, pension plan contributions, and employee rights of termination must be incorporated into business plans and discussions.

However, like the Northwest and Central European cultural groups, the Canadian, Australian, and New Zealand cultural groups consider the task at hand to be of primary importance. Getting the job done, as efficiently and effectively as possible, is critical and always is a key measure of success. In business situations, that translates into getting to the job at hand quickly and eliminating time spent on irrelevant matters.

Because of the similarity of Canadian, Australian, and New Zealand philosophies with those of Northwest and Central Europe, many similarities in business exist. Although surface behaviors might be recognizable or even similar, fundamental values and beliefs of the culture are distinct and must be identified and respected.

Mediterranean Europe

The group of countries referred to in our model as Mediterranean Europe include the non-Parisian French, Iberian, Italian, and Greek cultures. Using task orientation with facility and skill, businesspeople in this region are entirely able to do business with representatives from Northwest and Central Europe, North America, Australia, and New Zealand. However, the concept of the "extended tribe" begins here. If an individual is considered to be part of the same clan, ethnicity, country, or cultural group, some effort during the business activity will need to focus on developing a connection between relatives by establishing a common bond, personally.

The recognized nation-states of this region generally describe these extended "tribal" boundaries. Italians, although quite diverse within Italy, will attempt to establish some degree of commonality between/among themselves if two or more Italians are present in any larger European business meeting. This may be done in advance. If no premeeting occurs, these individuals will go out of their way to meet in brief asides or on breaks to establish some common bond.

As each party probes for personal connections, the subtleties of culture will come into play, including quality of language, slang, educational experience, other work experience, or personal connections—all playing important parts in determining the individual relationship and its value to participants. Similarly, people from Spain, France (ex-Paris), Greece, and Portugal will put forth some effort toward finding a common tie with one another within their own culture, based on common language and culture. Although each cultural group in this region behaves similarly, there is no sense of kinship outside one's home country; for example, a Greek will not usually connect with an Italian on this level.

For non-natives of a given country, extending the opportunity to develop an individual or personal relationship is a powerful way to change the dynamics of a business situation. For instance, this change of business relationships can be facilitated by arriving in advance of the scheduled meeting and inviting individuals for meals; touring the host location to find historic points of interest for possible discussion with hosts; learning the rudimentary parts of the local language, such as appropriate greetings or a formal thank-you; or learning what is being discussed in local politics. Expressing a similarity of attitude or opinion or simply an interest in the people or subject at hand—identifying similar connections—makes the foreign businessperson more approachable. Making the effort distinguishes you from others who do not try or do not know how to establish a personal connection. Once the link is established or reestablished, the parties can turn their attention to the task at hand. Often, the business activity will be more effective for both parties because your new relationship serves as a foundation for task accomplishment.

Another difference is the polychronic attitude toward time. While the task is still held to be most important, time is more flexible than in those groups farther to the left on the continuum. Important tasks come first. If that requires attending to an important personal or business problem until it can be resolved at the expense of being late for another meeting, not completing another job on time, or delaying delivery of a product, that is a reasonable trade-off when the reasons are communicated in a clear manner and in a timely fashion to the individuals concerned. The tasks agreed to be most important must be given adequate time. Each important task, in its time, will be given the same focus and attention. Completed tasks remain the measure of success and are viewed in a sequential pattern; time is viewed as the flexible variable; relationships among one's own cultural group must be maintained to execute tasks and to build future connections.

Approaches to business transactions using a Northwest European or North American perspective can be effective; however, the timing of the process may be very different and include other items, including some socializing. In addition to longer lunches and/or later dinners, appointments may be delayed or rescheduled.

Eastern Europe and Russia

The cultures of Eastern Europe and Russia have developed from a broader base and different set of assumptions. Ownership of the land and form of rule changed hands over time from the Visigoths, Holy Roman Empire, Mongols, Byzantine Empire, Ottomans, Hapsburgs, Romanovs, and Communists. With this unpredictable yet consistent and violent change of government, people never developed a trust in government, structure, and systems. Trusting the government for protection was tricky business because you may have been on the wrong side when it changed.

In these countries, the sense of an in-group and out-group appears (Figure 2).

Task completion is certainly a most important goal, and systems do exist with procedures to follow to complete a task. However, there is always an "informal" way of doing things. Trust is given to people, not to systems, structure, government, or laws. Family, close business associates, or school friends form the group from which the small in-group is created. When a task needs to be accomplished, there is a formal way to go about it following all of the procedures. That may or may not work well. There is always

Figure 2 Inner-Outer Circle of Contacts

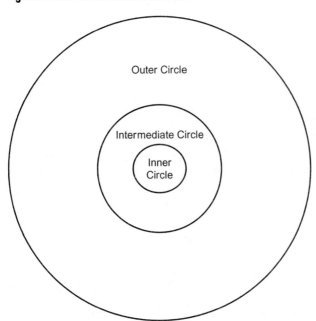

Outer Circle

Intermediate Circle

Inner Circle

an alternative mechanism. You may know someone who knows someone working in the department from which you need a permit. With the right introduction and connections, the task can be accomplished. The personal connections within your in-group are used only when accomplishing the task is going to benefit you. These connections are not generally used to accomplish a company's or an organization's job. If the companies or organizations do not have the connections, then who are you to change the company dynamics?

The Eastern European countries had centrally controlled economies after the end of World War II and are now in transition to free market economies and democratic governments. Russia and the Commonwealth of Independent States, individually and together, are also beginning to move from the centrally controlled economy of the Soviet Communist era to a free market economy and democratic government. A number of these countries have joined or will soon join the EU, creating government and business systems that are consistent with those of Northwest, Central, and Mediterranean Europe.

With mixed religious backgrounds, political structures, and forms of government, people in this area of the world have learned to live and accomplish their tasks in spite of and around all obstacles. Getting the job done is still paramount. However, there are usually parallel systems: a formal set of procedures and an informal process. Using connections among members of their in-group is often the vehicle that local businesspeople use to make things happen exercising the informal process, when accomplishing the task is important to the individual. Trust is not given lightly to outsiders. Suspicion is more common.

Northwest and Central European systems of government, law, and finance had an influence on the development of this area of the world. However, with the past two centuries of development in the parallel regions having had such divergent tracks, today's legal, political, and financial structures do not necessarily match those of Northwest or Central Europe, North America, Australia/New Zealand, or Mediterranean Europe. As some of the countries in this region work to join the EU, they need to create or re-create structures and systems that will allow their political, legal, and monetary regulations to harmonize with those of the EU.

Central and South America

The Central and South American cultural groups increase the importance of relationships and broaden the notion of extended tribe to include any other

Latin, Spanish-speaking country and, in some cases, other Romance-language countries. This cross-boundary kinship is a result of common colonial and independence-movement experiences and similar political and economic histories, as well as linguistic and religious commonalities. Again, members of this cultural group are quite capable of doing business using the North American or Northwest European assumptions of business, but clearly this is **NOT** their preferred method. This bicultural understanding is a signal to the foreigner of sophistication and knowledge that will affect the business process.

Identifying a personal link is important, even when one of the negotiators is not from a Spanish-speaking or Portuguese-speaking country. If the foreign businessperson has demonstrated trustworthiness, credibility, or an interest in getting to know something about the host people or the country, a relationship can begin to develop over time. With the increased importance of relationship, businesspeople from the North American and Northwest or Central European tradition find that rules of business have changed—persuasion and influence are directly related to the quality of the relationship between the two parties, and the nature of relationships is quite different from that in their native country.

For the purposes of the Classification of Cultures Model, relationship is the development of a connection with another person over time that includes certain obligations and duties. It requires that meetings with the Latin representative occur more than once; include meals with the local people; or involve time spent discussing general business conditions, during which participants begin to know and appreciate each other as individuals. When the visitor shows genuine interest in the host culture, history, language, business, cuisine, arts, religion, or politics, the Latin representative is allowed to share information that is of personal importance and to express national pride. As a result, participants begin to know one another—not as business associates, but on a deeper, personal level. This connection provides a richer and more meaningful context for the relationship to develop, with multiple dimensions from which to draw as the business dynamics of the relationship develop.

By making deposits in the "emotional bank account" (Covey, 1989) of the business partner over repeated interactions, the local Central or South American develops a sense of whether a potential business partner is a trustworthy person and the kind of person with whom he or she would like to do business.

India

At this point in the model, the sense of clan as an identifying factor is extremely important mainly due to the historical ties to locale, an agrarian-based economy, and reliance on local community networks. Entry into the group provides identity, protection, and conscious as well as unconscious preference while, at the same time, requiring adherence to emerging group norms. Success in business is extremely difficult for someone who is not part of the group or does not have a product or service that is in great demand but unavailable elsewhere.

Time must be spent developing a relationship with those individuals who are either decision makers themselves or who can provide access to decision makers. The interdependence of business, government, and social leaders creates a network within a particular geography or industry. Developing a relationship with influential network members, or an "intermediate circle," determines whether a potential business partner passes through the gateway and thereby has an opportunity to do business.

India has a legacy of many tribes, several religious groups, British colonialism, a caste system, and democracy. Different religious traditions and languages within a large geographic area create a strong clan-like sense with family groups. Layered together, the sense of clan, British legality, language, and government systems create a bicultural society that can be difficult for the foreigner to penetrate.

Legal systems and procedures that are familiar to North Americans or Northwest and Central Europeans are in place and can be followed. However, there is another informal system that is preferable to the locals that can be invoked at any time and can be penetrated only by trusted outsiders. Becoming part of the intermediate group takes time and adherence to the norms of local behavior.

Because of great distances, disparities in education, an uneven distribution of wealth, and many languages, doing business in India is very complex. The coexistence of a British style and a local style of business means that while the British style is transparent and easy to understand, the foreign visitor should remember that the British approach is only one layer. To be successful doing business with the local businesspeople, you need to develop personal relationships and learn the preferred business practices of a particular location. For example, working with highly educated and experienced staff in Hyderabad or Lahore may be quite different from trying to finalize contract details with the government functionaries in New Delhi. Simply showing up with an expectation of completing the deal will not get the hoped-for results in most cases. Time needs to be devoted to creating and nurturing personal relationships that will withstand the difficulties of long-distance work.

China and Overseas Chinese

Just as the Eastern European and Russian cultures were significantly different from the rest of European and North American cultures, so, too, are the Asian cultures significantly different from all of the groups farther to the left on the continuum. Despite centuries of effort by Christian missionaries, the Asian religions continue to dominate the values in China and the Overseas Chinese regions, with little fundamental change from outside religious or philosophical thinking. The religious and philosophical traditions of these countries, primarily of local origin, are distinctly different from the Judeo-Christian influences of the West. The most dominant religions in these countries are Hinduism; Buddhism; Animism; and, in several areas, Islam.

The philosophical writings of Aristotle, Plato, Descartes, Kant, Popper, Jung, or Freud do not represent the philosophical traditions of the Asian countries and, in fact, have little relevance in the development of the values of the peoples of these countries. Rather, the philosophies of Taoism, Shintoism, and Confucianism are more predominant and germane to understanding how and why individuals may conduct business. For instance, the Taoist tradition perceives time as circular rather than linear. While results are essential, the process of achieving the goals is more important. Deadlines for reaching agreements are not as important as taking time to reach a good agreement, and an agreement will be made only when the parties agree that the goals can be achieved. As a result, more time is allocated to the critical task of preparing an agreement, and the amount of time spent reaching an agreement is less important and more flexible, which is a significantly different perspective from the other cultural groups discussed thus far.

The Buddhist tradition teaches a predetermined fate or destiny whereby karma determines what happens in this life. Certainly this teaching affects the way in which individuals view the importance of decision making, their level of control over events and circumstances, and the timeliness of decision making. Events will or will not occur depending on what karma has in store, not whether a specific decision is made. In addition, individuals cannot control their future. Future events are to be seen in the future, not determined by actions in the present. On the other hand, fortune-telling has an important place in some countries, such as China, whereby knowledge of the future can allow individuals the opportunity to avoid problems or change their luck. For instance, feng shui is the ancient study of the proper alignment of objects with air, earth, and fire to ensure good fortune and harmony. By examining air, earth (environment), and fire, people can choose offices and apartments with good luck and propitious fortune. While the future cannot be controlled and destiny is predetermined, efforts are often made to increase good luck.

One of the fundamental beliefs consistent across Confucianism, Hinduism, Buddhism, Taoism, and Shintoism is that no one human being has the truth. Different views of a situation, different perceptions, and different philosophies can and do all exist at the same time. Different perspectives do not compete to determine which one "wins" and becomes the dominant point of view. They all exist at the same time, inconsistencies and discrepancies notwithstanding. This causes individuals to be able to accept differing interpretations of the truth or to see alternatives that often elude "win-lose" thinkers. This frequently leads to misunderstanding of a negotiator's intentions or perspective on issues.

The assumption of universal truths or a set of universal principles does not exist. The Asian philosophies are highly pragmatic: Each situation is different, and it is important to determine what will work and how it will work in a particular situation. The principle of precedent does not guide decision making. As a result, a problem solved a certain way in one situation may not be solved in the same manner in another similar circumstance involving other individuals and different relationships. Operating within this framework of different, sometimes contradictory, views of a situation to create a common goal is a significant challenge. However, the ability to accomplish tasks in this cultural environment is a strategic advantage for those people capable of working effectively across the diverse cultural groups of the world.

Another characteristic of Asian cultures that is based on the Confucian value of creating order and harmony among vertical relationships is the concept of "face," which can be defined as the ability to keep and enhance one's dignity, self-respect, and prestige. Thus, the ability to behave in ways appropriate to one's status and to preserve harmony, even at an individual's expense, is a fundamental belief. Losing face makes it difficult for an individual to operate effectively within the relationship-dominated business environment. Those who contribute to a loss of face are isolated from the network, relationships are weakened or broken, and those individuals must work their way back into the network on a very personal level with the person who was offended. Therefore, you must pay attention to the implications of this concept in all interactions.

One similarity between the Eastern European and Russian cultures and the Asian cultures is the interdependence of government and business. The People's Republic of China (PRC) also had a Communist government post–World War II and is now creating a "socialist market economy" in which the economy is market driven but the government maintains central planning, preserving broad socialist doctrines rather than moving to a democratic form of government. On the one hand, more business dealings are conducted with private business owners without governmental participation. On the other hand, when and if the local, regional, or central government wants to intervene, it is free to do so. The relationship between the business community and the government continues to evolve in this socialist free market.

Cultural variation is clearly evident within the PRC and throughout the overseas Chinese communities in Southeast Asia, North America, and Europe. As the Chinese emigrated to new locations, they worked to adapt to the new culture. However, total assimilation usually does not occur since the local Chinese immigrants tend to maintain strong bonds with their family and network in China. At the same time, the local population never permitted total assimilation, always maintaining a distinct distance with the people of Chinese extraction. The resulting Chinese orientation to work creates a perspective such that the accumulation of wealth and the ability to run a profitable business are widely regarded as an example of a smart businessperson who is accorded respect and face among all Chinese subcultures. Two legacies of Chinese emigration and the practice of maintaining strong relationships with family and networks are that the Chinese have a strong impact on the local economy wherever they settle and maintain contacts throughout the world wherever their family and network members reside. In many locations, the Overseas Chinese number in single digits of the total population but control major segments of the local economy.

Japan and South Korea

One of the characteristics of Japan and South Korea that makes them distinctly different among the Asian cultural groups is that they were not colonized or controlled for long periods of time by either the Europeans or the Chinese. As a result, each country developed cultures that are Asian but distinctly different from the Chinese.

While government and business are interdependent, the forms of government differ. North Korea is Communist and has not made the same commitment to developing a socialist market economy as China has. South Korea and Japan have a democratic form of government and continue in their transition of developing stronger financial, legal, and government systems. However, the government in both countries maintains a strong tie with the business community, setting policies and establishing priorities for economic development.

Given the evolution of each country through wars, economic downturns, political upheaval, and wealth creation, the acceptance of continuous change is a significant part of their culture. The process of being exposed to new information, sifting through it, and deciding which parts to incorporate into their way of life during the last century has created a dynamic evolution in everyday life as well as in business. As a result, South Korea and Japan's culture is much like a stereo component system with many separate pieces comprising a finely tuned and coherent whole. The Japanese and Koreans see change as inevitable and exhibit a fundamental need for adaptation. As new ideas and practices are discovered and adapted, they seem to accumulate one upon the other, with each one as a distinct but interdependent part of the whole. While some beliefs appear to be contradictory, they coexist as part of the larger culture.

This openness to change enables natives of the region to view individual events as parts of a recurring cycle. Events are not viewed as discrete activities, but as parts of a whole. Therefore, time has a longer-term focus, with individuals and events always being viewed as part of a larger dynamic. As a result, specific tasks, in and of themselves, do not have as high a priority as they do in the United States or Northwest and Central Europe. Completion of tasks is viewed as part of the overall objective and can be executed only by people in an ever-changing environment. Cycles of events and individual tasks work through people, so time must be taken to understand the people with whom you will work and to work within the cycle of change.

With the lack of strong governmental, financial, or legal systems in previous years, *chaebols* and *kereitsu* developed, creating networks of companies that worked together. With financial ties to one another, these organizations form strong horizontal and vertical business chains. These groups are networks that are very difficult for foreign businesses to penetrate. Developing the relationships necessary to be accepted as a business partner at any level takes a great deal of time. Whoever agrees to do business with you or introduce you to other members of the group must feel comfortable with you personally as well as professionally and trust that you will do nothing to cause a loss of face.

Language in these countries is implicit or high context, according to Hall's (1981) classification. Words do not represent a specific, single idea; rather, words represent many ideas, and the appropriate word depends on the circumstance, people, and relationships involved. The ambiguity of this form of language reinforces the Confucian principles of hierarchy, deference, and harmony.

Middle East

The people from Middle Eastern countries also operate from within a paradigm that puts relationships first. However, an important difference from the other groups is that blood relationships are distinctly more significant than other relationships and form the "inner circle." Deriving partly from the "clan" or "tribe" concept and partly from the religious tenet that emphasizes the importance of being responsible for and taking care of family members and others of the same faith, family relationships are a fundamental element of doing business. Business activities will be more productive when conducted between family members or if a family member is part of the negotiating team for the foreign company.

When products or services not available from family members are needed, members of the Middle Eastern cultural group can and do conduct business with people outside their family members. However, as with some of the previous groups, establishing a personal relationship is essential before attending to business. Introductions by trusted relations carry great significance and imply an opportunity to do business. After a solid trust relationship is established and appropriately maintained at a personal level, businesspeople must discuss the constraints and parameters of the situation. If the objective is mutually agreeable, the local representative will, of course, grant the favor, go along with the deal, or give permission to the project, to help a friend. "Western" standards of conflict of interest, nepotism, and integrity cause confusion and harsh judgments between the two parties when fundamental issues and values conflict.

In this environment, learning how to establish and maintain relationships, how to become part of an appropriate family network, and how to present your needs are absolutely critical aspects of doing business. Getting to the task in the least amount of time is considered rude and disrespectful. This behavior is inappropriate in the Middle East, where an introduction from a family member is necessary before time is taken to develop a relationship, which is the gateway that must be passed before a lasting business partnership can begin.

Africa

Africa is a large continent with many variations in geography, people, languages, and philosophies. However, a strong tribal culture has a significant impact on business practices throughout the continent. People in northern Africa have much in common with the people of Mediterranean Europe and the Middle East in terms of religion, history, language, and art. People in the perimeter countries in northern, western, and southern Africa have much in common with the people of the United Kingdom, France, Belgium, and Netherlands. In each instance, however, the fundamental culture is based upon local tribal beliefs, language, history, and industry.

Strong forms of government were not associated with particular geographies until the colonizing nations began to lay claim to specific territories. Before that time, each tribe had its own norms, laws, and established practices that existed within an agrarian or pastoral tradition, whereby the means of making a living and daily activities were inherently part of the fabric of life in the local community. A particular tribe may have stayed in a general geographic area or may have been nomadic. However, the culture and accepted forms of behavior stayed with the tribe. Thus, the tribal elders, chief, or king held immense power and influence. Today there is still a "big man" tradition in which things get done through the influence of a dominant or influential person in a country or region. Without overarching systems of government, law, or finance holding the tribes together, personal relationships within tribes were the primary means of protection, business, and social activities.

Because of agrarian-based economics and reliance on local community networks, the sense of clan or tribe as an identifying factor is extremely important but is generally overlooked by foreigners. Entry into the group provides identity and conscious as well as unconscious preference while, at the same time, requiring adherence to emerging group norms. Doing business with members of a clan or tribe is extremely difficult for someone who is not part of the group or does not have a product or service that is in great demand but unavailable elsewhere.

Many people in African countries have had experience working with people from Europe, North America, Latin America, or Asia and have the skills to do business within those cultures. However, those ways of conducting business are not necessarily the way local businesspeople do business with one another or how they prefer doing business. Those cultural groups that hold time to be of greatest importance find it difficult to invest the time necessary to develop a substantial relationship before addressing the task at hand. Delaying the discussion of task is not compatible with the assumptions of business practices common to people from North American or Northwest and Central Europe. Any delay in task accomplishment is typically seen as wasted time, inefficiency, inability to get the job done, or worse. Many unproductive value judgments are made by both parties, who simply have no cross-cultural context to deal with each other and, instead, end up failing to come to terms based on cultural gaps that cannot be bridged. Time must be spent identifying the appropriate network, getting known in the network, and establishing appropriate relationships with individuals in the network. Only after this is accomplished can the task be addressed.

An exception is when the businessperson has a unique product or service needed by the local party. Recognize that initial success may well evaporate if and when a competitor appears who has developed a relationship with the local representatives that is sustaining in nature. Once the competitor has an "equitable" product or service and has the trust and relationship developed, the contract or agreement is transferred as soon as possible to the local or relationship-based competitor. Often the original individual and/or organization never understands why the business was lost.

Discussion

Assumptions regarding the importance of task, time, and relationships significantly affect business practices. The Classification of Cultures Model presented here is used to classify cultural groups in relation to these three concepts, each pulling in a different direction.

Perceptions of the importance of the task affect how quickly participants want to begin addressing the task at hand, how interruptions will be tolerated, how the issues or products should be presented, and how the finality of a contract will be perceived.

These perceptions range from those that assume that time is the same as money—highly valued and to be managed efficiently to accomplish jobs—to those that assume that time is flexible; is to be devoted to the most important activities first, including relationships; and that other things, including business, will be accomplished in their own good time or as willed by a force outside the control of the participants.

Perceptions of relationship affect how much time is spent getting to know the other person, what topics are important to share with the other person, how to treat the other person, and what obligations are involved. These perceptions range from the idea that relationships are a means to an end—that is, the conduct of business—to the idea that relationships are foundational in nature—that is, the very basis of conducting business. The implications of these perspectives affect how individuals relate to one another. The relationship-oriented cultures generally have a very tight "inner circle" network composed of blood relatives in some areas, extended family and close friends in other areas, or family and trusted business associates in other areas. Potential business clients, customers, partners, social acquaintances, and everyone else form a large "outer circle." People in the outer circle are most often viewed with suspicion. Those associates with whom you have some business involvement and/or with whom you have formed a personal relationship may be part of the "intermediate circle." Specifically, individuals need to consider how important it is to value networks; establish and maintain relationships; meet required or implied obligations; determine the right timing for an appointment and appropriate topics to discuss during formal meetings; and decide how and when to present their issue, product, or service in an acceptable way.

Given the diversity of cultural groups, an expectation that one approach to doing business will be successful everywhere is naïve. The next section presents the Global Business Practices Model, which depicts elements affecting business practices in each cultural group.

Global Business Practices Model

Every culture has a unique perspective on the world; every community or organization within that culture has its own system of operation within that culture; every individual has his or her own personality and set of values. While successful businesspeople adapt to individuals in specific business situations, viewing the world as billions of individuals is not possible for people involved in either government or commerce.

Anthropologists investigate beliefs, values, attitudes, and behaviors when attempting to describe the culture of a group. That is not the purpose of this book. The purpose of this book is to describe the impact that a set of core elements has on business practices (Figure 3).

Based upon the work of anthropologists, social scientists, and research experts, the core elements discussed in this book are related to structure, process, and communication. Structural elements are the role of government, rule of law, and sense of hierarchy. Process elements are a sense of punctuality,

Figure 3 Global Business Practices Model

Areas of World	Gov't	Law	Hier.	Privacy	Punct.	Flow	Truth	Words	Style	Logic
Northwest & Central Europe										
North America, Australia, & NZ										
Mediterranean Europe										
Eastern Europe & Russia										
South & Central America										
India										
China & Overseas Chinese										
Japan & Korea										
Middle East										
Africa										

LEGEND

Role of Government: White = the government sets parameters and constraints to create the environment for doing business. Black = Direct involvement of government in business as a business partner.

Rule of Law: White = Reliance on systems and procedures. Black = Pragmatism or situational considerations.

Sense of Hierarchy: White = Assumption of equality. Black = Assumption of status difference.

View of Privacy: White = Business and private matters are separate. Black = Business and private matters are all part of one reality.

Punctuality: White = Fixed time. Black = Flexible or "rubber" time.

Flow of Activities: White = Time works in a linear fashion. Black = Time works in a cyclical fashion.

Truth: White = Universal truth. Black = Many truths exist at once.

Words: White = Words have explicit meanings. Black = Words have implicit meanings.

Style: White = Communication is direct and forthright. Black = Communication is indirect.

Logic: White = Formal deductive reasoning. Black = Alternative heuristic.

flow of activities, and the separation between public and private life. Communication elements are a view of words, style, truth, and logic.

Each of the core elements forms a continuum and will be described briefly in the following section. The chapters devoted to each cultural group will describe how the core elements affect the business practices of that group.

Structure

The governing philosophy in a country determines the degree of freedom businesses have for their activities resulting from the government's adoption of a free trade or central control philosophy or some variation. Within that overarching structure, the legal system creates laws that specify either what business must do or what business cannot do. Enforcement of the laws determines the reliability of these systems. In countries with unstable governments and legal systems, the informal hierarchy among citizens in that country provides the constraints and guidelines for doing business. A businessperson must become familiar with these concepts in each country to understand the practice of business in each cultural group.

Role of Government On one end of the continuum are those countries, such as the United States, Australia, and Canada, that were founded on Adam Smith's view of a laissez-faire government that creates policies to allow business activities to flourish in a free marketplace. On the other end of the continuum, the government in some countries, such as the PRC, is directly involved in business activities. The government in some countries, such as Japan or Taiwan, develops policies, goals, or directions for the business community.

Rule of Law Some countries, such as Germany or Great Britain, at one end of the continuum, believe that systems and procedures created by an approved process establish the guidelines that govern business transactions. These systems and procedures are rules that can be relied upon and enforced, thereby creating transparency in business practice. Other countries, such as Russia, Indonesia, or Nigeria, that have not created systems and procedures that are routinely enforced throughout the country rely more on a situational or pragmatic approach to conducting business.

Sense of Hierarchy Countries such as Australia and the United States espouse the value of equality, meaning that each individual has the same of set of rights, obligations, and duties. No one has special privileges because of position. Individuals are empowered to make decisions, take risks, undertake new ventures, or solve problems on their own. At the other end of the continuum, countries such as Argentina and Japan have hierarchical systems in which people of high status are expected to have special privileges. Individuals know their position within the hierarchy and adhere to the norms of the group.

Process

Some cultures view time as monochronic—moving forward in a linear and sequential fashion with segments clearly defined. Some cultures view time as polychronic—moving forward in a non-linear and simultaneous fashion. Some cultures view time as flexible—there's always more time to be used on a given activity. Some cultures view time as cyclical—events happen in phases with each event receiving the amount of time it needs. Some cultures use a mixture of these types. Knowing how a particular culture views time is important for understanding how business practices will flow. In addition, the attitude toward the separation of public and private life is important for understanding which activities and conversations are appropriate in which situation.

Punctuality Some countries, such as the United States and Netherlands, view time as fixed; time can be segmented into discrete blocks. Time is valuable, and maintaining a tight schedule by staying on time is the mark of a professional. On the other end of the continuum, in countries such as Indonesia and Saudi Arabia, time is flexible and stretches like rubber to cover all important or predestined tasks.

Flow of Activities In considering flow, on one end of the continuum are countries such as Germany or Canada that view time as linear, looking backward to the beginning of time and forward to the end of time. Activities are divided into discrete blocks of time with specific activities relegated to certain time periods: meal time, bedtime, family time, or study time. In other countries such as Japan or Chile time is seen to be cyclical, with time devoted to each phase of life: birth, growth, death, and rebirth or regeneration.

View of Privacy On one end of the continuum, in countries such as Germany, Netherlands, and Japan, individuals keep their private life and business life totally separate. Time for family is spent with extended members of the family or close friends and does not impinge upon time set aside for work. On the other hand, family obligations can be a reason for closing business deals in Brazil or Thailand. However, that does not mean business discussions end, because most business is conducted with family members and close friends in these countries; the separation between business and family does not exist.

Communication

Understanding the languages of a particular cultural group is valuable for learning how people view the world. Learning about the philosophical orientation toward concepts of truth is critical for determining the meaning of the words used. If the orientation is strongly relationship oriented, then words need to be interpreted in light of how they have been used to maintain harmony within the group. Some languages use words in a very concrete way, while other languages use words in a more ambiguous manner. Given the characteristics of a particular cultural group, the conversation style may be direct or indirect; therefore, the meaning of what is said needs to be interpreted differently. Cultural groups use different forms of logic. Using only one form of logic will not result in success everywhere. Understanding these differences and making the required adaptation will result in more successful communication in business.

Truth Countries that have a dominant Judeo-Christian-Islamic religious tradition, such as Israel, Italy, Iraq, or Canada, also tend to believe in a universal truth—things are either right or wrong, and some truths are always true. Countries with a different religious tradition, such as India or Japan, have a pragmatic view of truth, with every situation and each person's perspective being different. Depending upon the situation and the people involved, saying the correct thing will preserve harmony.

Words Countries in which English or a Romance language is spoken use words to refer to specific objects, people, or ideas. Precision requires the use of the correct words to convey thoughts efficiently. On the other end of the continuum, languages such as Japanese or Chinese use groups of symbols to convey thoughts, ideas, and objects. Individual symbols have significantly different meanings depending upon the combination of symbols, relationships between speakers, or context of the situation.

Style Countries such as Sweden or the United States value language that is direct, to the point, and concise. People should "say what they mean and mean what they say." On the other end of the continuum, in countries such as the PRC, Indonesia, and Japan, "saving face," maintaining harmony, or respecting the other person's honor requires the use of an indirect form of communication in which there are many ways to convey information without stating it literally or directly.

Logic Forms of logic, on the one hand, are formal, syllogistic deductive arguments used in Western countries such as France or Great Britain in which it is critical to have sound premises, or inductive arguments such as those used in the United States, in which objective evidence and representative examples are critical. On the other end of the continuum, alternative forms of heuristics are legitimate, such as circular logic or arguments based on honor or relationship.

Discussion

Each of the concepts in the Global Business Practices Model is a continuum. In the following chapters, the Global Business Practices Model will be used to place each cultural group on the continuum for each element. That framework provides a way of thinking about billions of individual people, preparing for business activities, and interpreting behaviors and communication of business partners. With this understanding, you can make informed choices about how to adapt your behavior effectively.

Beliefs regarding each of these elements create a particular view of the world. The unique combination of beliefs makes each cultural group distinctly different from any other cultural group. The succeeding chapters will examine the implications of each cultural group's view of the world on business practices. By incorporating this knowledge and making it part of your behavior, you will be better able to plan more effectively for business activity with members of other cultural groups, interpret what you see and hear in the ensuing business exchanges, and adapt more successfully to the unique individuals involved in each exchange.

CHAPTER 3

NORTHWEST AND CENTRAL EUROPE

Classification of Cultures Model

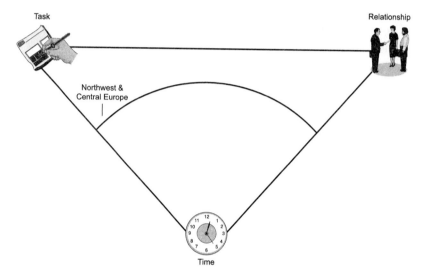

Task

Relationship

Northwest &
Central Europe

Time

Categorizing a group of countries as "European" can involve a great deal of debate. Opinions vary, and every system is different and legitimate in its context. Trompenaars (1991) suggests that the dividing line between Northwest Europe and Euro-Latin countries runs somewhere between Netherlands and Belgium. Laurent (1991) divides Europe into North (Sweden, Netherlands, and Denmark), South (France and Italy), and Middle (Great Britain, Germany, Switzerland, and Belgium). We classify Northwest and Central Europe as Switzerland and the European countries to the north and west, with the exception of France. Paris is included in this discussion, but the prefectures outside Paris are generally more compatible with the orientation of Mediterranean Europe.

The group of countries in Northwest and Central Europe is not homogeneous by any means. Differences in culture do exist and may be even more important as harmonization in the EU moves forward. Differences among the countries clearly exist, but the common thread is stronger than the differences. What, then, are the common threads binding these European countries together? How does their orientation toward time, task, and relationship influence business practices?

The European tradition is conquest and domination. Wars occur frequently from one century to the next, involving some type of collective action by armies, political parties, religious groups, or classes of people (Miller, 1987). As a result, the world is seen as an unsafe and painful place with war as a normal condition, or certainly a good possibility. Therefore, continued defense is critical. Having seen empires crumble, individuals tend to have modest aspirations characterized by a certain level of accepting an inevitably less-than-ideal solution. Knowing that the result of all their efforts could be disaster, people are prepared to risk very little. Instead, they prefer the small but guaranteed gain, if successful, to the great risk of knowing that it could all be lost.

The attachment to one's country is strong, and people usually do not relocate. In this local environment, people develop a strong sense of family and community; they tend to suffer indignities in silence for a long time for the sake of maintaining continuity and stability within the family or community. While they suffer in silence, the anger simmers beneath the surface and, after a period, bursts out and violence returns. This recurrent violence is a fundamental part of European tradition that contributes to a pessimistic outlook.

As the history of the United States (winning its war for independence, conquering the frontier, becoming a world power) engenders a general air of optimism, the history of Europe (recurring wars and transient dominance) results in a general sense of pessimism. People habitually prepare for the worst. Defeats and humiliations are accepted outwardly, but the frustration festers. Periodically, sudden rushes of hatred and anger explode on a national or ethnic level.

Continental nations and cultures, which have contiguous borders, have developed an ability to accommodate stronger and more influential neighbors in a way that is clearly distinctive from their island neighbors. In NW and Central Europe, the changing hegemony of invaders, rivalries between royal families, and intermittent alliances have passed through the history of the Continent and have created a desire to establish the EU. Sometimes countries were allies as a result of intermarriage between royal families. At other times, countries were at war because of enmity between royal families. As a result, governmental authority and outward loyalty may differ from time to time even though people remain in their home location.

Throughout the development of European countries, the United Kingdom and Ireland have remained separated, both in fact and in spirit. The ability to accommodate the viewpoint of others, which is critical for peaceful existence on the Continent, is not a notable characteristic of an island nation, safely isolated over the centuries by unpredictable navigation and relatively isolated by the primitive technology in past ages. It is more difficult for the Continentals to penetrate these nations, even today, due to the islands' historical isolation and relatively ethnocentric perspective.

The implication of the common European background is that the Northwest and Central Europeans have a similar orientation to time, task, and relationships. Tradition demands that tasks be finished within the scheduled amount of time. Because of the general attitude of pessimism, tasks are approached conservatively, usually with modest ambitions—thereby ensuring successful accomplishment of limited expectations. Social class, status, and hierarchy are important norms requiring adherence to specific forms of business behavior. People work together in groups and teams, but personal relationships are not very important in the workplace. It is not unusual for colleagues to work together for years and never discuss personal circumstances or meet socially outside the workplace. Unnecessarily revealing information is not a norm. Keeping some important information to oneself is a matter of course rather than an exception.

This chapter describes the impact of cultural characteristics on the business practices in the countries north and west of Switzerland, including Metropolitan Paris but not the rest of France. Anthropologists, sociologists, and psychologists, as well as management and marketing researchers, have explored concepts, assumptions, and characteristics that define and explain culture. That is not the purpose of this book. Our empirical observations and field work over a combined 35 years focus on how these concepts, assumptions, and elements of culture translate into business practices that are unique to each cultural group.

Some of these elements of culture (role of government, rule of law, and sense of hierarchy) provide a structure for business activities. Some elements (punctuality, flow of activities, view of privacy) create the process for the normal conduct of business. Some elements (truth, words, style, and logic) create guidelines for the communication process used in business activities. The Global Business Practices Model creates a matrix that represents the role of each element within each cultural group. The rest of this chapter will explain how these elements translate into business practice in Northwest and Central Europe.

Global Business Practices Model

Areas of World	Gov't	Law	Hier.	Privacy	Punct.	Flow	Truth	Words	Style	Logic
Northwest & Central Europe										

LEGEND

Role of Government: White = the government sets parameters and constraints to create the environment for doing business. Black = Direct involvement of government in business as a business partner.

Rule of Law: White = Reliance on systems and procedures. Black = Pragmatism or situational considerations.

Sense of Hierarchy: White = Assumption of equality. Black = Assumption of status difference.

View of Privacy: White = Business and private matters are separate. Black = Business and private matters are all part of one reality.

Punctuality: White = Fixed time. Black = Flexible or "rubber" time.

Flow of Activities: White = Time works in a linear fashion. Black = Time works in a cyclical fashion.

Truth: White = Universal truth. Black = Many truths exist at once.

Words: White = Words have explicit meanings. Black = Words have implicit meanings.

Style: White = Communication is direct and forthright. Black = Communication is indirect.

Logic: White = Formal deductive reasoning. Black = Alternative heuristic.

Structure

Harsh weather, marauding tribes bent on conquering new lands, political intrigue, and the size differential of countries created a climate of watchfulness and preparation in Northwest and Central Europe. Systems, processes, and procedures are highly valued in this area of the world because they maintain order and create predictability—necessary goals in a world in which survival requires hard work. This section examines the role of hierarchy, government, and legal systems in the practice of business.

Hierarchy

Organization of society in this area of the world evolved from a system of conquering tribes (for example, Vikings, Goths, Anglo-Saxons, Huns) prior to the Holy Roman Empire, to a system of nobles, peasants, and serfs during the Middle Ages, to an aristocratic form of government in most countries beginning in the late Middle Ages. As members of the peasant class and trade class gained wealth and stature in the nineteenth and twentieth centuries, they began to assert their rights and demands for freedom and participation in government.

Social class has a strong tradition in Europe, affecting the role of government as well as relationships among people. Kings, queens, feudal lords, knights, landed gentry, and the military are all part of the historical hierarchical system of social classes in Europe. Knowing how to behave appropriately given one's social position and how to treat others who are above or below you in the hierarchy is essential. Depending upon the conclusion of a specific war and resulting domination by the conquerors, however, one's place in the hierarchy could change drastically.

The legacy of an aristocratic society is evident today in the formality of business activity. Appointments are necessary as a courtesy and to allow time for proper preparation. Individuals expect to be addressed by their title, such as *Doctor, Professor, Herr, Frau,* or *Director.* Use of proper etiquette in social situations is a sign of refinement and evidence of belonging to a class of society that is appropriate for someone eligible to conduct business at high levels in an organization. A quick e-mail using informal spellings such as *ttyl* is not considered appropriate business behavior and will not open any doors.

Role of Government

The bureaucracy and decision making of governments and corporations have some grounding in the traditions of social class. For instance, the *noblesse oblige* attitude of the aristocracy was the sense of responsibility and regard for people of lower status. Ensuring that the lower classes had the tools, education, shelter, and clothing necessary to fulfill their tasks enhanced the worth of the socially elite. The lower classes came to expect that someone would provide for them. In return for the security and protection provided by the ruling class, the lower classes followed the directives of the aristocracy. Security and stability that provide a predictable life are seen as a reasonable trade-off for living with a bureaucracy that is slow to change and oriented toward corporate or national interests.

Contemporary European governments lean more toward a social industrial democracy. In the post–World War II period, the social welfare state developed throughout Northwest and Central Europe, partly in response to the diminuation of control of the royal families after World War I and the destruction of the upper classes' cartel-like control of the wealth of the countries. The middle classes exerted their new-found strength and institutionalized their power via the structure of the government and the taxation of the very wealthy to the benefit of the lower and middle classes.

Within the system, government and business work together for the good of society and to increase the competitiveness of their country by protecting their companies. Democratic socialism in Europe varies across countries but embodies the fundamental assumption of providing for the basic needs of citizens. As a result, taxes are high so that government can ensure a basic standard of health care, education, and living conditions for the vast majority of its citizens. Corporations also help achieve social objectives by advocating long-term jobs and providing social benefits. For instance, Belgium has some of the most stringent laws in the world regarding the hiring and firing of employees (Copeland and Griggs, 1986). Another consequence of the high level of services to citizens is a stringent and long-term immigration system that makes citizenship a difficult and time-consuming process. This is done to protect the nation from poor immigrants who try to take part in the relative wealth of this region without having been born in the country.

Rule of Law

Daily life in these countries through the ages meant protecting one's space, territory, and way of life from a variety of threats. It has also meant conducting daily activities in the face of harsh temperatures and storms; meeting the challenge of travel by land or sea; living with neighbors when boundaries change; and dealing with the possibility of changing rules, taxes, and loyalties when overlords or boundaries change through war, marriage, or political variance. Therefore, in this region, predictability and security became increasingly important. To survive the vagaries of nature, preparation is even more important on the Continent than in Great Britain and the Scandinavian countries, which are more isolated and protected by geography. The rule of law establishes the rules, guidelines, and terms for how activities will be conducted and who has responsibility for completing the activities.

Adam Smith promoted a laissez-faire approach toward business by government. Great Britain espouses this philosophy more than any of the other Northwest and Central European countries and is often at odds with decisions made by the EU. However, Great Britain is basically in agreement with the EU's principles of harmonization. While Great Britain may debate the form of specific laws or regulations, there is a fundamental belief that agreed-upon systems, processes, and rule of law are important structures for society.

In the tradition of Roman law, broadly understood and practiced throughout this region, the contract is the instrument that actually creates the legal rights and duties of both parties in a business deal. What is explicitly stated and agreed upon is precisely what will be executed, with no room for interpretation or further discussion. The written contract is binding, with the expectation that the parties are obligated to perform according to the conditions of the contract. The goal is to create written contracts that are precise and explicit, leaving as little room as possible for ambiguity and interpretation.

The legacy of this worldview of the role of government and the rule of law is evident in the business practices of today. For instance, the government does involve itself in creating and maintaining a system that protects local companies, fosters a competitive environment for them, and establishes the framework for harmonizing business activities throughout the EU. People who want to do business in this area of the world need to be aware of the active role of government and the central philosophy of creating an environment that protects the competitiveness of local companies. Contracts are traditionally restrictive, dictating terms and agreements. The Roman law concept specifies which party will do what by what deadline, with no ambiguity or interpretation permitted.

Process

The European tradition of preparedness influences the way people use time. Assuming that time occurs in a linear fashion and that the future can be predicted based on the past, it is possible to identify the seasons of the year and predict rainy seasons, snowfall, storms, and temperatures. Observation of past events leads to prediction, which allows individuals to prepare adequately for future events. From the Swiss watchmakers to the German engineers, being precise about time, measurements, and construction is part of the process of business. Attitudes toward the importance of time and the flow of activities have a direct bearing on business practices. Attitudes toward the separation of private and public life have a direct bearing on what topics and forms of communication are appropriate in which situations.

View of Privacy

Changing boundaries, rulers, and position in society meant that the citizenry had to be accommodating. Outward loyalties may have to change. Personal loyalties may not need to change, so people separated their public life from their private life. On a personal level, family, friendships, and business ties remained strong whatever the public requirements were. To facilitate this dichotomy, public relationships remained formal and polite at all times. People did not let down their guard, have informal conversations, socialize with business or government officials, or become personally attached. Then when it came time for a change in authority, life could carry on with the same formality and polite behavior.

The implications of this dichotomy, developed over years of responding to changing circumstances, are that business practices are formal and impersonal. Personal relationships are not part of the business environment. Within the hierarchy of the organization, bosses give up their power to the system, which establishes objective, rational processes with clear criteria for decision making in order to eliminate personal subjectivity. Therefore, managers perform business activities in accordance with the policies and procedures of the organization. Businesspeople avoid personal familiarity to preserve privacy, and long-term business relationships are usually between organizations rather than individuals. Therefore, personal lives can be kept separate from public lives.

One way of keeping personal and business relationships separate is to keep a distance between employees and associates outside of work. Northwest and Central Europeans tend to be quite private, with strictly segmented business and personal lives. In general, managers keep their distance and reinforce their authority by maintaining proper decorum; for example, showing a "stiff upper lip" in the face of a difficulty or keeping relations on an impersonal or formal level.

In this way, personal relationships between businesspeople, which might interfere with business, can be avoided, enabling managers to follow procedures objectively with no personal prejudice. In this legalistic society, nepotism is frowned upon. Personal issues should be left outside the room during business discussions; the only relationship that matters is that of the business organizations.

Punctuality

Throughout this region, business activities are expected to function in a precise manner. Meetings begin on time, last for a specified amount of time, and cover the required subjects. Being late is considered rude, inconsiderate, and unacceptable. Professional behavior requires that agendas be circulated well in advance of a meeting so that all parties can adequately prepare for the designated discussions. Discussions proceed in a formal manner, with topics and time designated by the agenda. The closer the meeting and discussion stay to the agenda, the better the European group will feel about the level of professionalism of the process.

For instance, during a presentation at one meeting in Germany, several U.S. participants began to ask questions. After politely responding to two questions as a courtesy to the U.S. businesspeople and seeing that more questions were coming, the presenter stopped, pointed to the agenda, and explained that *question time* came later and that "this was *presentation time*, so it would be best to proceed now, holding questions for the appropriate place on the agenda." Structuring interaction through the agenda is common throughout Northwest and Central Europe, although strict adherence to the agenda may vary from country to country.

Arriving late, not being able to cover the required subjects in appropriate detail, trying to introduce new topics, or assuming that the meeting can last longer than the specified time reduces your credibility and calls your professionalism into question. When prepared individuals arrive promptly for a business meeting, engage in formal introductions, and quickly review the agenda, the discussion itself will progress in an orderly manner.

Flow of Activities

In business, agendas are used to provide the framework of the meeting. As new issues outside the scope of the current agenda are identified, they will become topics to be addressed in future meetings. In this way, business functions in a very orderly fashion. Businesspeople know ahead of time what will be discussed, have the opportunity to prepare their best arguments, and will assign the discussion of new business to another meeting rather than discuss it at the current meeting.

Life, in general, appears to have a distinctive pace in Europe, with an emphasis on higher quality in fewer areas of interest. Europeans value in-depth knowledge, demonstrated skill, and expertise in work or specialized areas of interest. It is not unusual to meet businesspeople who participate in the arts or in their specific hobby to the extent that they have original works of their own. A fairly rigid line separates work and personal activities so that business receives the attention it deserves at the appropriate time and vice versa. For example, compared to the United States and Canada, people will schedule fewer activities so that sufficient time can be devoted to each activity. Time is linear, can be segmented, and is scheduled for efficiency. This leaves little room for spontaneity or extemporaneous activities.

The slower pace is related to the cultivation of leisure time. Europeans insist on taking time off from work and have some of the longest vacation periods in the world. The value and use of leisure time is not only the result of a well-scheduled calendar, but also a legacy of the aristocratic social classes. The aristocracy had time to cultivate refined tastes in art, travel, music, and fine cuisine. Today knowledge and appreciation of the arts and epicurean pursuits continue to be an indicator of class distinction. Taking time to cultivate these interests is valued.

Time continues in a linear flow, with a specific amount of time assigned to each activity. Since the world is a predictable place (as a result of vigilant observation and records), people can count on what will happen when. Adhering to the proper order of events and conforming to the systems, procedures, and regulations are all expected in a business setting. Time outside of work is preserved for family and the pursuit of art, hobbies, or special interests.

Communication

When business partners from different cultures are conducting business, they may speak different languages, one or both parties may use a translator, or they may use an agreed-upon third language that is native to neither party. The potential for misunderstanding is very high. Obviously, proficiency in using the language is a major factor in successfully communicating ideas. Unfamiliar vocabulary is an obstacle to clear communication of ideas, as is the use of idioms.

Misunderstanding and misinterpretation can also occur because people from different cultures have a different worldview, provide and use different contextualization cues, differ in the way they say things, or express values in a different way. This section describes how the conceptualization of words, use of style and logic, and perceptions of truth impact business communication in this cultural group.

Words

Languages in Northwest and Central Europe are classified as low context, according to Hall (1981), which means that words have explicit meanings representing specific ideas or objects. Words are chosen very carefully to represent certain ideas, describe expected behaviors, motivate individuals, create a mood, or establish parameters. The words are most important; what you say and how you say something determines the nature of the agreement. In fact, the words are so important to the details of an agreement that writing the contract often becomes a separate negotiation.

Once two business partners agree to the wording of a contract, all parties know what to expect, when things will happen, and what the consequences will be if the agreed-upon event does not happen.

Logic

The explicit nature of words is part of the language, but it does not define the communication process by itself. In Northwest and Central Europe, the philosophies of Aristotle and Plato are the foundation for typical European processes of argumentation, which are heuristic—that is, given to disputation, turn-taking, creative argumentation, and the use of all available evidence.

Two kinds of logic dominate the writings on logic and argumentation: deductive and inductive. When businesspeople work to persuade partners to agree to an idea, deductive (using valid assumptions that lead to a conclusion) or inductive (using specific instances supported by evidence from which a conclusion can be inferred) forms of logic are acceptable. Both require objective data, precision in thinking, and the use of words that have specific meanings.

An example of a deductive argument is as follows: Federal Express always delivers packages overnight. This package needs to be delivered overnight. Federal Express always should be used to get a package to its destination overnight.

While formal, deductive logic is an accepted form of argument, participants in conversations must scrutinize all assumptions for accuracy. For instance, if Federal Express does not always deliver packages overnight or if the package does not need to be delivered overnight, then the conclusion of always using Federal Express is no longer valid. This form of argument is powerful, but the listener must be diligent in testing all assumptions before accepting conclusions.

When trying to transfer inferences from one situation to a new situation, inductive forms of argument, espoused by Aristotle, are more appropriate. In these cases, the person making the argument needs to establish the similarity between situations and provide data to support the conclusion. For example, the system of one-way streets around the courthouse in Town A has been effective in controlling traffic accidents. Since Town B has a similar configuration of streets around the courthouse, a system of one-way streets would be effective in diminishing traffic accidents.

The person making this argument must provide credible data demonstrating the decrease in traffic accidents as a result of the system of one-way streets and that the configuration of streets around the courthouse in both towns is similar. The data presented must be unbiased, accurate, and relevant. Gathering the data and establishing its credibility and relevance are activities that are an important part of the preparation for the person presenting the argument.

Knowing what topics will be discussed at a business meeting makes it possible for participants to gather the relevant data and construct their strongest arguments. Knowing that the other side is not to be trusted, that others probably intend to frustrate your efforts, and that information might be hoarded, each person must defend his or her position so nothing more will be lost. Listeners need to evaluate the credibility of the data being provided and the consistency of arguments being presented. Wrangling over positions is commonplace; criticizing the positions of the other side is expected; "giving in" to the other side's argument is unthinkable; holding one's ground at all costs is essential. After the fact, upon due consideration, good points from your opponent's arguments may be acknowledged and incorporated into your arguments. However, the good points from your opponent's arguments are not likely to be acknowledged during the discussion.

This approach to argumentation rarely leads to a higher synthesis or compromise of positions. The more likely results are concessions, with the weaker party yielding more and the stronger party making fewer concessions. When this process begins, the foreigner must either have a prepared position or stop the process and regroup. To do nothing may well result in a major concession, unanticipated in the agreed-upon expectations.

Truth

Objectivity, credible data, and consistency are important elements for creating logical arguments. The point of using structured forms of logic and words with specific meaning is to arrive at the "truth," according to Aristotle and Plato. This philosophical perspective is also consistent with the Christian religious traditions of Northwest and Central Europe.

Under the Holy Roman Empire, Roman Catholicism was the dominant religion throughout most of Europe, clearly establishing itself as the dominant religion and promulgating a set of universal truths regarding right and wrong, with the Pope as the head of the Church. During the Reformation, several factions broke away when they disagreed with some of the practices of the Catholic Church. However, each faction had its own set of accepted beliefs. Belief in the existence of a universal set of truths or values about right and wrong remained consistent across all the Christian churches. Belief in a "universal truth," the soul as a uniquely human characteristic, and a sense of "right behavior" has implications for business behavior.

Using credible data and accepted forms of logic, businesspeople will arrive at "correct" or "right" decisions. Therefore, specifying business systems, processes, and rules that everyone will follow allows all parties a structured way to conduct business properly, and business transactions become transparent.

The assumption that human beings are different from any other element of nature is important for two reasons. One reason is that this concept is a universal truth, taken for granted that it is the "correct" way to view humankind. The second reason is that the concept has implications for how people are treated in business settings; for example, what rights, dignity, or status accrue to individuals as distinct from machines or other forms of life. In Northwest and Central Europe, human beings are separate from every other form of life or element of nature and have distinct rights to life and dignity that are universal and to be protected.

Style

With tasks, systems, specific rules of logic, rights of human beings, words with precise meanings, and the use of objective evidence as a foundation for communication in business, an appropriate style is presumed for successful business activities. Formality and a sense of place are critical, so conversations are usually formal and follow a prescribed pattern. While there may be small talk at the beginning of the conversation, it will be short, will not include any overly personal comments, will use formal titles, and will focus on objective events such as travel or accommodations. Asking a general question about someone's personal activities is fine, but it is not acceptable to probe. Polite discussion is the limit of the range, and anything more is considered rude.

Quickly the conversation will turn to the topics on the agenda. Business situations such as job performance, salary, terms of a contract, or work processes related to results can be addressed directly. Everything related to business (for example, productivity, turnover, sick days, salary, terms, or responsibilities) can be discussed in a forthright, direct, objective manner. However, the strict separation of business and private life means that topics related to what illness someone had, use of familiar or informal forms of address, or an expectation that an individual should relinquish vacation time for work are unacceptable and will result in unsatisfactory relationships.

Remember which language is the recipient's native tongue, and refrain from using the colloquialisms and shorthand of your own language; for example, we want to hit a home run with this ad. Asking for a response ASAP is likely to get no response. Using correct forms of language, discussing appropriate topics, following an agenda, using accepted forms of logic, and being prepared with relevant information are all important style elements for creating a professional image.

Conclusion

One legacy of the monarchical system in Northwest and Central Europe is that governments and businesses have a social responsibility toward their citizens and employees. Taxes are high to support the social benefits of providing health care, education, and job protection. A second legacy of the aristocratic system is a sense of protocol and formality in business relationships. Many topics characterized as personal in other cultures are considered acceptable topics of conversation in Northwest and Central Europe, but the style and form of communication needs to be formal, tactful, and polite.

Preparation for doing business in this area of the world is critical for success. Data needs to be gathered, agendas need to be circulated in advance to provide an opportunity for preparation of strong logical arguments, and time must be managed according to the published agenda. Business proceeds in a structured manner, and activities need to be adjusted to the flow of this orderly process.

Within this environment, business activities are transparent, are easily learned, and proceed in an orderly fashion within established parameters. Those who live in this area of the world believe that this orderly, transparent approach to business is the correct and best way to conduct business and are willing to share this knowledge with businesspeople from any other culture.

CHAPTER 4

NORTH AMERICA, AUSTRALIA, AND NEW ZEALAND

Classification of Cultures Model

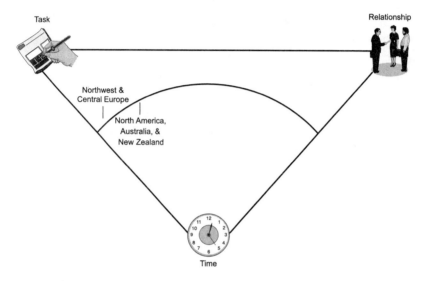

Australia, Canada, New Zealand, and the USA have a similar language and some obvious differences in government, climate, and internal political philosophy. When originally claimed by the English, native tribes were already established in all four countries but were swept aside by a combination of disease, colonial zeal, and technology once the colonies were able to survive their initial period of adjustment.

Whether the colonizers were members of the aristocracy representing the government, missionaries coming to convert the indigenous peoples, adventurers interested in finding treasure, people fleeing religious persecution, or prisoners being expelled to the colonies, they brought their version of the European home country culture with them. In any case, the colonizers claimed the new land for their home country, whether it was England, Holland, France, or Spain.

The form of government and many social values of the home country were transferred to the colonies in this process. The European colonial powers with lasting influence in the formation of Australia, Canada, New Zealand, and the USA as countries were from England and, to a lesser extent, in Canada, from France. Their legacy still stands—that of English as the dominant or one of the official languages of the country, democracy as the form of government, capitalism as the method of business, and Christianity as the primary religion. The Western, Christian, free trade, hierarchical, and democratic values replaced or were superimposed upon the values and philosophies of the native populations. Although there were clearly other colonial and trade influences in these parts of the world, the lasting effects on language, government, business practice, and religious perspective are from the English colonial era.

Each country did develop a unique blend of cultures, due to the relative isolation, primitive communications, and distance from England. As a result of these differences, as well as variations in patterns of immigration and local traditions, business practices in all four countries evolved in slightly different directions. The legacy of the British colonial system regarding the legal, language, business, and government structure, as well as the current relationship with England as members of the The Commonwealth of Nations (the current designation of the older British Commonwealth), create a similar orientation toward doing business in Australia, Canada, and New Zealand.

The king or queen of England was the reigning monarch and official head of the government of all colonies. Regardless of where they settled, immigrants from England, Ireland, Scotland, Germany, the Netherlands, Greece, Italy, and China braved the danger of perilous ocean voyages, confrontation with the unknown, and separation from families because of their belief that life in this new land offered a better, more lucrative future. With such a diverse group having various motivations, loyalty to the Crown was not standard practice among these immigrants. Official representatives of the government—owing their position, livelihood, and status to the colonial system—had strong loyalties. Those who were persecuted for religious reasons, exiled to a new land as prisoners, or had fled to escape persecution had much less loyalty to the Crown. Those who were from countries other than England did not have any loyalty to the British Crown.

English colonial practices established the need to create flexible approaches to laws, reporting requirements, representation at court, government structures, and business practices. Representative democracy evolved as a way of creating a voice for the commoner to be heard, as a balance to the aristocratic and authoritarian rule of the colonial system, and resulted in the implementation of "home rule" in geographically distant colonies for an often unruly group of citizens who were not strongly committed to upholding decisions of the Crown or of the British ruling class.

Canada and the United States of America were not as distant from England as Australia and New Zealand, so people and news traveled more frequently between these colonies and England. Therefore, settlers to Canada and the United States were under closer scrutiny. This eventually led to an increasing resentment toward the colonial establishment, which habitually failed to account for specific concerns expressed by the colonial representatives to the home country, resulting in sovereignty and the end of colonial rule.

In 1931, the Statute of Westminster granted legislative equality to certain self-governing countries, including Australia, Canada, and New Zealand. The statute took immediate effect in Canada, was approved by Australia in 1942, and by New Zealand in 1947. These three countries continue to be members of the Commonwealth of Nations of which Queen Elizabeth II is the Head of State, but each country has its own constitution that establishes its version of parliamentary democracy. A representative parliament is elected to govern the country with a system of checks and balances among the legislative, executive, and judicial elements of government. Australia and Canada continue to have bicameral houses of Parliament; New Zealand abolished its upper house in 1951 and currently has a unicameral parliamentary form of government.

In Canada, the bilingual status of Quebec was created for French-speaking Canadians as a legacy of the French attempt to colonize this area of North America. Quebec remains a province of Canada but has a unique bicultural approach to business, which the astute businessperson must acknowledge when conducting business there.

In the United States, groups of immigrants from France, Germany, Italy, and Spain were never satisfied with being governed by decisions made in England without sufficient local representation. Many of the people who left England because of religious differences or as prisoners also did not like being governed remotely by the English. This tension culminated in the American Revolution and resulted in the United States of America becoming an independent country that owed no loyalty to the British Crown. There was no aristocracy, so the parliamentary form of democracy with a member of the royal family as head of state did not make sense. After much debate and discussion, a federal government was created using representative democracy to select a president as head of state. Further, a federalist system was adopted in which the decisions made at the federal level superceded decisions made at the state and local levels. Many issues, however, were left to be decided and enforced at the state and local levels. Local representation and decision making was kept as a key operating principle, with the states agreeing to abide by the principles established in the Bill of Rights, the Constitution, and federal laws.

All four of these countries share similar beliefs in individual human rights, representative democracy, and the rule of law, based on English common law with wide interpretation given to local judicial agencies. Having common experiences in survival and trials in an unknown land, the successful creation of these countries resulted in an optimistic view of the future, whereby individuals have great confidence in their ability to achieve goals through their own effort. Change is viewed as improvement; taking informed, calculated risks is acceptable; constant reinvigoration is desirable; and the ability to think and act in new ways is seen as necessary. Therefore, businesspeople are naturally entrepreneurial, innovative, and interested in short-term recognizable, attributable results.

The rest of the chapter will address the implications of this heritage of adventure, optimism, and self-reliance for the structure, process, and communication of business practices.

Structure

The position of North America, Australia, and New Zealand on the Classification of Cultures Model indicates that less attention is given to relationships, while completing tasks is extremely important. Within this framework,

Global Business Practices Model

Areas of World	Gov't	Law	Hier.	Privacy	Punct.	Flow	Truth	Words	Style	Logic
Northwest & Central Europe	▓		▓							
North America, Australia, & NZ										▓

LEGEND

Role of Government: White = the government sets parameters and constraints to create the environment for doing business. Black = Direct involvement of government in business as a business partner.

Rule of Law: White = Reliance on systems and procedures. Black = Pragmatism or situational considerations.

Sense of Hierarchy: White = Assumption of equality. Black = Assumption of status difference.

View of Privacy: White = Business and private matters are separate. Black = Business and private matters are all part of one reality.

Punctuality: White = Fixed time. Black = Flexible or "rubber" time.

Flow of Activities: White = Time works in a linear fashion. Black = Time works in a cyclical fashion.

Truth: White = Universal truth. Black = Many truths exist at once.

Words: White = Words have explicit meanings. Black = Words have implicit meanings.

Style: White = Communication is direct and forthright. Black = Communication is indirect.

Logic: White = Formal deductive reasoning. Black = Alternative heuristic.

using time effectively and efficiently to accomplish the task is the preferred *modus operandi* of the Anglophone style. Although variations exist among the four countries, across regions in each country, and, of course, among individuals, observation and data do clearly identify predictable behaviors that characterize successful business practices in these countries. Differences specific to the Francophone style in Canada and major differences among the four countries will be addressed as they become relevant.

Hierarchy

Since the role and status of royalty has diminished since World War II globally and no royal family ever established residence in any of these countries, status and hierarchy was locally realized, not conferred by birth. Australia moved to have Australians appointed as local governors in 1936; New Zealand made that change in 1963. While supporting the monarchy for a longer time, New Zealand has moved more quickly than Australia to reconcile the monarchy with a modern multicultural society, and has twice had a woman as governor-general and once had a person of Maori origin in that office. Status is important in these countries, but the source of status comes from wealth or personal accomplishments in the local country.

Many immigrants in these countries were indentured, debtors, prisoners, or people fleeing religious persecution. None of these people wanted someone else telling them what to do, making decisions for them, or controlling their lives. Survival in a new land with few resources forced them to rely upon one another for survival. While not completely broken, formal class boundaries became less clear and less important. As a result, informal introductions can serve to initiate a business relationship in any of these countries. Once an initial contact is made, the burden is upon the individual to get the potential client's attention and generate enough interest for further discussion.

Hierarchy, of course, still exists; a chain of command within organizations is important for decision making, reporting purposes, and assigning responsibility. While not as rigid as in western and central Europe, hierarchy still needs to be recognized and respected. Especially in Canada, Australia, and New Zealand, the traveler needs to use titles and last names until asked to use first names, defer to the person in charge for decisions, and use the chain of command. Individuals must always be treated with the deference due their position, but it is predictable that individuals will make decisions based upon the authority prescribed by their status in a hierarchical structure rather than wait for a group consensus to emerge.

With the value of equality as a fundamental basis of government and society in the USA, the formality associated with position in the hierarchy is less obvious. As a result, bosses often advocate an "open-door" policy, stating that employees are free to make an appointment with them without going through the chain of command. In addition, in conversations, employees often use first names without titles. With titles being more of an indicator of an individual's function or position, there is little use of ceremony, tradition, and formal rules during business meetings. Participants can get right to the business at hand and focus on the task without taking time for a lot of formal preliminaries. When people sit down and talk with others on an equal basis, the focus of the conversation can be on problem solving. Regardless of the appearance of equality, prior to a final agreement, the hierarchy will need to be involved in all decisions related to final outcomes involving strategy, financial commitment, or resources.

The high scores of these countries on the Individualism dimension in Hofstede's system[1] reinforce the notion that one's place in the hierarchy depends upon one's own success and accomplishments. The hierarchy that exists in the USA, Australia, Canada, and New Zealand is not based on bloodlines of nobility, but rather on position, wealth, and accomplishments in the local country. Any citizen can become president, prime minister, chair of the board, or business owner.

Role of Government

As part of the Commonwealth of Nations, the role of government in Australia, Canada, and New Zealand is similar to the role of government in Britain in philosophy, but each country retains it sovereignty. With a strong legacy from the British system, the role of government in the USA is also similar to that of England. All four countries have an underlying free trade assumption that government's purpose is to ensure an environment in which competition can flourish. While some regulations do control, constrain, and regulate specific business activities, managers and owners generally are free to run their businesses without government involvement.

The Northwest and Central European legacy of a strong social policy orientation is more apparent in the Canadian, Australian, and New Zealand

---

[1] Geert Hofstede began collecting data at IBM in 1967 and continues to collect data from managers and students around the world. The research identified four primary dimensions to assist in differentiating cultures: Power Distance, Individualism, Masculinity, and Uncertainty Avoidance, with a fifth dimension added after conducting an additional international study with a survey instrument developed with Chinese employees and managers. High scores in Power Distance demonstrate the degree to which members of the society recognize inequalities of power. High scores in Individualism indicate that individual rights are paramount. See http://www.geert-hofstede.com.

forms of government than in the USA. Regulations governing business practices of health coverage, pension plan contributions, and employee rights of termination are stronger in these countries. Business plans need to take these requirements into consideration when developing budgets for doing business in these countries.

The distance from England resulted in a decentralized approach to government because adaptation to local conditions was necessary and the time needed for consultation, guidance, and implementation made local initiative a recognized requirement. Decentralization continues to the province or state level in Canada and Australia, resulting in a somewhat confusing level of bureaucracy to the new businessperson. Identifying the true decision maker in a bureaucratic structure may be difficult, but time spent making this identification is essential. Formal guidelines for decision making create several approval steps before decisions can be made. The bureaucracy entails a formidable array of federal and provincial or state regulations that must be considered, requiring time for the necessary paperwork to be completed, processed, and approved. Normally, it is prudent to find local resources to ensure compliance with legal and contractual requirements.

The federal system adopted in the USA resulted in an overarching set of regulations aimed at creating an environment in which free trade can flourish. Federal regulations govern business activities that take place across state lines. Individual states can create regulations for doing business in that particular state as long as there are no conflicts with federal regulations. Lobby groups from all sectors are constantly negotiating to create regulations that are appropriate for their particular industry, company, or issue. As a result, regulations do change. By partnering with those capable of working within current guidelines, there will be no need to involve government officials in your business activities in the USA except in matters involving the national Department of Defense or the Office of Homeland Securities. The assumption is that government creates the parameters for business activities but is not directly involved in business decisions.

Rule of Law

The British system of common law is the foundation of the legal systems in Australia, Canada, New Zealand, and the USA. Three assumptions of this approach have important implications for business: (1) the use of precedent, (2) the assumption of transparency, and (3) the requirement for impartial enforcement.

Based on the belief that it is not possible to cover every contingency, circumstance, or action, laws are intended to create a standard or guideline by which specific actions can be evaluated. The judicial system is responsible for interpreting the application of legal doctrine in specific circumstances. Court cases continually push to redefine the limits, standard, or interpretation of the law. Legal decisions interpret the application of laws, creating precedents that are then applied to new situations. In this way, the legal system evolves to encompass new technologies, new practices, new circumstances, and new situations.

Transparency involves establishing a set of common standards that everyone follows to ensure fair access to fields of competition. If all players know and follow the guidelines, companies can compete on the merits of their products and services. By creating guidelines for reporting earnings and costs and making those reports publicly available, business activities can be tracked, compared, and valued, thereby facilitating free trade and investment.

The rule of law works only when there is unbiased enforcement. Every company and individual is assumed to be equal in the legal system. Widely publicized cases in the USA—such as the impeachment of a sitting president, Richard Nixon; the censure and removal of politicians on ethics violations; and the conviction and sentencing of well-known business executives such as Bernard Ebbers (former chairman and CEO of WorldCom), Dennis Kozlowski (former chief executive of Tyco International), Kenneth Lay (CEO of Enron), and Martha Stewart—demonstrate that the law applies equally to all individuals.

One implication of these assumptions for business activities is that in these high-task-oriented countries, the goal of business interaction is to obtain a signed agreement that specifies who will do what within what time frame with what consequences if the activities are not performed. The written agreement is expected to be quite specific and provide details on all aspects of the agreement: specification of the product, details of delivery, quality standards, payment schedules, liability, performance standards, and sometimes reward or punishment for compliance or noncompliance. The written agreement offers security because all parties are then expected to live up to the terms of the agreement. As would be expected in a low-context language (Hall, 1981), the wording of the contract is extremely important. Legal advice from the province or state and country in which you are doing business is critical for long-term success when negotiating contracts in these countries.

Contract law and the precedent set by many court cases establish the binding nature of agreements. All parties agree to live by the terms of the agreement. Penalties for not completing the required tasks are specific. Fulfilling the terms of the agreement is extremely important; businesses that do not live up to these terms are viewed as bad business partners and lose their credibility in the business community. The judicial system is the recourse for enforcing compliance with the terms of the contract.

Since the law on contracts and torts is under primarily provincial jurisdiction in Canada and state law in Australia, a contract negotiated in one province or state may not necessarily use the same legal guidelines in other provinces. Issues affecting the conduct of business are assumed to be more local, so the provinces enact laws to govern those activities. Therefore, while a contract in the USA that abides by federal regulations is generally accepted throughout the country, this system is not consistent with business practices in Canada or Australia. Contracts must adhere to the local regulations of the province in which business will be conducted. In New Zealand, the provinces were abolished; currently, there are 12 regional councils and 74 territorial authorities. The legal system is uniform for the country, with localities having only the power conferred upon them by parliament.

The Role of Government and Rule of Law approaches in these countries are consistent with the scores on Uncertainty Avoidance on the Hofstede scale.[2] Structure is desirable for providing direction, but there must also be latitude for interpretation. Interpretations may vary, so differences of opinion are inevitable. The judiciary is the final word on interpreting the law, and lawmakers have the recourse of creating new laws and regulations when it is deemed necessary.

Process

In North America, Australia, and New Zealand, time is viewed as a precious commodity that is expected to be managed efficiently, spent well, divided as appropriate, organized to accomplish goals, and not wasted. Because of the emphasis on task accomplishment, businesspeople strive to use time as efficiently and effectively as possible to achieve their goals. Therefore, a minimal amount of time is spent on small talk; and conversations proceed to the heart of the matter as quickly as possible. This trait is even more pronounced in the USA than in the other countries. Formal introductions and acknowledgements continue to be an important part of meetings in Canada, Australia, and

---

[2] High scores on Uncertainty Avoidance indicate that there is a low tolerance for ambiguity and uncertainty. http://www.geert-hofstede.com.

New Zealand. The following discussion examines the topics of privacy, punctuality, and flow of activities as elements of the process of doing business.

Privacy

As in Northwest and Central Europe, public and private life is separated as much as possible. How non-working time is spent on each is up to the individual. The assumption is that during working hours, you spend time on company-related work and that on personal time you do not need to be responsible for work-related matters. As technology blurs the distinction between company and personal time, more and more business in these countries is being conducted outside of normal business hours. The old boundaries are eroding, and work can take place at any time in any location. However, people are expected to handle their personal matters outside of work and not take away from work results. The presumption is that as long as no laws are broken and you show up on time, ready and able to work, what you do on your own time has nothing to do with your job.

The emphasis on individualism is strongly related to the system of meritocracy. Individuals are hired, promoted, and rewarded based upon their efforts. Family ties, friendship, or background usually have no bearing on work-related decisions. If personal relationships develop, questions of conflict of interest and unethical behavior arise and must be addressed to maintain business integrity and individual credibility. Nepotism is illegal in these countries, and many companies have policies against a family member supervising another relative.

With an increased emphasis on just-in-time delivery, seamless supply chains, and collaboration, the relationship between companies is changing. Many firms are establishing long-term relationships with their business partners. Two important factors are that (1) the focus of the relationship in these countries is between the businesses—not the individuals—and that (2) the successful performance of activities may result in personal friendship—rather than personal loyalty resulting in increased business. The individuals facilitate the relationship between the business organizations, but these relationships emphasize the task rather than the individuals. As such, people have no responsibility to these relationships outside of work-related issues.

Punctuality

Since time is a valuable commodity not to be wasted, punctuality is essential. Arriving at the specified time demonstrates respect for the other party and your ability to control your activities. Generally, there is a five- to ten-minute grace period depending upon traffic conditions or extenuating circumstances.

However, if a delay is likely to be any longer, then it is appropriate to notify the other party, apologize, and identify your situation and anticipated time of arrival. Keeping someone waiting is considered unprofessional or may be interpreted as a demonstration of power on your part. Neither situation creates good rapport for a productive business meeting.

The legacy of a pioneering spirit and strong sense of optimism is consistent with a sense that humans not only are separate from nature, but also are masters of nature who can achieve their goals with determination and perseverance. The implication for business practices is that businesspeople believe they have the power to shape and control events, activities, and processes. A true professional ensures that events happen on time and as scheduled.

Flow of Activities

When an appointment is scheduled, the participants presume that the purpose is to work toward the goal of creating an agreed-upon solution at a meeting that begins on time, proceeds in an orderly and linear fashion, covers all necessary topics in the time allotted, and arrives at an agreed-upon course of action by the end of the meeting.

Starting from the premise that individuals and companies earn status based upon their accomplishments, there is a strong motivation to succeed in any business situation. As a result, concessions and compromises do not happen easily. While the bargaining process usually begins with each side stating his or her position and arguing for a fair outcome, neither side wants to give in to the other. While outright or prolonged conflict is not a desired goal, it is preferable to losing. As a result, compromise, with an expectation that both sides will have to give in to some degree, is generally more desirable than conflict.

The approach taken when working toward concessions is to proceed sequentially, considering one issue at a time until a decision is made on an issue and then moving on to the next issue. This flow for decision making follows from a linear, segmented view of the world. These discussions usually take place in private, with only members of the immediate business team present. The interaction proceeds in this manner until each issue has been discussed and resolved, with appropriate concessions and compromises. Pursuing a compromise and making decisions at the table with individuals who have the authority to make decisions on behalf of the company is the expected process of business activity.

One major difference in this process occurs among the French population in Canada. French Canadians are less time conscious and more open to sharing personal information than Anglophones are, so they are likely to spend more time getting to know you and your business. The French Canadians may ask questions about the history of your company, the quality or specifications of the products, your business experience, the company's business record, your family, or your background. Because personal relationships are somewhat more important, time may be spent in social settings, taking time to get to know the people. The French Canadians tend to be more laissez-faire, less intense, and more family oriented once you get to know them. While personal relationships are more important, they are not necessarily directly related to business opportunities.

In general, business activities take place on time and proceed to address items one at a time until agreement has been reached on all issues. Professionals are then expected to manage the process within their own company to ensure that all parts of the agreement for which their company is responsible occur on time as specified in the contract.

Communication

Examining the way words are used, how truth is viewed, preferred styles of interaction, and forms of logic helps facilitate understanding how to communicate effectively when conducting business.

Words

As mentioned earlier in this chapter, Hall (1981) categorizes the English language as low context, implying that words have specific meanings, specific words are chosen carefully to convey a desired meaning, and the meanings of words remain the same in most cases regardless of context. Every field and every large company has its own jargon, using special terms to convey specific information. Learning the appropriate vocabulary of your partner's business is important to demonstrate that he or she is part of the group and to participate effectively in conversations.

While this is true in Australia, Canada, New Zealand, and the USA, an interesting phenomenon is that the vocabulary is different in these countries. *Boot* and *trunk* refer to the same spot on an automobile; *nappies* and *diapers* are the same important piece of clothing for infants; *lift* and *elevator* both refer to the equipment that transports people between floors in a building. In British English, a motion to "table" a topic means to add it to the list of topics for discussion; in American English, the same motion means to remove the topic from the list. The words have specific meanings, differ between British English and American English, and must be used correctly.

Taking time to learn and understand the vocabulary or the form of English being used in the country is critical for success. The wording of contracts is a time-intensive task because choosing the correct words is the essence of the contract, which specifies who will do what, within what time frame, and with what consequences.

Style

Because accomplishing the task is emphasized over building relationships for Anglophones, time is not used to build relationships. Rather, time is spent on business topics with a direct, frank, open discussion of issues progressing in a linear fashion. Typically, the most important issues are addressed first, the desired results are identified, a reasonable opening offer is made, and relevant concerns or objections are discussed. Value is placed on brevity, specificity, relevance, and the ability to stay focused. Reaching agreement, preferably in the form of a signed contract, is the primary objective; and little time is spent on any issues not directly related to the task.

Employees in these countries typically have a specific functional job with defined areas of responsibility. In most cases, these employees do not like bureaucratic structure because they prefer to take individual responsibility and make decisions within their functional area. Dealing with bureaucracy within their own organization or the other side's organization is frustrating because their expertise might be questioned, bureaucracies take time, and someone with little expertise in the area might second-guess their decision. Businesspeople in these countries perceive themselves as experts in their functional area and expect the person in authority to make decisions relative to the functional area. Therefore, it is important to have areas of expertise, tasks, authority, and decision processes clearly defined.

Initially, business behavior in Canada, Australia, and New Zealand is likely to be somewhat more reserved, formal, and polite than in the USA. Using titles and last names is appropriate, and discussions usually begin in a more formal manner until the local person signals a move to a less formal style. In addition, there is a tendency to play with words, to use a dry sense of humor, and to downplay accomplishments.

In the USA, participants in business activities are assumed to be on similar levels, so conversations are frank, direct, and open using simple, commonly understood language. Discussions are likely to be straightforward, with much of the relevant information revealed so that the participants on opposite sides can work together to solve the problem. In the USA, status is less important, titles are more useful as an indicator of an individual's function or position rather than as an indication of status, and the emphasis on local participation emphasizes face-to-face decision making. The assumption is that when people sit down and talk with others on an equal basis, they can find solutions to problems.

With some variation, the important style across these countries is a focus on establishing agreements, resolving issues according to prescribed procedures, and completing business activities in a timely manner.

Logic

For Anglophones, business discussions aimed at resolving differences and creating compromises rely heavily on the ability to create persuasive arguments. With a high value placed on systems, processes, and objectivity, rational appeals accompanied by objective information are perceived as most persuasive. Presenting information about the features and/or price of a product is often a successful form of appeal. Test results, objective data, and testimonials by recognized experts are accepted as strong evidence that can be used to build persuasive arguments.

Typically, first offers may be a little higher than the expected outcome, but are fair, nonetheless. The expectation is that the ensuing discussion will include arguments over alternatives, that the pattern of revealing information is part of the process of influencing people, and that an unyielding stance will result in small concessions. Aggressive, goal-oriented tactics are often used successfully, especially by those engaged in distributive or competitive bargaining. This bargaining may include tactics such as exploiting the weaknesses of opponents, making more offers, or rejecting more concessions. However, the integrative, or win-win, approach uses more of a problem-solving technique with communicative patterns that induce cooperation, which can result in higher profit in some cases.

French Canadians have a stronger interest in personal relationships. As such, evocative appeals that stress the benefits of a product or service, particularly the benefits to individuals, are likely to be successful. However, success is more likely when personal influence is accompanied by strong logical arguments.

Successful businesspeople spend time evaluating which approach, communication style, forms of argument, and influence technique are likely to be most effective in a given interaction. During the interaction itself, successful businesspeople continually refine their plan and adapt their behavior. In some situations, an aggressive, hard-bargaining, competitive approach is more successful; in other situations, a cooperative, problem-solving approach will be more successful. Choosing the appropriate form of argumentation and presenting it in a persuasive manner is the essence of success in business.

Truth

Establishing credibility is essential for success. To be credible, you need to be honest and trustworthy. Honesty is usually judged in a straightforward manner because Anglophones tend to hold absolute principles of right and wrong, true and false, good and bad, or right and wrong. Subtlety, nuance, and variations of truth are seen as violating the right-and-wrong dichotomy.

Establishing a reputation as honest and trustworthy can take a great deal of time. Destroying it can happen in an instant. Anything that creates doubt, suspicion, or skepticism about any business behavior, such as discovering a discrepancy in a statement you made, missing a promised delivery time, or not adhering to one of the terms of the contract, means that all your behavior is now viewed with suspicion.

Trust is earned over time by demonstrating that you can be relied upon, are dependable, have expertise, and make true statements. Words alone are not enough; **words** *and* **actions** demonstrating that promises made are kept are necessary to earn the other side's trust and respect. When promises are honored consistently, if your statements are accurate, and if your word can be relied upon, then you are credible.

Conclusion

Differences in business practices occur within all four countries (Australia, Canada, New Zealand, and the USA), within companies, and between individuals. Not all individuals in all situations adhere to the descriptions presented in this chapter. However, the general principles broadly apply. While personal relationships may develop as a result of doing business together, or perhaps even provide entry to potential customers, they are not a prerequisite for doing business, do not necessarily have any effect on the process, and are ***not*** expected to interfere with business.

Time and task are paramount in these countries. This emphasis affects the process of obtaining an agreement and is the focus and goal of business activities. Participants are expected to use time efficiently in pursuit of the goal by spending as little time as necessary on the less important parts of the process. Decisions are made by individuals influenced by the presentation of sufficient evidence as support for a particular point of view or position. With as few concessions as possible, the partners reach a final agreement that includes detailed specifications on all relevant issues. The contract not only is the goal of the process, but also contains the guidelines that govern the future behavior of all parties involved in the agreement.

CHAPTER 5

MEDITERRANEAN EUROPE

Classification of Cultures Model

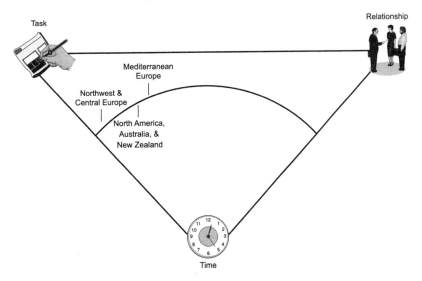

Living well, with time to enjoy the benefits of hard work and productive output, is important in Mediterranean Europe. Mediterranean Europe includes those countries bordering the Mediterranean Sea. France shares that coastline and is considered part of Mediterranean Europe, with the exception of metropolitan Paris, which operates more like Northwest and Central Europe. Tasks continue to be very important but no longer have overriding precedence. Differences between North America and Northwest and Central Europe are, generally, of degree and style, with basic agreement that tasks are more important than relationships. In Mediterranean Europe, there is a fundamental shift in attitude, behavior, and orientation toward the development and maintenance of personal relationships.

Quality in all aspects of living is more important here than in North America, Australia, New Zealand, or Northwest and Central Europe. Important tasks will receive sufficient attention and are completed in their own good time, but will be balanced with other equally important social expectations. Both task accomplishment and relationships will receive attention when necessary, but task issues are not always placed ahead of relationships in these countries. Be assured, there is certainly variation among the Mediterranean countries and within each country. However, the orientation toward task and relationship is more similar among the Mediterranean countries, as a group, than it is in other European or Latin American countries. This chapter explores those similarities, realizing that each individual with whom the foreign businessperson interacts will exhibit characteristics representing this region, a specific country, a section within a country, a particular company, and his or her individual background.

Developing relationships among circles of friends and business colleagues is more important in Mediterranean Europe than in previously discussed groups. These relationships are relatively structured and formal, requiring an understanding of how they function. Your position in society—derived by a combination of family background, education, and personal accomplishments—allows access to key decision makers or to those who can provide access to key decisions makers. The amount of power developed through connections and individual accomplishment determines your position of leadership in the community, which is significant in a society with a tradition of hierarchy and class distinctions. While not overtly acknowledged, class and privilege are undercurrents in many business transactions and must be analyzed and understood prior to entering into agreements. In other words, the distinction between "old money" and "new money" exists in this region and, while not discussed, is an element the businessperson must recognize when dealing with business partners.

Participating in conversations and discussions is an important vehicle for establishing your identity, creating a connection with others, and accomplishing business objectives. The positions taken, arguments made, and strength of convictions presented during discussions define who you are and how you relate to others. These articulated positions also become the basis for your connections and positions in future business dealings. A flexible attitude toward time is necessary because the use of time is not organized around task accomplishment. Rather, it is balanced between accomplishing tasks and personal goals, whichever is most important at the moment. The following discussion about the characteristics of this approach to business will include the elements of structure, process, and communication characteristics in business situations.

Structure

With class and privilege creating a strong sense of distinction in these countries, it is just as important to determine how the informal hierarchy

Global Business Practices Model

Areas of World	Gov't	Law	Hier.	Privacy	Punct.	Flow	Truth	Words	Style	Logic
Northwest & Central Europe										
North America, Australia, & NZ										
Mediterranean Europe										

LEGEND

Role of Government: White = the government sets parameters and constraints to create the environment for doing business. Black = Direct involvement of government in business as a business partner.

Rule of Law: White = Reliance on systems and procedures. Black = Pragmatism or situational considerations.

Sense of Hierarchy: White = Assumption of equality. Black = Assumption of status difference.

View of Privacy: White = Business and private matters are separate. Black = Business and private matters are all part of one reality.

Punctuality: White = Fixed time. Black = Flexible or "rubber" time.

Flow of Activities: White = Time works in a linear fashion. Black = Time works in a cyclical fashion.

Truth: White = Universal truth. Black = Many truths exist at once.

Words: White = Words have explicit meanings. Black = Words have implicit meanings.

Style: White = Communication is direct and forthright. Black = Communication is indirect.

Logic: White = Formal deductive reasoning. Black = Alternative heuristic.

functions as it is to understand the role of government and the rule of law. Understanding all three of these elements is critical for practicing business successfully in this region.

Hierarchy

This region is the heart of the ancient and pre-Enlightenment empires, including Greece, Rome, France, Portugal, and Spain. Each country has been the center of vast empires during its history. Each country had ruling aristocracies, vast wealth, and political influence that have left a distinct imprint on the national character of its people. Part of the legacy of these empires is a sense of cultural identity and self-importance that may not manifest itself immediately, but is a national characteristic broadly shared within each country. The accomplishments attained in a broad range of fields, including philosophy, engineering, navigation, commerce, industry, and the arts, have left each nation with a deep sense of achievement and national pride.

As empires developed, they created an imposed peace and official network for commerce. Imperial governments collected taxes. At the same time, sectors of the economy were developed as a result of the stability within the empire, and individuals amassed huge fortunes. Fundamental to the creation of wealth during the era of widespread illiteracy and harsh living conditions was the development of reliable, long-term personal relationships.

Emperors changed; boundaries flexed as rivals grew in power outside the empire; trade and commercial relationships developed that were independent of imperial politics. Each group consciously worked to preserve its power and add to its historical influence.

Regardless of who ruled, these relationships have been passed down, in these cultures, as the best way to conduct business in volatile, changing political circumstances. The traditional wealthy class has power in politics, commerce, and industry based upon its inherited or attained social position. For instance, for centuries, the Spanish have been doing business through networks involving close personal relationships built through intermarriage. In this region, the boss is often viewed as a patron—a father figure who may be severe but loving, handing out rewards and punishments. In Italy, finding someone with *enshufismo*, having the right connections, throughout this region is essential because that person can initiate a meeting between important parties. These relationships are based upon social standing, status, and power rather than personal friendship; and they continue today.

Compared to Northwest and Central Europe, the stronger belief in hierarchy in Mediterranean Europe has been documented by Hofstede (2005).[1] An appropriate educational and family background is necessary for social standing, as is self-assurance related to individual achievements. Power can come from leadership and accomplishment in financial, political, entrepreneurial, managerial, or intellectual endeavors, with the intellectual endeavors being highly respected because they are indicative of that individual's superior knowledge, another respected way of attaining status, position, and power.

In this hierarchical system, the person at the top has the authority to make decisions, is supposed to know the answers to questions, and is not open to criticism. As a manager you need to be aware that the person you put in charge of a proposed activity has important business implications in this region. For those who operate from a more egalitarian system, in which people are evaluated based upon their individual accomplishments, this may not seem to be a decision of consequence. However, within an environment in which hierarchy is so important historically, time must be taken to ensure that the *proper* person has been asked to be in charge of the activity— someone with appropriate status, background, and connections.

Prior to beginning business, it is important to analyze the power, social standing, and hierarchical position of your contacts. You need to know

---

[1] Geert Hofstede's research identifies five dimensions of culture. High scores in Power Distance demonstrate the degree to which members of the society recognize inequalities of power. See http://www.geerthofstede.com.

where your contact is in the local hierarchy. At the same time, your contact needs to know your status, reputation, etiquette, power, and ability to manage relationships. That evaluation determines whether or how quickly you may obtain access to the next level in the hierarchy, because your contact will determine *if* and *when* to introduce you to others at higher levels in the hierarchy. By making an introduction, your contact takes a risk by implicitly conveying an assurance that "my friend is your friend." The implication is that your contact is certifying you as an *appropriate* individual to do the job *and* is creating an obligation for you to perform as promised.

Entering a network is not straightforward in Mediterranean Europe. Determining who has the authority to make a decision and finding a respected individual who will provide a proper introduction to the decision maker is invaluable to the person new to the region. Having a respected individual "certify" you as a legitimate business partner is extremely valuable. Networks are an important part of day-to-day business, and informal methods of behavior are assumed and used. Status and hierarchy create networks that are not easily penetrated. Members of the network are loyal to one another, but they also rely upon the specific words in the contract for complete protection.

Role of Government

The role of government is to protect domestic businesses and keep them competitive. Governmental bureaucracy is the basic means through which official decision making takes place. Authority tends to be centralized at the top of business organizations and within government. With decision-making power retained at the tops of organizations and close ties within networks of status, there are key individuals from government and business who have a great deal of power. In some cases, the structures of businesses are so intertwined with government that major shareholders *and* government officials must approve major research and development (R&D) projects, partnerships, or mergers. As part of the EU, the role of government in Mediterranean Europe is more similar to the rest of Europe than different.

Rule of Law

Legal regulations are similar throughout the EU. Like other European groups, a dominant attribute of Mediterranean Europeans is risk avoidance. The purpose of contracts is to provide protection, resulting in lengthy discussions to ensure full protection. Positions and agreements need to be represented accurately, which also involves lengthy discussion.

Any laws enacted in Mediterranean European countries are more likely to follow the Napoleonic or Roman code of law rather than the British system of common law. An important distinction is that code law specifies what activities should be carried out; anything unspecified is illegal. This system discourages the use of precedent, as in the British legal system, and interpretation by judges. The necessity of identifying specific steps to be followed and providing documentation regarding the acceptable performance of each step results in the need to acquire many permits and approvals from different agencies. Working in this milieu means that time must be reserved for obtaining the required permits and approvals before doing business.

Process

The structural elements determine what businesses have to do and who in the hierarchy is responsible for making decisions or granting approvals. Process elements impact the pace of business activity. Punctuality and the flow of activities regulate when and how activities move through time. The separation between public and private lives determines what topics of conversation are appropriate at which events and which events are important to the successful conduct of business.

Punctuality

Anyone coming from an area operating with a monochronic time orientation, in which everyone focuses on tasks sequentially with little or no interruptions, will have their expectations of how time works challenged. Mediterranean Europeans use polychronic time, meaning that interruptions are common. People who are not from this region may find interruptions to be disconcerting and frustrating. It can be especially unnerving to visitors when these interruptions are for personal and not business reasons.

Family and personal relationships as well as tasks are often equally important in Mediterranean Europe and are all legitimate reasons for interruptions. Whatever personal or business tasks the locals deem most important at a particular time will be given preference. Having your meeting interrupted because something else is considered more important is likely to be frustrating to the visiting foreigner. Being interrupted for a personal or family matter is likely to be quite surprising to someone from a task-oriented culture.

This flexible approach to time results in meetings that may take longer than expected or scheduled, less work being accomplished within a given time frame, and a lower sense of importance for deadlines. The flow of time proceeds in a more flexible manner than in task-oriented countries.

Flow of Time

Time needs to be taken to establish each individual's social standing, contacts, power, and status. The process of assessing an individual includes professional, formal, business, and social activities. You will be expected to use correct manners and behave properly in a number of situations. Can you choose an appropriate wine? Do you know the proper silverware or drinking glasses to use at dinner? Can you participate in social conversation, without conducting business, during introductions? Do you know when to begin business conversations?

Several people are likely to be in and out of an office during a meeting and create a number of interruptions. Can you be gracious about the interruptions and seamlessly steer the conversation back to your topics? Or, are you obviously frustrated by the interruptions, immediately returning to whatever you were saying before being interrupted?

The conversations that take place do not necessarily progress in a neat, orderly, sequential manner. The presence of several people who enjoy conversation leads to lively discussions encompassing many points of view, often with more than one person talking at the same time. Suppressing disagreement is not desired behavior; full discussion of various points of view is encouraged.

Progress toward agreement is slow because compromise is not viewed as the appropriate vehicle. Because individuals seldom change their position based upon the arguments advanced by others, at least not publicly, these discussions rarely lead to resolution at that meeting. Generally, meetings are adjourned without resolution, but with an agreement to work on a solution that can be discussed next time. After everyone has had an opportunity to ponder the debate, refine their arguments, and accept any points from the preceding discussion that seemed particularly useful or relevant, positions shift, making agreement more or less difficult to obtain. Problems may be resolved after two or three of these adjournments—only to result in more argumentation over the wording of an agreement. Resolution occurs from general consensus after some time has passed; agreements appear to be almost a by-product of the discussion.

With interruptions during meetings and a process involving public engagement and private reevaluation, the flow of activities generally takes more time than in task-oriented cultures.

Privacy

In Mediterranean Europe, personal relationships do not necessarily imply personal friendships. Respect in public life is important, so conducting activities in a manner that reinforces your social status is expected. During an initial meeting, the conversation may touch on topics that would be considered personal and off limits to someone from a task-oriented culture. The Mediterranean, however, wants to determine your educational background, social standing, family background, and professional experience. These topics may seem presumptuous so early in the conversation, but your responses are important for determining what levels of obligation might exist, what level of status you deserve, or what level of authority you might have.

As the conversation continues, you are expected to express strongly held positions, because in that process you reveal your attitudes, values, and beliefs. Knowing what you believe and how you think is critical for any negotiation that will take place later. While expressing strongly held opinions is expected, doing so in a way that does not create personal animosities is also an important point of etiquette. Points of view are argued vigorously but not with comments directed toward any individual. Differences of opinion are often expressed loudly and vehemently, but they are expressions of ideas not considered to be personal. These complicated and involved discussions and the need for universal participation result in lengthy meetings.

These types of discussions are an expected part of establishing business relationships and not personal friendships. People guard their privacy and keep their personal lives separate from their public lives. Discussion of personal lives is reserved for family and very close friends. Those topics are not part of social conversation and would not be considered appropriate in a public setting.

Communication

During business and social meetings, a visiting businessperson is expected to demonstrate good etiquette and participate in discussions. Many of these social conversations, while not addressing specific business issues, will form the foundation for future business discussions. Understanding how words are used, what kind of logic is persuasive, the predominant view of truth, and the appropriate style of communication is critical for the successful practice of business in this region.

Words

The languages of Mediterranean Europe are in the middle of Hall's (1981) high/low context continuum and have properties of both the high and low context languages. High context cultures are those in which the words get meaning from nonverbal cues and the relationship between individuals, as in

China or Japan. Low context cultures have more defined, absolute words and derive less meaning from the speakers and more from the words, as in Northwest and Central Europe. In the Mediterranean area, words *and* nonverbal aspects of conversations are important.

Nonverbal cues—from facial expressions to clothes to the use of gestures—are all important for establishing status, conveying information, and creating emphasis. Eye movement, facial expression, body posture, hand gestures, and physical expression are all more widely used in Mediterranean Europe than in the more task-focused cultures. So conversations can be loud and lively as various points of view are presented. Emotions and opinions are strong and often reinforced with many gestures.

On the other hand, words, especially in contracts, are used in a very precise manner for protection. As a result, negotiations over the wording of a contract are serious and will take a long time, just as they do in task-oriented cultures. Social conversations often appear to be rhetorical, general, and even somewhat unfocused. However, these conversations define issues, determine parameters of the questions, and identify main principles. This seemingly informal social conversation forms the basis for formal arguments that are presented at a later time. This process should not be taken casually because it forms the core of substantive discussions.

Truth

The foundation of Western philosophy comes from the Mediterranean region. The writings of Aristotle and Plato form the basis of the definitions and pursuit of *truth* in the Western world. The concept of a universal truth is that regardless of time, place, or point of view, truth can be identified and is a constant. Assuming that the correct forms of argumentation are used (see the following section on logic), truth will be revealed. Honorable businesspeople are honest and truthful and will arrive at correct decisions when using the rules of logic. The Roman Catholic and Greek Orthodox religions, which have been a central part of the cultures that developed in these countries, promote precepts that are consistent with this view of honest, truthful, honorable behavior. An expectation of businesspeople throughout the region is that people will be truthful in their dealings and honor agreements reached through discussion and negotiation.

Logic

People from Mediterranean Europe love discussion and find what they say to be most interesting. Everyone wants to be involved. From the French perspective, the form of argumentation most often used is Cartesian logic, arguing from what is known to a logical conclusion. Facts are important—all of the facts—including both negative and positive information and statements. Once all of the facts have been presented and their veracity debated, rational arguments, based upon previously accepted premises, lead to conclusions.

Thorough preparation is necessary before engaging in this form of argumentation. The principles agreed upon during earlier conversation become inflexible bases of agreement from which a person's position is justified. The argumentative discussion is an important vehicle for learning more about the other side's position and the quality of his or her thinking, for establishing premises that can be used when creating logical arguments, and for demonstrating that a particular conclusion is *right*. Conflict resolution is often win-lose or distributive.

From the Spanish perspective, exaggeration is often substituted for logic, with the favorable evidence multiplied by 1,000 and the damaging testimony divided by the same factor. Often, people from more task-oriented cultures characterize this kind of discussion as hyperbole and then miss the point of hearing what is important to the Mediterranean European businessperson. Although it is convenient to dismiss exaggerated positions as unrealistic, doing so does not get to the core of the issues being discussed. Listening and clarifying are key skills during these discussions.

Business conversations can be viewed as logic problems requiring careful preparation and attention. Gathering all the relevant facts and precedent-setting cases or decisions is necessary as a first step in resolving issues. Quickly agreeing with principles to get to the heart of the discussion may not be a wise strategy. What is agreed to in this step forms the logical basis of *a priori* arguments presented later.

Style

Style is extremely important in establishing status, demonstrating competence, and establishing authority. You will be expected to use correct manners and behave properly in business *and* social situations. Trust develops over time and depends upon your task performance, sensitivity to people, and appreciation of the local culture. You need to present an appropriately formal demeanor, especially during introductions and formal meetings. You also need to know how to give and accept hospitality on a social basis, in which you need to demonstrate formal behavior while also being able to relax, enjoy the surroundings, demonstrate your appreciation, and be enthusiastic without being too personal. Showing sensitivity to and appreciation of social traditions is important for earning respect and developing trust. Developing trust is most important, not necessarily developing a lasting personal friendship.

Do not be surprised or intimidated by loud or apparently volatile discussions. Both parties present their points of view in a strong manner that may seem combative, competitive, and confrontational to an outsider or someone used to discussions aimed at compromise. Direct personal confrontation is avoided, so individuals are not insulted or challenged. Mediterranean Europeans are comfortable with conflict. The French, for instance, perceive little virtue in compromise and are usually willing to compromise only when their reasoning is demonstrated to have been faulty. Participants are not likely to agree to a new idea in public. Rather, they will leave the meeting, think about the ideas discussed, and incorporate any new ideas that seem reasonable into their position. At the next meeting, they will present a new position modified by their thinking between sessions and you will find yourself engaged in another lively, loud discussion punctuated by interruptions, both business and personal.

Conclusion

Networks, status, formality, and hierarchy highlight some of the nuances of difference in the role of government, rule of law, and hierarchy between Mediterranean Europe and Northwest and Central Europe. Networks and families of influence are important. The acceptance of hierarchy in Mediterranean Europe endows a good deal of power to those individuals within the network who have demonstrated knowledge, success, and experience. Establishing relationships that result in introductions to those people of influence and power is time-consuming, but critical for success.

A polychronic approach toward time permits interruptions, both business and personal, during business activities and allows for time to be diverted to whatever is identified as most important at the moment. Argumentation is perceived as enjoyable and involves the use of formal logic. Preparation is critical for active participation in this process. Active participation in the arguments, social activities, and business discussions must demonstrate social grace to establish trust without becoming too personal.

With the interruptions, lengthy discussions, and necessary pacing of meetings, the time needed to achieve success in business is longer than in the task-oriented cultures. The pacing, style, and forms of argumentation require careful preparation before meetings and careful attention to what is being said when conducting business.

CHAPTER 6

EASTERN EUROPE AND RUSSIA

Classification of Cultures Model

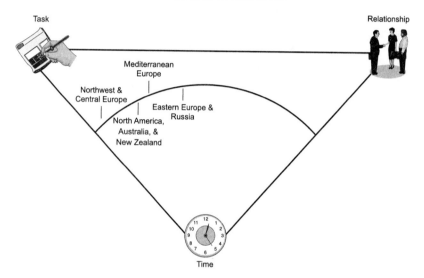

Eastern Europe and Russia are in the midst of a major transition. Throughout the history of the region, the location of these countries made them a focal point for economic development and trade, power shifts and war, as empires expanded and contracted, as armies battled for control of new lands, and as traders traversed the region. With the ebb and flow of history, the region became a mixture of ethnic groups and religions, creating significant differences in points of view. Post–World War II, the Eastern European countries and Russia were incorporated into the Soviet Communist system, which was organized around four principal elements: the hierarchy of the Communist Party, ethnic federalism, state socialism, and Russian dominance. Business activities took place within a framework of central planning and control, rigid direction, and imposed regulation. For at least two generations, business practices in these countries were conducted in essentially the same manner.

Amid unrest and dissatisfaction with this system, countries eventually began to assert their independence, challenge the Soviet system, and demand changes. Beginning in 1988, individual countries broke away from the Soviet

Union's control—until 1991, when the Soviet system was dissolved. By 1992, all Soviet institutions ceased to exist and all countries were transitioning from a centrally controlled economy to a free market, multiparty economy.

Some countries, such as Croatia, the Czech Republic, Estonia, Hungary, Latvia, Lithuania, Poland, Romania, Serbia, Montenegro, Slovakia, and Slovenia, chose to be independent from Russia while establishing their free markets. Others, such as the former Soviet Republics of Azerbaijan, Armenia, Belarus, Georgia, Kazakhstan, Kyrgyzstan, Moldova, Russia, Tajikistan, Uzbekistan, and Ukraine, chose to maintain their sovereignty but continue their affiliation through the Commonwealth of Independent States. Emerging from the Soviet Union, each country had experience with and the traditions of practicing business from a command economy perspective. Transition to a free market economy has not been identical across these countries, but does share some common patterns that will be explored in this chapter.

On the one hand, the northern European attitude toward task accomplishment is present to some degree. On the other hand, within the former Soviet countries, there existed a well-used network system, through which many things were able to be accomplished without having to go through the approval process of the central system. In this way, relationships among trusted friends and colleagues established a ready-made business network in these countries with more of a relationship orientation like that of Mediterranean Europe. The countries that were part of the Silk Road trading route historically have been influenced in culture and business by the Middle East and Asia. Given the amount of conflict, turmoil, and transition seen by these countries throughout their histories, time is clearly flexible—in time, all things will change. All of the countries are in the process of creating legal systems, a form of government, and financial systems, using a number of different European models that have been proven successful. The level of complexity of the region is daunting to the outsider at first glimpse.

One aspect of society that is important in these countries is the concept of an inner circle and an outer circle of contacts (see Figure 2 in Chapter 2). With governments in transition and consequent governmental structures and expertise being created, relationships are critical in the conduct of business. Suspicion has been the primary response to strangers and officials during the past several generations. Relationships beyond the family take a long time to build, and trust is not given lightly. Those trusted members of the inner circle were the only stable factor in a changing world, so trust was not given until you were confident that the individual was completely worthy of your trust.

Global Business Practices Model

Areas of World	Gov't	Law	Hier.	Privacy	Punct.	Flow	Truth	Words	Style	Logic
Northwest & Central Europe										
North America, Australia, & NZ										
Mediterranean Europe										
Eastern Europe & Russia										

LEGEND

Role of Government: White = the government sets parameters and constraints to create the environment for doing business. Black = Direct involvement of government in business as a business partner.

Rule of Law: White = Reliance on systems and procedures. Black = Pragmatism or situational considerations.

Sense of Hierarchy: White = Assumption of equality. Black = Assumption of status difference.

View of Privacy: White = Business and private matters are separate. Black = Business and private matters are all part of one reality.

Punctuality: White = Fixed time. Black = Flexible or "rubber" time.

Flow of Activities: White = Time works in a linear fashion. Black = Time works in a cyclical fashion.

Truth: White = Universal truth. Black = Many truths exist at once.

Words: White = Words have explicit meanings. Black = Words have implicit meanings.

Style: White = Communication is direct and forthright. Black = Communication is indirect.

Logic: White = Formal deductive reasoning. Black = Alternative heuristic.

Habits developed over lifetimes under an oppressive and suspicious system are difficult to eliminate, and the businessperson must demonstrate both trust-worthiness and patience before trust will be granted reciprocally.

Since both task accomplishment and relationship are almost equally important in this area, Eastern Europe and Russia fall near the middle of the Classification of Cultures Model, resulting in a unique approach to the structure, process, and communication aspects of business practice.

Structure

With countries in transition, the structure is not necessarily stable and predictable. Determining the direction of change, underlying philosophies, and commitment of individuals to the change process is essential. Hierarchy is more important when the structure is unstable. This section explores the impact of hierarchy, form of government, and rule of law on business practices in this area of the world.

Hierarchy

Under Communism, everyone was accorded the same rights, all contributions were deemed equal, and everyone had access to the same benefits with the exception of the Communist Party and the military. Rank in the Party or the military bestowed levels of power, influence, and special treatment beyond those of the ordinary citizen. Thus, a system of ins and outs has a natural counterpart in current business expectations. In a centrally controlled command economy, the government decided what would be grown, where, and by whom; what would be manufactured, where, and by what company; and what would be taught, where, and to whom. For several generations, citizens were expected to follow orders without taking initiative. The centralized decision-making process and bureaucratic structure created a paternalistic system, with the government providing for all of the material needs of the citizens, creating regulations, and administering discipline to both formal and informal organizations when necessary. One major consequence of this *cradle-to-grave* system was to sap individual initiative. The legacy today is that there are multiple generations of workers who have never been given or taken responsibility for their careers, have never saved for their future, or have never developed their talents. These people still wait to be told what to do. Hierarchy is still extremely important to these people.

Another consequence of this system was that all business was done through government functionaries. Within this system, informal networks of families and friends made it possible to circumvent the government system of controls and obtain goods, permits, or services. Another legacy today is that those who were enterprising under the old system and managed to find extralegal ways of getting around systems, rules, and procedures thrived and are taking advantage of the opportunity to take responsibility to do business on their own. This group wants to take charge and be in charge.

Today many businesspeople from these countries will offer their services and present themselves as able to cut through the system's red tape. The foreign businessperson needs to take time to determine the authenticity of the individual's claims, the actual ability of the individual to facilitate successful business activities, and adherence to the legal structure required by the home office. In the Soviet system, officials had a difficult time determining when people from countries outside the Soviet Union were acting as official representatives of the country or as private citizens representing corporations or themselves. Even today a local businessperson may expect you to have the same access to government officials and important businesspeople in your home country.

Cultivating personal relationships within the bureaucracy was a requirement for entering into business relationships in the Soviet system. Because the structures and institutions of business such as the banking systems and the legal systems are not well developed, local businesspeople continue to rely upon individuals they know and trust. Some people are learning the process of doing business in a free market while they create and operate their businesses. They are willing to take charge and take the risk. At the same time, the fluid change in regulations, tax laws, and government policies as the economy evolves makes it incumbent upon the visiting businessperson to have strong relationships with informed and accomplished local business-people. Flexibility and adaptation are most important as legal procedures and government policies change.

In many cases, an intermediary, trusted by both sides, is the key to doing business successfully. When faced with a choice between a product with a recognized trademark sold by a stranger and a product without a recognized trademark sold by someone familiar, a distributor will choose to carry the product with the less recognized trademark because the seller is known. Identifying those intermediaries who are trusted by the local businesspeople and with whom you can develop trust takes research and time.

As these countries go through their transition, the government in each country retains more or less power to control business practices, creating more or fewer restrictions for doing business. Individuals vary in their willingness to follow directions, take responsibility, take risks, and make decisions. Visiting businesspeople will find it worthwhile to take time to determine the power and authority structure in a country, city, or company before committing to do business. In addition, determining an individual's ability to take risks, to make decisions, and to be loyal to someone outside his or her in-group is also essential to success in this region.

Role of Government

Russia and the Eastern European countries were Communist, with centrally controlled economies from the end of World War II to the early 1990s. While the transition process differs in speed, philosophy, and direction across the former Commonwealth of Independent States, they have a shared assumption: that the economy of a country should not be totally controlled by the central government and that citizens will have some level of participation in the process of government. A key decision on the part of the visiting businessperson is to determine the level of government involvement needed to meet business objectives.

The countries in this area have adopted some form of parliamentary democracy or constitutional democracy or have created a federal republic. The president or prime minister has been granted more or less power depending upon the country. Not all countries have created equality between the executive and legislative branches of government; many countries have retained more power in the executive branch. Some countries have bicameral legislative bodies; some countries have unicameral legislatures. Some, like Russia, are in the process of determining the appropriate balance among central, regional, or local authority. They are, however, creating the mechanism for free elections of the president or prime minister and members of the legislature. International observers have reported fewer problems in each succeeding election.

Movement is toward a democratic government, but the form may differ from country to country, so time taken to learn the local reality is essential to understanding where the country is in the transition toward its new government system.

Rule of Law

Personal relationships and *backdoor* deals were standard operating procedure for accomplishing tasks in the centrally planned economies of the former Soviet Union. Transparency was not routinely practiced, primarily because the government officials, who controlled every sector of the economy, including business, knew everything about your business. The best way to keep government officials out of your business was to withhold information from them. Habits developed to survive in such an environment are difficult to discard in an environment with evolving systems.

Each of these countries is in the process of reforming the legal system and the system of government. Laws pertaining to property rights, ownership, contracts, the banking system, insurance, and the stock market are being created. The pace of reform has been different in each country depending upon its status before World War II, its level of industrialization, its connection with the EU, and its ability to halt corruption. Progress is being made; however, it is not always linear, not always forward. The visiting businessperson must be up to date on the current legal situation related to the business at hand.

Once the laws are created, autonomy and enforcement are important issues. In some countries, the court system is controlled by the president. In some countries, judges see themselves as government officials charged with protecting the state's rights. In some countries, the judges are subject to manipulation by political authorities. In some situations, offering the right person a favor or bribe can result in a favorable decision. As a result, businesspeople in these countries do not necessarily rely on the legal system for protection. Protection comes from doing business with trusted individuals. Before entering a situation that might be questionable, ensure that your legal status is sound and your business and government are aligned with your planned activity. In some situations, payment of "finder's fees" or "facilitation services" is condoned and will get the results that would otherwise involve difficult legal processes.

Four of the Commonwealth of Independent States—Armenia, Georgia, Moldova, and Ukraine—are members of the WTO, as are Albania, the Czech Republic, Estonia, Hungary, the Kyrgyz Republic, Lithuania, Latvia, Poland, Romania, Slovenia, and Slovakia. A group of these countries are now members of the North Atlantic Treaty Organization (NATO): Bulgaria, the Czech Republic, Estonia, Hungary, Latvia, Lithuania, Poland, Romania, Slovakia, and Slovenia. Tajikistan is a member of NATO's Partnership for Peace, and Ukraine has specific agreements with NATO. Membership in the WTO and NATO demonstrates each country's efforts to meet the goals of democratic government, common defense, and international legal standards.

Many of the countries have directed their reforms to meet the standards required by the EU's political, legal, and government institutions. Currently, Bulgaria, Croatia, and Romania are applicants to the EU and are in the process of making the necessary reforms. In May 2004, the Czech Republic, Estonia, Latvia, Lithuania, Hungary, Poland, Slovakia, and Slovenia became members of the EU. To be granted membership, each country had to meet specific standards in the areas of government, law, finance, and human rights. Membership does not mean that all reforms are complete, but that the countries have met the minimum established standards.

Rule of law, transparency, free markets, and democracy are a different way of operating than had been in place for the prior era. Each country's evolution has taken a different path, and each country is at a different place on the change continuum. What all of the countries have in common is that individuals do not necessarily give their full faith and trust to the systems. Creation of these systems is new, independence of enforcement is progressing, and transparency is a goal. However, keeping current and having trusted advisors are requirements for successful business in this region.

Process

While the structures are being created, they are not yet stable, trusted mechanisms for doing business. Business continues, however, using a combination of new structures and reliance on old networks. This section addresses how the separation between public and private life, importance of punctuality, and the flow of activities affect the conduct of doing business.

Privacy

Since an inner circle of family members and close friends has been an important part of getting things done in a hierarchical, centrally controlled economy, outsiders are viewed with a level of distrust, which takes time to overcome. Most of the countries in this region were invaded and inhabited by nomadic tribes at some time in their histories. One of the traditions of many nomadic peoples is hospitality, in terms of sharing food, drink, conversation, and is a highly valued part of the local tradition and culture. This characteristic has been widely retained in this region. However, hospitality and conversation do not necessarily include sharing personal information. Information that could be construed as antigovernment or illegal will not usually be discussed in social settings. Questions trying to elicit this information will raise suspicion.

In this environment, public life and private life are kept separate. Little information about one's private life is shared with any outsiders. It is important to determine what topics of conversation are appropriate for social occasions and what personal topics to avoid. Is it appropriate to talk about family members, holidays, politics, professional sports, or personal hobbies? Probably not for the first-time visitor. While any of these topics may be appropriate for conversations between friends, they may be too personal and, therefore, inappropriate for formal social conversations.

Trust develops over time. Initially, private but safe information about your family or the business environment might be shared, and, if the other person is appropriately discrete about using that knowledge, more information may be revealed over time. Progressing to a more informal style of interaction takes place very slowly and only if the foreigner can penetrate the intermediate circle while moving toward inclusion in the inner circle.

Continued adherence to local protocol and reliable performance on initial projects may result in movement toward inclusion in an intermediate circle, one reserved for trusted business partners. Oral agreements are considered binding, and you are only admitted to the intermediate circle if you uphold those agreements. Private information is shared only with members of the inner circle.

Punctuality

Since much of the infrastructure is under construction or reconstruction, electricity, heat, and transportation do not always function dependably. In this kind of environment, expectations for punctuality are not as stringent as in those countries on the task-orientation side of the Classification of Cultures Model. The commonly stated expectation is that meetings and activities will begin on time and be completed within the allotted time. The reality is that meetings and activities begin as soon as people arrive and are continued or postponed if not completed within the allotted time.

Flow of Activities

Most of these countries had an agrarian-based economy before becoming integrated into the Soviet system. As such, activities take place in a cyclical process, each with its allotted time, and can't be rushed. In addition, *efficiency* was not an important concept in the centrally controlled economies. Therefore, accomplishing tasks in the most efficient and effective manner has not been a criterion for measuring success. These tasks are only one part of life, a life over which individuals have little control. Tasks will be accomplished in their own good time, depending upon the tools available and whether systems are working.

Controlling the environment has not been a central concept, and taking individual responsibility for accomplishing tasks has not been a central value. Rather, workers followed directions, working to achieve goals imposed upon them and realizing that that they could work only within the confines of their environment depending upon whether the electricity or water was available or the heat was working. Increasing efficiency was not an issue if the basic requirements for doing their job were not reliable. On the other hand, high educational standards meant that people had the ability to do precise scientific work if and when the tools were available.

Communication

The former Soviet Union included 100 nationalities and more than 130 languages. The number of ethnic groups, religions, and the geographic expanse resulted in diverse world views within this region, directly affecting the communication process. This section examines the concept of truth, role of words, style, and form of logic that impact the practice of business.

Truth

Nomadic invasions, conquering armies, and changing boundaries resulted in the introduction of a number of religions into this area, including Greek Orthodox, Christian Orthodox, Bessarabian Orthodox, Old-Rite Russian Orthodox, Roman Catholic, Protestant, Sunni Muslim, Jewish, Calvinist,

Lutheran, Baptist, Pentecostal, and Unitarian. Monotheism is a common theme in all of these religions. Followers of these religions all have a strong belief in right and wrong and a universal truth.

In Russia during the Soviet era, participation in religious activities was banned. Not everyone abandoned their religion, but participation in religious celebration was severely curtailed. In an effort to protect one's self and family, not all information was readily shared in a straightforward manner. As a result, the concept of universal truth shifted. Truth is important; honesty is valued; protecting oneself and one's inner circle has an even higher priority. As a result, context is critical when presenting or challenging truth.

Words

With 130 different languages used in these countries, it is difficult to make generalizations. Most of the languages, however, are part of the Indic group, which views words as having specific meanings. Choosing words carefully is an important skill. Crafting the language of contracts is a serious discussion involving much detailed work that is best accomplished with native speakers and lawyers. The words identify who does what, when, and where. Determining the specificity of those concepts takes time.

Arguments over the interpretation will also take considerable time if there are disagreements later. When a disagreement occurs, the local partner is likely to go back to the contract and either rely upon the literal interpretation of the words in the contract or will talk about the intended meaning of the words in the contract. Whichever approach best provides an opportunity to defend the local partner's position will be taken. The result is that while the crafting of the contract was done with great care using words in a precise manner, disagreements will also be prolonged by arguing over which interpretation is more appropriate.

Style

These countries had large bureaucracies and slow decision-making processes when part of the centrally controlled economy. This vestige of the past economic system has not been completely eliminated, and there is a sense of formal protocol that needs to be observed. Determining a person's rank and age is important because proper protocol must be observed in both business and social meetings. Knowing the proper protocol for both occasions is important. New business and government structures, institutions, and agencies are being created that require a knowing partner to guide the visiting businessperson through the new system.

Determining who has the formal authority to make specific decisions, can authorize specific decisions, can authorize specific activities, and what set of protocol apply is a difficult but critical task. The informal network continues to exist, making it important to determine who the *information gatekeeper* is or to identify the person who influences decisions. Since strangers are not welcomed until relationships have been established, having an introduction from a respected intermediary is often a very valuable way of getting access to people who wield power.

If chosen carefully and if effective personal relationships are established, these contacts may even become mentors or allies as you continue to work in the country, and provide valuable advice and knowledge about business practices and methods, and help find new networks. Business needs to be conducted face to face in these countries. While a preliminary introduction may be done by letter, you will need to meet personally with the network, business, and government representatives. At these meetings, mentioning that you know other members of the network or their relatives can facilitate your acceptance into the group. As unfamiliar businesspeople, foreigners must demonstrate their patience and trustworthiness to the locals before trust will be given back. This process may seem time-consuming and difficult, but it is necessary and will usually result in attaining the objectives outlined at the home office.

Providing introductions is, at times, an opportunity for members of a network to earn additional income or favors in the former Soviet republics. When connections or contacts are important, *facilitation* or gratuity payments are common. However, these services and/or payments may be illegal depending upon the country in which the activity takes place, the country where the participants or companies are headquartered, or the country in which the individuals involved live and work. Therefore, determining the laws and regulations of the country in which your company is based, the country of your citizenship, and the country in which you will be doing this kind of business is absolutely essential before engaging in any of these activities. Further, your socialized values and judgments of the intentions of the participants requesting favors simply do not apply as long as no legal prohibitions are violated.

The agenda for initial business meetings is generally flexible. In the former Soviet Union, however, the agenda was usually controlled by the host in the country where the meeting was held. The initial discussions in any of these countries are generally relaxed and the participants cooperative, with questions, opinions, offers, and counteroffers being made. If the relationship between the parties develops well, the meetings might even be relatively informal or accompanied by informal meetings held after the formal meetings are adjourned.

As meetings progress, businesspeople from these countries generally seek a great deal of information about products, services, financing arrangements, warranties, and/or service. However, they are reluctant to provide much information. The outsider must be prepared to explain or expand on the outline of what is stated and to seek as much information as possible from the local businessperson. Because of scarcity in the past, purchasers from the Eastern European countries and Russia did not have much experience with making decisions when faced with a variety of choices. During the transition process, they have rapidly gained experience with making decisions among choices. However, what counts as a necessity in these countries is different from what counts as a necessity in developed countries; frugality in thinking is an ingrained value.

Logic

Making concessions and coming to an agreement in these countries does not happen easily. In Russia, the word for *compromise* was borrowed from another language. Suspicion can lead to confrontation. Inflexible views can also prolong the process of doing business. Resolving differences on substantive issues while maintaining a positive relationship requires a great deal of skill, effort, and time.

Negotiators can be competitive, confrontational, uncompromising, and inflexible. Relationships are often adversarial, with each side needing to win— or at least save face. However, confrontational words should be avoided to keep the exchange from becoming combative or personal, perhaps resulting in your potential partner walking away from the negotiation. Concessions are made slowly and cautiously and with great deliberation. Time away from the formal meetings, allowing both sides to seek opportunity from their partner's positions, is a part of the negotiation process and needs to be built into the planning for meetings.

Conclusion

While the ethnic, linguistic, and religious traditions in Eastern Europe and Russia include great diversity and while the agrarian tradition of countries was replaced by an industrial base at different rates, the centrally controlled economies of these countries created a similar set of institutions, policies, and procedures. The transition to a democratic form of government and free market economy is proceeding at a different rate in each country. As such, the laws, policies, and regulation change and need to be revisited frequently.

Finding trusted help when entering networks is essential for the visiting businessperson. The complexity of newly developed governments with the consequent evolution of regulations and practices is difficult to understand from the outside. Establishing trust, both within networks and with outside help, requires time and investigation, using both in-country and home country networks. While the difficulties of doing business in this region cannot be overlooked, the people are willing to work hard, look for opportunity to be recognized and valued, and can become long-term assets to a business. The work it takes to do business successfully in this region is often long and hard; but to those who have persevered, it has been rewarding both professionally and personally.

Chapter 7

Central and South America

Classification of Cultures Model

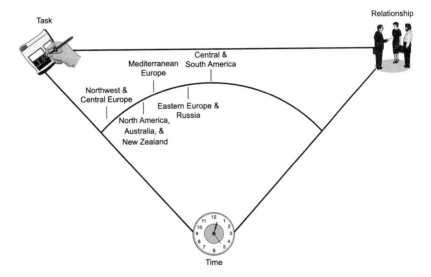

From Mexico to Ecuador and on to Chile, from Cuba to Guyana, from Costa Rica to Brazil, from the Bahamas to Peru and on to Argentina, Latin America is a diverse region of distinctive and unique countries. British, French, Dutch, Spanish, and Portuguese colonial cultures influenced the traditions, laws, and customs of highly developed Native American civilizations, creating a different culture not only in each country, but also in regions within many of these countries. As a result, an expatriate who is successful in one Latin country may not necessarily be successful in another country in this region. Developing effective business practices in one country does not automatically qualify an individual as a regional expert because of the breadth and diversity in this area.

At the same time, there is a distinctly identifiable "Latin" culture, developed over the last five centuries, that has common characteristics with local applications. Sophisticated Native American civilizations were thriving when European explorers arrived. Almost all of the countries share their primary cultural, political, educational, and spiritual heritage with the Mediterranean European countries. The colonial system flourished during the fifteenth to eighteenth centuries. This era concluded with wars for independence and attempts at feudalism during the nineteenth century. Internal and external conflicts arose early in the twentieth century as countries matured, while the latter half of the twentieth century has seen relative peace and economic progress in Latin America.

The Roman Catholic religion is a major historical and cultural force in almost all of these countries, influencing both thinking and way of life. While the late-twentieth-century social justice doctrines of Pope John XXIII had a profound effect in the region, the *Evangélico Pentecostal* or born-again philosophy is increasing. This philosophy moves away from the more tolerant *traditional* Roman Catholic orientation, with its tragic sense of life and death, toward a self-reform, self-empowerment view that emphasizes taking personal and group responsibility for life now, not just in the hereafter. As this movement develops, there may be significant social responses to this effort.

The commonality in history, religion, and political development is reflected by the inclusive nature of relationships in Latin America, whereby the other Spanish-speaking and, in some cases, other Romance-speaking countries are considered to be part of the *extended tribe*. Personal relationships are fundamental throughout Latin America, but differ significantly from relationships in other countries on the Task side of the Classification of Cultures Model and are closer to relationships in Eastern Europe and Russia. Relationships are not primarily between businesses and are not established on the basis of business friendships, but are **personal** links between individuals. Tasks serve as important measures of success, and Latin Americans are able to conduct business using a Task approach. The common European heritage of government and economic systems creates a thorough understanding of how to work on a time and task basis. However, the widely held preference is to conduct business using Latin American norms, in which time and personal relations are gauged differently. Interruptions for personal concerns are not viewed as a nuisance, but as an essential part of doing business. Tasks will be done well, but in accordance with a more flexible timetable.

The following sections will discuss the structure, process, and communication characteristics of conducting business in Latin America, remembering that diversity in this region creates different local working environments in each country.

Global Business Practices Model

Areas of World	Gov't	Law	Hier.	Privacy	Punct.	Flow	Truth	Words	Style	Logic
Northwest & Central Europe										
North America, Australia, & NZ										
Mediterranean Europe										
Eastern Europe & Russia										
South & Central America										

LEGEND

Role of Government: White = the government sets parameters and constraints to create the environment for doing business. Black = Direct involvement of government in business as a business partner.
Rule of Law: White = Reliance on systems and procedures. Black = Pragmatism or situational considerations.
Sense of Hierarchy: White = Assumption of equality. Black = Assumption of status difference.
View of Privacy: White = Business and private matters are separate. Black = Business and private matters are all part of one reality.
Punctuality: White = Fixed time. Black = Flexible or "rubber" time.
Flow of Activities: White = Time works in a linear fashion. Black = Time works in a cyclical fashion.
Truth: White = Universal truth. Black = Many truths exist at once.
Words: White = Words have explicit meanings. Black = Words have implicit meanings.
Style: White = Communication is direct and forthright. Black = Communication is indirect.
Logic: White = Formal deductive reasoning. Black = Alternative heuristic.

Structure

The transition period of creating new government, financial, and legal systems began in Latin America long before Eastern Europe and Russia began the process. In fact, managers who were successful during the tumultuous times of excessive inflation in Latin America are now being sought for advice in Eastern Europe and Russia. As in Eastern Europe, Latin American countries are not all at the same point in the transition process. This section will address the hierarchy, role of government, and rule of law as structural elements that have an impact on business practices.

Hierarchy

Latin American society is stratified depending upon whether an individual is born into a family that is a member of the wealthy class or the struggling class. Despite the growth of a middle class in the latter part of the twentieth century, social class boundaries remain fairly rigid with regard to everyone's *place* or status. In addition to an individual's family, factors such as religious background can also determine a person's place. For instance, being a member of the Catholic religion is an indicator of character and respectability. Education can provide entry into the higher classes, and has certainly contributed to the growing middle class. However, coming from a "good family" is probably more important than having an MBA—since neither merit nor potential is as critical to success as old money and traditionally valued characteristics. An individual's power and influence comes from social position, personal qualities, and *ubicacion*, where one is plugged into the network of personal relations and how effectively these relations are maintained and nurtured.

With the exception of Argentina, Costa Rica, and Jamaica, Power Distance[1] scores for Latin American countries are significantly higher than those in North America or Northwest and Central Europe, meaning that hierarchy is well established, accepted, and respected. In accordance with a formal class structure, organizations rely on an entrenched hierarchy and centralized decision making. For instance, governments control political parties, industrial monopolies, and large private sector firms through their roles as dispensers of permits, operating licenses, jobs, and contracts. However, in many instances, people are more important than position in the hierarchical structure because authority resides more in the person and his or her connections than in the position. Having the *right friends* means knowing someone who can open doors and get appointments with the proper authorities to obtain authorizing papers or allow permissive circumstances for the business. For example, Brazilians are noted for *jeitinho*, that is, the way they get around impersonal bureaucracies.

Meeting and being accepted by someone who has influence within a particular business sector is a critical step for entering the network unless, of course, a product has no equivalent competition or needs no permits. In these cases, the product will create a local demand that will eventually be satisfied by a local competitor who is better connected than the foreigner and who has taken the time to develop the local network to work to local advantage.

People and network relationships come first, with job and organizations being second. Both levels must be developed for long-term business to take place in Latin America. As a result, nepotism is a common practice, and people often are more loyal to their immediate bosses than to the organization. Superiors are accorded respect and loyalty from their immediate subordinates and, in turn, bestow *favors* on their subordinates, expect their

---

[1] Geert Hofstede's research identifies five dimensions of culture. High scores in Power Distance demonstrate the degree to which members of the society recognize inequalities of power. See www.geert-hofstede.com.

decisions and orders to be followed, and have subordinates do much of the groundwork before meetings take place. Since each person with power builds a group of loyal followers, the large, complex, and highly sophisticated organization with many departments working toward a shared goal is not common. A more common arrangement is to have organizations comprising many small units, subgroups, or companies of different sizes, each loyal to its own boss, working together when it is in the best interest of a person's immediate boss.

Two kinds of managers are typical. A *caudillo* is the owner-manager, almost exclusively male, who holds all of the power and authority for a company and is master in this domain. The *caudillo* is a strong man who gives orders to his subordinates but is ready to do the bidding of someone more powerful. A *patron* is a man of power or wealth who receives loyalty from those of lesser status. The *patron* may be an important political official, a traditional landowner, a moneylender, or a merchant. The patron is not only extremely powerful, but he is also considered to be knowledgeable on a wide variety of subjects. Therefore, those dealing with the patron must be respectful, never openly questioning his opinions or decisions.

Decisions, generally, are made by the person of highest authority. In the postcolonial past, the Catholic bishop or priest in the area often had a role in making decisions for the community. As Catholicism decreases in importance in the daily lives of people, especially in urban areas, church officials are no longer an integral part of the decision-making process.

Delegation and teamwork are not normal ways of doing business. Typically, bosses decide what is to be done, and subordinates follow directions without asking questions. The person representing the company in a meeting may have been assigned because of individual charisma or power, not necessarily because of personal knowledge. Therefore, decisions are not likely to be made during the meeting, especially if the central decision maker is not present or if the decision requires technical expertise.

Although this chapter presents a Latin American perspective, it is important to remember that each country has its own distinct culture—of which its citizens are justly proud. Businesspeople in these countries not only identify with each other as fellow Latin Americans, but also value their own heritage as the best. Therefore, hiring someone who has been forced to depart from one of the Latin American countries because his or her *patron* lost power or influence and has not developed the appropriate personal relationships or networks with the current leadership is not a wise step for improving your company's business in the local country. In addition, hiring a Portuguese-speaking Brazilian manager to be in charge of an operation in Spanish-speaking Chile or Honduras is not likely to be successful, unless some unique relationship with people in the appropriate network or family already exists. Similarly, employing a native Spanish speaker from Peru to run the Brazilian operation is also likely to be fraught with potential difficulty.

Specific individuals have access to power in the network; individuals make decisions and enter business deals on behalf of organizations. The relationships are formed **between individuals**, not necessarily between organizations. Those individuals with the power to make decisions are of a higher class and expect deference from those who have a lower status. Therefore, demonstrating the proper respect to these individuals is essential.

Government

Even in those cases in which a Latin American country continues with the colonial power's head of state as the official leader, as in Aruba, where the governor is appointed by the Queen of the Netherlands, the local countries have sovereignty and elect their representatives to the legislature. The remaining countries instituted constitutional democracies or a form of parliamentary democracy with the executive, legislative, and judicial branches of government being independent. This process has not been smooth, without setbacks, or completed in all countries. The Organization of American States and the Carter Center consistently find improvement in the election process of most Latin American countries.

Some countries retained more power in the executive branch of government, but most established three independent branches of government. One major problem in this region has been the history of favors and bribes. As a result, the three branches of government and the elected officials do not always make independent decisions. Knowing that officials' decisions can be influenced means that people do not yet have confidence in the system operating independently in a transparent manner. Progress is being made, but the stability of government continues to be fragile in this region. Businesspeople new to the region must find facilitators, lawyers, or trusted partners in the local country and in the home country to negotiate the legal system and remain in business.

Rule of Law

Because interpersonal relationships are so important and because success depends upon the exercise of power through an interdependent network of people, agreements must be made during face-to-face meetings. Titles and job functions are not relevant; individual power and influence are the critical issues. Contracts are often awarded on the basis of family and personal connections. Because decision making is centralized, the most powerful individuals make the decisions, and these individuals are part of an interdependent network. Therefore, trade-offs among industries, companies, and government agencies are often possible. For instance, an individual could orchestrate a trade-off on tariffs for vegetables in return for permits to build a manufacturing facility. Sometimes Latin American negotiators do not understand why businesspeople representing a foreign company operating within a hierarchical, bureaucratic society are not able to make similar deals involving government agencies or other companies since this is routine business practice for them.

Initial agreements at these face-to-face meetings are oral and, while those agreements are a good sign, obtaining a signed, written contract is verification that the agreement was more than a face-saving tactic. The written, signed contract embodies a meaning that is substantially different from its significance in Australia, Canada, Northwest and Central Europe, and New Zealand.

A contract in Latin America is perceived more as a work of art than an immutable agreement and should be appreciated as such. That statement includes a number of *silent assumptions*. First, the contract expresses an ideal and should not be expected to cover the detailed, practical world in *all* cases. Second, the specific agreements are goals rather than absolutes. For instance, the times specified in the contract are desirable objectives, not binding promises. Third, the promises made are fewer than those in contracts from countries with low-context languages, such as the USA, the United Kingdom, or Germany. Fourth, the agreement is on goals and not necessarily on the means to reach those goals. Issues such as time, place, or division of labor are not specified or resolved in the contract.

Therefore, many agreements are made with good intentions but not necessarily complied with in every detail. Why would a businessperson enter into a contract, knowing that the probability of fulfilling the terms of the deal is low? How is that considered making a deal in *good faith*? Because much of the legal and governmental system is unpredictable in many parts of Latin America, businesses retain a certain flexibility in delivering on contracts, a concept that is difficult for non-Latins to appreciate or understand.

The pessimistic or fatalistic perspective that comes from living through major shifts in government, systems, and currency fluctuations accepts the premise that wealth can come and go or that chance guides destiny. Given that attitude, a businessperson may agree to a contract in good faith, knowing that the probability of fulfilling the terms is low because everyone knows that the future is indefinite and any of the following can happen: (1) The buyer may renege on the contract, thereby ending the transaction; (2) other work that has priority may be canceled, making it possible to fulfill the order after all; (3) the buyer may wait until the day after the deadline to call, using sickness or an emergency as an excuse, thereby giving the seller an extra day and the opportunity to set a new date; (4) the buyer may die, thereby relieving the seller of any obligation; (5) the seller may die and, therefore, will not be required to fulfill the obligation; and (6) who knows? A miracle might happen, and the work will be completed on time. Even if the probability of fulfilling the contract is low, the possibility of fulfilling it still exists; so the contract is signed in good faith with good feelings toward all participants.

Interdependent relationships include an assumption of giving and returning favors; what is considered corruption by North American or Northwest European standards is seen as natural and normal in this setting. Independent legal systems are being created and established in Latin America. However, given the influence of powerful *patrons* and historically pervasive corruption, the legal system cannot be depended upon to enforce agreements. The rule of law is not the established norm for business practices throughout the region. As a result, relationships are relied upon as the vehicle for resolving problems, either directly among participants or indirectly through the use of intermediaries.

Businesspeople agree to contracts as a moral bond to please the other side, to bestow a favor, to engender an obligation, to exercise power, or to acquire power. Understanding the *silent assumptions* of what a contract means in Latin America is critical for determining appropriate follow-up activities after the contract has been signed. Since the contract may not include the specificity of who does what, when, and where or since the details may not be met precisely, signing a contract is not the end of the deal. A more appropriate perspective is to immediately begin to plan for the follow-up activities necessary to manage the implementation of the contract.

In addition to regular, formal communication tools, the informal, personal interdependent networks are an essential component for determining the ultimate success not only of the specific contract for a particular project, but also for the possibility of developing a long-term working relationship. As a result, having different levels of people from your organization—for example, technicians, engineers, salespeople, marketing research specialists, top management, or accountants—periodically spend time with their counterparts and friends in Latin America is absolutely necessary. As the socializing and conversation take place, the company representative has opportunities to listen for relevant information and attend to the silent assumptions of the situation to determine what, if any, problems have occurred, might occur, or are being handled.

Early detection of potential problems makes it possible not only to solve problems, but also, if done in a culturally sensitive manner, to enable local contacts to be successful in overcoming problems, thereby increasing their respect, status, and power. This process can have significant, long-term advantages in building a successful working relationship. Relationships can be established only by personal contact and social interaction. Electronic communication is not a relationship, merely a tool for the minimal maintenance of relationships.

Process

Without a well-established rule of law and role of government, the practice of doing business uses a different sense of timing. This section will examine business practices related to the separation between public and private lives, punctuality, and the flow of activities.

Privacy

Personal relationships are fundamental to any Latin American business, organizational, or societal function. In the United States, casual friendships can develop quickly without much substance, but personal relationships in Latin America take longer to develop and involve a greater depth of understanding, caring, and mutual responsibility. Relationships emphasize the total person and are based on respect and trust, which is developed over frequent interactions characterized by warm conversations in both business and social situations.

The fundamental set of relationships is the family unit as the center of economic, political, social, and religious life. The family provides not only companionship and a common set of values, but also protection. The family exists to support and protect all its members as they pursue individual goals. Therefore, privacy is important. Meetings are usually conducted in private behind closed doors; homes are generally surrounded by fences or high walls, and many have personal guards. It is customary for visitors to come by invitation, rather than dropping in unexpectedly. A sense of distrust of and distance from those outside the family is very common. In particular, foreigners are considered members of the *out-group*; that is, they do not enjoy the same privileges as members of the in-group and receive different treatment. Penetrating the barrier and becoming a trusted friend or member of the family takes time and effort and great consideration. Once allowed inside, the foreigner assumes obligations to maintain the relationship, even when no longer responsible for the business that brought about the opportunity for the relationship in the first place.

The connection between family relationships and business groups is so strong that it is difficult to separate the two. Although individuals are unique, they are not considered equal in Latin American society. Holding power is a major objective, and individuals strive for personal power, which is translated into *palanca*, or leverage. Those individuals with *palanca* have a strong network of contacts, are respected by other influential leaders, project an aura of personal significance, are forceful with their opinions and decisions, and mete out rewards and punishment as appropriate given their status.

Having selected representatives from the Latin American operations visit your facilities, offering your hospitality with ceremony and appropriate protocol, publicly praising the effort and accomplishments of those individuals, and listening for cues to any potential problems during business *and* social activities are important to developing business in Latin America. The status and power of these individuals is increased, sensitivity to their needs has been demonstrated, and the personal relationship has been significantly strengthened, preparing the way for future possibilities.

Another essential dimension of personal relationships is *machismo*, which has many connotations: attitude of men toward women, power and virility, competitiveness, a zest for action, a need to demonstrate forcefulness, self-confidence and courage, and a strong sense of pride in family and country. Any word, deed, or attitude that might be a slight to a person's self-esteem or dignity is considered a grave provocation and can irretrievably damage a personal relationship. Business associates and coworkers need to be treated with a warm, personal approach that respects their self-esteem and pride. People from Northwest Europe, Canada, or the USA are often viewed as *insensitive* because they avoid any discussions of an insightful or emotional nature.

A warm, personal approach in Latin America is not the same as a warm, personal approach in other regions of the business world. For example, in the USA, speaking with a subordinate as an equal may be a sign of respect, but doing so in Latin America not only causes a loss of respect for the superior but also violates the other person's privacy. When the non-Latin is circulating through the workplace or is socially visiting with workers, the conversation needs to demonstrate understanding and caring for Latin people as individuals. Social competence is as important as technical competence for developing a warm, personal relationship. Addressing the person by name and talking about the person's family, health, hobbies, or interests is appropriate. In addition, asking questions about special interests, local sports teams, museums, architecture, local art, or historical monuments would all demonstrate an interest in the other person and make room for expressions of pride without violating an individual's privacy. Discussing business, asking questions that require more than superficial self-disclosure, or asking someone to identify areas of weakness is not appropriate. Humorous remarks about local people, sights, politics, religion, or events are considered inappropriate in almost all cases.

This sense of privacy and general level of conversation is accompanied by a much closer physical distance between people than is considered appropriate in countries that do not value personal relationships as highly, such as the USA, the United Kingdom, or Germany. Typically, men stand or sit closer together and touch more often, usually with a hand on the other person's shoulder or arm. Greetings among friends often include the *abrazao*, or embrace. The emphasis on personal relationships includes physically recognizing the other person as well as demonstrating an interest in that person. However, handshakes, the use of titles, and formal conversation remain the norm until the Latin initiates a more personal approach.

Punctuality

Latin Americans have a strong sense of family and enjoy working with people. Spending time with people and making a connection is important, as is viewing time as flexible, which affects scheduling, the completion of tasks, and the ways Latin Americans relate to others. Completing tasks in accordance with specifications and on time is a priority and a measure of success, but is not the highest priority. Personal relationships are often the highest priority and a measure of success; therefore, time spent interacting with others is viewed as a critical business activity. Given this orientation to time, task, and relationships, businesspeople must consider the implications for conducting business.

The Latin American's polychronic sense of time, similar to that of the Mediterranean European's, can be disorienting for the business partner from a culture with a monochronic view of time, such as Germany or the USA. Important tasks will be addressed first; however, important tasks may be family issues. A polychronic orientation assumes that there is always more time available for completing a task. Attention must be given to important issues first—those that affect the network. If those issues are not satisfactorily resolved, no tasks will be completed. The network members are personal friends, all of whom need to receive attention.

Someone of great influence has many demands and is attending to many important issues. Expecting that person to be on time for an appointment is unreasonable. If someone does not come to your appointment on time, it may be a sign of respect—an acknowledgement that you are too important to be expected to be on time. As Latin American businesspeople engage in business with representatives from multinational companies, punctuality is less often an issue. Videoconferences begin and end at prescribed times. Requests are often made about whether the scheduled meeting is "North American" or "British" time or local time so participants know whether they are expected to be "on time." However, given infrastructure challenges or unavoidable personal emergencies, having flexible expectations regarding punctuality is reasonable in Latin America.

Flow of Activities

Developing personal relationships with the *right people* takes time, so the business process automatically slows down. Cold call selling is not normally an effective technique, unless a product is the only one of its kind on the market. Patience must be exercised to spend the time necessary to simultaneously develop relationships with those individuals who have the connections necessary to allow access to the decision makers and to determine which permits, licenses, or contracts may be necessary to do business. Entering the network is a formidable barrier to the non-Latin, but one that must be addressed to do business successfully. Learning whom to contact, how to contact that person, what to ask, and how to ask are necessary skills for successfully penetrating the confusing barrier of networks in Latin America.

As the fundamental unit of society, families come first, even before business. Business schedules and public appointments are not allowed to interfere with activities involving family or close friends. These personal relationships are interdependent and involve a set of responsibilities. As a result, interruptions for personal reasons can delay business conversations until the personal problems are resolved. Since Latin Americans view time as circular rather than linear, more time is always available for task activities. Attending to the personal issues enables participants to gather information, influence decisions, resolve disagreements, grant favors, and exercise power.

Another area of significance that affects the character, worldview, and flow of business activities in Latin America is the role of carnivals and holidays, which have their origin in feast days celebrated in the Catholic religion. On the one hand, the events include solemn ceremonies, receptions, and processions accompanied with pomp and circumstance marking anything from the opening of a new factory to a traditional feast day. On a much deeper level, these celebrations depict emotional events involving death, rebirth, and new beginnings. During these carnivals and fiestas, people have an opportunity to attack authority figures, which offers an opportunity to diffuse hostility by poking fun at some aspects of daily life. Masked and costumed figures provide an opportunity to express emotions through dramatic forms, such as dance or poetry. People relax and enjoy themselves in a public party or celebration atmosphere. In addition, these events mark the passage of time and the place of time; that is, life is perceived as a repetition of the life cycle patterns in nature, a circular rather than linear process.

Without understanding the historical and religious context, foreigners often miss the importance and significance of carnival time. Even today, in an environment in which the Catholic Church has less influence in some areas, carnival represents an emotional time of renewal in which the spirit is reinvigorated, dreams are renewed, and people remember their heritage.

These events are central to life in Latin America and take precedence over normal business activities. Without understanding the cultural significance of these kinds of events, the foreigner may interpret the Latins' willingness to stop work for parties as merely an excuse not to work. However, these celebrations are a time to vent frustration with the rigid social structure or with particular community leaders, to exercise creative talents, and to refresh the spirit before returning to more controlled daily activities. A popular Latin sentiment is that people work to live; they do not live to work. This is often misinterpreted in daily activities, by foreigners, as not being focused or as being easily distracted.

The business traveler also needs to adjust to the flow of the workday. Since both personal relationships and tasks are important, the business process includes both professional and social activities. Mealtimes are social activities—a time to get to know one another on a personal level, not for conducting business. This does not mean that the workday is shorter; rather that time is distributed differently. Work generally begins by 9 A.M., followed by a two-hour lunch break. Since people return to work later in the afternoon, they work into the evening. As a result, the evening meal, which is another occasion for developing relationships, begins late in the evening. This flow of activities can be a difficult adjustment for travelers who are not used to this schedule and who may be experiencing jet lag at the same time. Adapting to this pace of activities can take patience and will test your stamina.

Communication

The predominant languages in Latin America are Spanish and Portuguese. This section will address the role of words, forms of logic, style of communication, and role of truth in business communication.

The Role of Truth

Personal relationships are fundamental to any Latin American business, organizational, or societal function and are based on respect and trust, which is developed over frequent interactions characterized by warm conversations in both business and social situations. Language is often more *flowery*, taking time to show honor and respect to the other person. An individual's place in society determines whether that person has enough power to reward and punish others, the amount of respect due that person, and the proper tone of voice and manner to be used when addressing that individual. If proper respect is not demonstrated or something is said that is taken as a challenge to one's honor, the offense is not taken lightly and will affect business dealings.

Since informal meetings and the transfer of information occur continually at many levels within and across organizations, care must be taken when divulging information to ensure that the information being shared is consistently shared with everyone, because the grapevine is so efficient that everyone is likely to hear the information eventually. What is considered *honest* information and how it should be used varies greatly and is heavily influenced by culture. With the North American's value on equality, openness, and being direct, discussions include the exchange of much candid information. This perspective is viewed as being "too open" in Latin America. Not only is a frank exchange of views or information not viewed positively, it can also be viewed with suspicion. Words and data are used to present the most favorable view possible for your position, point of view, or argument in Latin America. Therefore, information presented by the other side is often considered to be suspect, presenting a view that is as favorable as possible.

Words

While a few countries in Central and South America have a colonial legacy of speaking French, English, or Dutch, the primary languages in the region are Spanish and Portuguese. These languages rely more on the context of the situation than do English, German, Swedish, or Dutch (Hall, 1981). Therefore, stated *and* unstated assumptions must be interpreted in accordance with the body language, gestures, and facial expressions of the participants as well as the assumptions associated with particular situations, such as time, space, patterns of activities, roles of actors, and rules governing the situations. If the interpretations are not thoughtfully considered and evaluated, trivial actions can lead to major misunderstandings. Insensitivity to actions, assumptions, and interpretations results in misinterpretation of motives, which can ruin a potential agreement.

The shared history of Latin American countries includes instances of mass oppression, failure, acceptance, and endurance. Accordingly, many people have come to expect inequality or oppression and have adopted a pessimistic or fatalistic view toward solving problems. Therefore, if a foreigner's approach appears to threaten the Latin American's position or perspective, the probability of success is very low. A more effective approach is liberally compliment Latin American participants, to give them respect, and to project an attitude that an attempt is being made to do things their way rather than imposing the foreigner's way of doing things. Words need to be chosen carefully. Erring on the side of demonstrating tact and respect is a good guideline.

Logic

Social conversations, aimed at getting to know one another and establish a personal connection, are also a preparation for discussions of business issues. As topics are examined in a social setting, each side is engaged in identifying principles, values, and considerations that are important to the other side. As in Mediterranean Europe, agreeing to main principles establishes a foundation from which later discussions evolve, and these principles rarely, if ever, change. Therefore, participants need to carefully consider the principles before agreeing to a vague, ambiguous statement with the intention of getting or making clarifications later. Urgency to move to a discussion of the task is not merely ill mannered; it is a tactical error. Time must be taken to develop a personal relationship and to understand the whole person and his or her view of the world.

When creating persuasive arguments, a primary consideration is identifying an approach that will benefit the other participants and their boss, remembering that these people are generally concerned about their family, personal friends, position of power, and personal influence. Self-interest is a significant motivator in societies that emphasize the accumulation of power and wealth as a major objective, measure of success, and indicator of the prestige of a person.

Compromise is not perceived as a virtue; not having to concede is often a matter of honor. Disagreements are not stated directly or pointedly, as that could be perceived as a challenge to one's honor. Since requests are often inflated and neither side wants to lose respect by making any concessions, achieving agreement among participants can be extremely difficult. When evaluating arguments to arrive at a decision, Latin Americans use an approach called *projectismo*, or development of plans without critical analyses based upon the assumption that, in due time, all will be eventually accomplished as best it can. The cultural inclination to pessimism or fatalism results in a boom-or-bust attitude. Without needing all of the details of *how* a plan will work, businesspeople usually rely on either agreement on general principles or the experience and advice of a well-respected individual in a particular situation. Power and influence, exercised during discussions at critical points, can be very persuasive.

One of the major factors affecting the conduct of business is the style of the individuals involved. Individual style includes not only one's personality, but also the verbal ability to project the force of one's personality. Latin Americans often use the word *no* preceding a statement of disagreement, followed by dramatic and patriotic persuasive appeals. Silent periods will be few and far between. As soon as participants understand, or think they understand, another's point of view, they tend to interrupt and fight for the floor or *airtime* to add to the conversation. Distributive, hard-sell, or win-lose bargaining tactics may be used quite effectively.

While conversations are likely to be loud and argumentative, participants must continue to defer to authority by using the appropriate tone of voice with superiors and subordinates. Disagreements often are carefully phrased to avoid embarrassing the more powerful people. Foreigners must pay particular attention to the indirect, often circuitous logic required to defer to superiors in discussions. Participants, coworkers, and friends will work hard behind the scenes by exercising their power and influence to grant concessions or to offer other attractive benefits to move to an agreement. Relationships will be maintained at all costs since today's adversary may be tomorrow's partner.

If backed into a corner, if everything else has failed, and if the other side has more power, one side will make a concession if the outcome is desirable. However, the concession must not be the focus of discussion. Rather, it would be more appropriate to acknowledge any concession in a positive manner, suggesting that it was a sound idea of the giving side instead of a demand by the receiving side.

Style

Initially, greetings and conversation are more formal and elaborate than those in North America. Business jackets will not be removed, even when the temperature is extremely warm; titles and last names will be used; norms of proper etiquette must be followed; hospitality will be offered and is expected to be cordially received; hearty laughter is inappropriate; and *flowery* forms of language will be used. Take time to learn about the other person.

Direct questions during face-to-face meetings with the other side generally are not effective in soliciting information. Communicating with friends of friends, who know the other participants and their boss, is an essential part of doing business and a useful way of gathering information. This method is an effective way of determining the self-interests of the individuals with whom you are doing business. The information gathered is necessary for personalizing appeals during discussions.

Formal meetings that incorporate the use of protocol, social activities, and official presentations do occur and are a measure of a participant's professionalism. Discussions are likely to become enmeshed in power plays among equally strong-willed people and can be effectively resolved only informally. Continuing the formal process would, in many cases, preclude resolution.

When difficulties, disagreements, or differences of opinion arise, the response, generally, is to rely upon personal relationships for resolving problems. Individuals, acting informally, call on friends, make contact at various levels within the organization, pass information to the organization, and use their ability to reward friends by influencing the process, or offer and request favors from friends. Informal meetings and the transfer of information occur continually throughout business discussions at many levels of the organization using whatever forms of communication are available. This practice can be disconcerting to foreign businesspeople, who expect more direct and explicit business practices.

Doing favors may be expected and has been an accepted part of business, but laws against bribery are very specific. Check with legal counsel in the home office to understand the constraints and guidelines that need to be followed in anticipation of being asked for favors. As the legal systems become well established, enforcement of all legislation will be more rigidly enforced.

Conclusion

On the one hand, formalities and protocol such as introductions, periodic visits, thank-you notes, and regular, *formal* communication are important for establishing and maintaining relationships on a personal level. On the other hand, given the assumption that contracts are an ideal that does not necessarily apply in day-to-day situations, given that much information is transferred between organizations by *informal* contacts at all levels through networks of social contacts, and given that loss of respect is a serious issue, businesspeople must find a way to fulfill the personal relationship requirements and achieve the goals of the contract.

The Latin American assumptions regarding time, task, and relationships create a complex business environment. Not only are personal relationships more important, but they are also inherently different and require that a caring, understanding personal bond be developed over time. Power, status, and connections are core concepts dictating the relationship between individuals and determining the parameters of business relationships. The importance of personal relationships and the polychronic approach to time not only allow for but also encourage the interruption and/or delay of business conversation until personal issues are resolved.

Discussions are often volatile and intense. People enjoy expressing their opinions. After many long conversations to resolve differences, partners arrive at an agreement if the relationship is strong. A contract is viewed as a work of art representing ideal circumstances rather than a set of specifications governing future activities. The intentions of both parties, embodied in the agreement, are followed not because of the nature of the contract itself or fear of enforcement by the courts, but rather by the strength of the personal relationships that have developed. Attending to and maintaining these relationships allows for the successful accomplishment of the task and establishes the foundation for long-term business activity. In the meantime, businesspeople must manage the details of the contract effectively to meet the objectives of the agreement.

CHAPTER 8

INDIA

Classification of Cultures Model

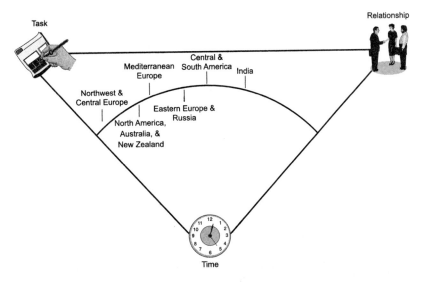

While India is part of the Commonwealth of Nations and was a former British colony, its historical development and culture are significantly different from that of Australia, Canada, New Zealand, and the USA. All of these countries had an aboriginal culture that was essentially tribal in nature. India had one of the most richly developed ancient civilizations even when Alexander the Great arrived in the third century B.C. The first of many successive invasions of India occurred around 1500 B.C., bringing the Aryans from central Asia. Over the subsequent centuries, a series of invaders, including Arabs, Afghans, and Turks, created a unique cultural blend of Hindu, Buddhist, and Muslim philosophies, which are major influences on Indian thinking today.

When the Europeans began exploring the Indian Ocean in the early 1600s, the first organized efforts from England were those of the efficient and ruthless British East Indian Company in 1619. After establishing control over the subcontinent, the Company eventually was forced to transfer political power to the British Crown. England administered most of India directly or through treaties with individual royal rulers. Efforts to establish sovereignty began in the late 1800s, resulting in independence in 1947 as part of the inevitable move from colonies to countries after World War II. Creation of independence led to the partition of the subcontinent, as the inevitable result of the unwillingness of two major religions to coexist as minorities. The enmity between Hindus and Muslims led to the creation of East and West Pakistan as Islamic states, where there were Muslim majorities. In 1950, India became a republic within the Commonwealth of Nations. With the unique challenges of addressing the concerns of such a vast population, India continues as the world's largest democracy and has made enormous internal changes to attain a competitive position in the global economy.

The mixture of Hindu and Muslim religions among the large native population is a significant difference in India from other former British colonies. These traditions, having been established in independent kingdoms and sultanates over the centuries before British rule, have local variations. Neither religious tradition has any relation to the philosophies of Aristotle or Plato, and was not substantially changed by exposure to the British administration in India. While the British encouraged the spread of Christianity, all of the major religious sects in India continued to coexist under British rule. Within this historical diversity, the local population has had significant authority for self-rule and has been a democracy since 1950.

Given the history of kingdoms and sultanates, well established before the introduction of modern communication and with 216 distinct languages, local regions naturally developed distinctive cultures. There are 15 recognized languages, with Hindi established as the official language and spoken by about 30 percent of the population. Certainly India can be described as a true mosaic culture—many distinctive local cultures existing within the framework of one country.

This chapter will discuss the impact of structure, process, and communication on business practices in India. However, any generalizations about India must always be checked with the local situation for unique or specific variations, and the visiting businessperson must be ready to adapt accordingly.

Structure

The role of government, rule of law, and hierarchy have a major impact on the transparency and conduct of business practices in India. This section will address each topic in more detail.

Global Business Practices Model

Areas of World	Gov't	Law	Hier.	Privacy	Punct.	Flow	Truth	Words	Style	Logic
Northwest & Central Europe										
North America, Australia, & NZ										
Mediterranean Europe										
Eastern Europe & Russia										
South & Central America										
India										

LEGEND

Role of Government: White = the government sets parameters and constraints to create the environment for doing business. Black = Direct involvement of government in business as a business partner.

Rule of Law: White = Reliance on systems and procedures. Black = Pragmatism or situational considerations.

Sense of Hierarchy: White = Assumption of equality. Black = Assumption of status difference.

View of Privacy: White = Business and private matters are separate. Black = Business and private matters are all part of one reality.

Punctuality: White = Fixed time. Black = Flexible or "rubber" time.

Flow of Activities: White = Time works in a linear fashion. Black = Time works in a cyclical fashion.

Truth: White = Universal truth. Black = Many truths exist at once.

Words: White = Words have explicit meanings. Black = Words have implicit meanings.

Style: White = Communication is direct and forthright. Black = Communication is indirect.

Logic: White = Formal deductive reasoning. Black = Alternative heuristic.

Role of Government

With limited transportation, limited communication, and the increased competition for scarce resources as the population rapidly increased in the preindustrial period, personal relationships evolved as a primary way to survive and thrive. Since personal relationships had proven successful prior to independence, it was natural to carry close personal relationships into the government-business dynamic. Due to the enduring influence of the British colonial system, elements of both parliamentary democracy and Adam Smith's philosophy of business are the foundation of today's system of government.

With 28 states and 7 union territories, there are 250 members of the Council of States and 545 seats in the People's Assembly, creating a large elected government that represents over 1 billion citizens. India has many more political parties than in less populous countries, resulting in many different views on what the government should do in any situation. Within this democratic structure, establishing a countrywide majority position on any issue or in a national election does not happen often. The ruling authority is derived as a result of coalitions of political parties. The authority to govern remains stable as long as the coalition is stable. When the coalition begins to unravel, a new configuration of parties creates a new ruling coalition. As in Latin America, loyalty is based upon relationships and connections with people rather than formal systems because those systems are subject to change and protection comes from people rather than systems.

With a central government and subordinate state governments, there are levels of bureaucracy that often result in difficult and tedious administrative requirements that are difficult to fathom by foreign businesspeople. With the significance of personal relationships in modern India, paperwork moves more quickly or slowly depending on how well you know the person doing the paperwork, whether someone intercedes on your behalf, or whether you offer gifts to gain the bureaucrat's favor. All of these characteristics erode confidence in the government as a reliable, transparent system.

Rule of Law

The Indian legal system is based upon English common law, creating a structure that is similar to that in Great Britain, the rest of the Commonwealth countries, and the USA. Separate personal law codes apply to Muslims, Christians, and Hindus. However, in business, written contracts are important, with long negotiations over the precise wording of the contract.

As in other areas of the world, the belief in the ambiguous nature of the future makes people in India wary of describing future events in absolute terms. To the people in India, the future is uncertain and unforeseeable and new coalitions will likely create shifts in policies and procedures. Therefore, the terms of a contract may need to be adjusted. The sense and intent of the contract will be upheld because maintaining one's honor is critical; however, the details of execution may no longer be possible. Depending upon current circumstances, people will rely upon their connections or the offer of bribes to make things work, to move approvals through the bureaucracy, or to get documents signed.

The networks in India are social in nature, based upon family ties, which means that people from different firms or organizations get to know each other first as people. Only after taking stock of the person, learning his or her values and attitudes, and developing personal ties, will business relationships begin to evolve. These personal relationships involve an obligation to provide personal favors and offer assistance when asked. These loyalties create bonds that are stronger than a legal document. Maintaining one's standing of honor in these networks is critical for success. If your honor is tarnished, the ability to develop future business is jeopardized. The intricacies of the social network, however, are difficult for an outsider to penetrate, creating a legal system that is not necessarily transparent to an outsider. The nature of the interconnected social network will be addressed in the next section.

Hierarchy

Hinduism, Buddhism, Jainism, and Islam have all had a major influence in India in different but sometimes overlapping areas of the subcontinent, at different times. Islam and Hinduism each believe in the existence of one God; a major difference is that Islam believes in one manifestation of God, while the Hindu God is infinite with many manifestations.

Currently, 80 percent of the Indian population identifies itself as a member of the Hindu religion, with the second highest percentage (13 percent) as members of Islam. The caste system, as described in Hinduism, is an attempt to create an efficient human society based on the strength of its educational/knowledge-pursuit system (Brahmin), its military and defense system (Kshatriya), its economical and business system (Vaishya), and a strong, happy, productive workforce (Shudras). The caste system evolved over an extended time until there were thousands of castes. This system gave each individual a place in the social structure, for both identify and reference, and guidelines for acceptable behavior. The system was more or less abolished when India declared its independence, and caste distinctions are beginning to disappear, but the legacy remains as a subconscious theme in business within India.

Traditionally, it was not possible to break out of one's caste during a lifetime. If this life was lived well, a person was reborn into a higher caste in the next life. The impact of this tradition on today's business practices is that, within networks, status is very important in determining the degree of respect due each individual. Bosses are expected to be strong, knowledgeable, confident, and able to give orders that workers follow without question. Bosses are paid to make decisions, not to have their subordinates make decisions. Empowerment has not been an established business practice. The scores on Hofstede's[1] scales of Power Distance and Individualism are consistent with a high acceptance of hierarchy and high degree of collectivism in India.

---

[1] Geert Hofstede's research identified five primary dimensions to assist in differentiating cultures. Power Distance high scores demonstrate the degree to which members of the society recognize inequalities of power. Individualism high scores indicate that individual rights are paramount in that society. See www.geert-hofstede.com.

Contacts can be used to learn about the available networks, determine which networks are most appropriate for your products, obtain introductions to the people within the right network, identify the decision maker, and be introduced to the decision maker. During this process, a great deal of time and effort needs to be spent evaluating the local person's contacts and the contact before deciding whether to do business with that individual and his or her network. Questions determining whether the local businessperson has influence, contacts, status, power, an appropriate style of business, authority, or any "hidden agendas" need to be addressed satisfactorily. At the same time, the local businessperson is going through the same process to find out as much as possible about the visiting businessperson.

During this process of providing introductions or information, many local businesspeople find an opportunity to receive gifts, favors, or money for their services, thereby cementing ties, building connections, or strengthening personal loyalties. This practice establishes an expectation and easy basis for bribery and corruption. While the expectation may exist, it is not a requirement. In any case, you need to check with the legal and ethical requirements of the home country and company as well as the local country before engaging in any activities that may be considered illegal in either location. However, if local contacts are chosen carefully, and if effective personal relationships are established, these contacts may become mentors or allies as you continue to work in the country, providing valuable advice and insight about business practices and networks.

Operating within the government, educational, and social systems created by the British, the local population learned to adapt to the colonial culture to survive and, in many cases, to do business successfully. The result is that many people in India are bicultural; they know how to do business comfortably in their native culture, and they know how to do business with equal facility in the manner of the British.

Another Hindu tradition is the emphasis on education. Certainly at the high levels of the caste system in the past and, as much as possible throughout Indian society today, parents work to provide educational opportunities for their children. Throughout India, there are many schools, technical institutions, colleges, and universities. British English is usually taught in these institutions. Many eligible graduates go to Canada, Great Britain, or the USA for college or advanced degrees. This legacy created a well-educated workforce that speaks English fluently. Since wage rates are lower in India, many global companies have outsourced engineering, architectural, computer programming, call center, or other technical jobs to India. These workers also become bicultural as they learn the systems of doing business from whichever country houses the headquarters of that company.

As the result of a long-standing strict hierarchical system, social networks created out of necessity, the British system of bureaucracy, the influence of global companies, and the strong local differences across the country, the process of doing business in India is necessarily complicated. Systems and procedures do exist and are followed. However, there is also a layer of social networks that determines how well and when the systems and procedures work. To succeed, the newcomer needs to learn to use both the established and the informal systems.

Process

The combination of a governmental system characterized by complicated bureaucratic approvals with social networks based on family and long-term personal connections creates a process of doing business that can be cumbersome and lengthy for the foreigner who has little or no experience in India. Understanding the separation between public and private lives, the sense of punctuality, and the flow of activities over time is important for determining how to practice business in India.

Privacy

Businesspeople in India who have not traveled or lived abroad are often bicultural and know how to be formal and informal, personal and professional. Newcomers need to determine which behavior is appropriate when and where. Erring on the side of formality is always a good way to begin. Business attire, use of titles, and formal speech is always a good first step. You honor the other side by assuming they have status that demands a formal approach by you or by providing them the respect they expect because of their social position. Becoming less formal is always an option but should be initiated by the local Indian businesspeople.

A warm, personalized approach is necessary for creating personal connections within the social network. Personalized in this sense involves being willing to answer questions frankly and forthrightly and demonstrating interest in your hosts, their area of the country, and their backgrounds as an active listener. Time may be spent on small talk, and the newcomer must resist the urge to assume familiarity or conduct business too quickly. The fact of being there and available is evidence of a desire to conduct business. A show of impatience may cause the opportunity to be lost. Willingness to wait to do so indicates respect of local practices and gains the foreign businessperson credibility.

Determining what topics of conversation are appropriate for social occasions and what personal topics are to be avoided is important. Is it appropriate to talk about family members? all family members? holidays? which ones? professional sports? personal hobbies? While any of these topics may be appropriate for conversations between friends, they may be too personal and, therefore, inappropriate for formal social conversations. This is the kind of advice and insight you must seek from your local contacts.

Progression to a more informal style of interactions takes place slowly as the foreigner moves from the outer circle to being a member of the intermediate circle and, possibly, to the fringe of the inner circle. Demonstrating the ability to respect local business practices and an interest in a partner's environment can facilitate movement toward the intermediate circle. Continued adherence to local protocol, interest in the local business environment, and reliable performance on initial projects may result in more movement. Over time, if the personal relationship between partners continues to grow, you may be invited to attend or participate in functions with members of the extended family or network. Key characteristics of success in reaching such an important stage in relationships are patience, rectitude, and dependability on the part of the foreigner who wishes to be included in an Indian network.

To develop proper rapport, time will be spent socializing at people's homes, birthday parties, sports events, dinners, or sightseeing. Generally, business matters are discussed in the office and not during social events. During social events, the foreigner needs to demonstrate interest in local customs, traditions, icons, architecture, and events. The goal of these activities is for the local businesspeople to get to know you as an individual and develop trust, respect, and confidence in you. As you become accepted into the network, your obligations to behave as a member of the network increase. For example, friends may be asked to extend the time of payment on a loan without any penalty or to make travel arrangements for a relative visiting your area of the world. Aspiring to and being accepted into the inner circle of relationships carries mutual responsibilities that must be considered prior to entering this level of relationship. Aside from the time involved, the expectations are demanding and long term. Becoming part of an inner circle, is rewarding, personally and professionally, but not something to be done without due consideration.

Learning what topics of conversation are appropriate for what occasions, developing connections with individuals, being introduced to other members of the social network, and earning their acceptance is time-consuming.

Once the network is established, its members can help speed other government approvals and business decisions, so time taken to become an accepted member of the network is a worthwhile long-term investment.

Punctuality

Bicultural local businesspeople can and do operate within the monochronic time orientation of North America and Northwest and Central Europe. As in other countries, the question of whether the meeting is being held in USA or British time or local time may be asked, with no slight meant or taken. Working with a linear approach to time is common, although it may not be the preferred approach when meetings involve only local Indian businesspeople.

The local infrastructure often makes punctuality a challenging goal. If the electricity goes out, the equipment necessary for a phone or video meeting may not work or data may not be sent when expected. Traffic, excessive rain, or roads in disrepair can make arriving on time at meetings impossible. Locals, living with uncertainty on a daily basis, learn to adapt. The outsider might find the adaptation to be more challenging. Knowing your business partners and the local conditions or determining which system of time is being used will help determine how punctual business activities will be. Social activities, however, are likely to use a local, more flexible sense of time.

Flow of Activities

Karma and rebirth are interrelated concepts in Indian philosophy. According to the theory of Karma, everyone is part of a cycle of births and rebirths. This cycle has no beginning or end. While good actions cause you to be reborn to experience the good effects, bad actions cause you to be reborn to undergo pain and suffering. The cyclical view of life, death, and rebirth carries over to day-to-day activities, with Indians seeing time as circular rather than linear. Results are absolutely essential; therefore, take as much time as necessary to achieve those results. Deadlines are not as important as taking time to reach a good agreement—an agreement will be made only when the parties involved mutually agree to the goals. As a result, the actual amount of time spent coming to an agreement is less important, more flexible, and allocated to the critical task of preparing an agreement. This is a significantly different perspective from a linear approach to time in which specific steps to attaining agreement are identified, addressed, and moved forward to inevitable conclusion within the allocated time frame.

Part of the cycle of getting agreement in India involves creating connections with people who are a critical part of the social network of life and of doing business. While getting agreement and attaining task completion is an identifiable accomplishment and goal, it is, at most, of equal importance to the relationship and not viewed as the only criterion for evaluating success.

Time is clearly flexible, with different criteria being used to determine which activities are deemed more important and thereby deserving of more time, whether time is a critical constraint for task completion, and how much time should be spent on various activities. Overall, time is viewed as cyclical, which implies that there is always more time for important activities.

Communication

With well over 216 languages and only 30 percent of the population speaking Hindi, communication is a major challenge in India. This section examines how the concepts of truth, words, style, and logic impact communication in India.

Truth

While Hinduism is a monotheistic religion, God is infinite and has many manifestations. While there is absolute truth in God, people know that truth from their perspective, their experience, and the intellectual capacity in their current life. Given that individuals have different capacities, experiences, and perspectives, any situation has a variety of views and they all exist at the same time, inconsistencies and discrepancies notwithstanding. As a result, people accept differing interpretations of situations and do not feel pressure to have everyone agree to only one interpretation. Deciding not to confront or disagree with the traveler's point of view displays respect and helps the traveler maintain honor, but does not necessarily mean agreement. With no need to have only a single, agreed-upon interpretation, there is no need to disagree.

Ethics, too, are tied to the situation. Wanting to maintain harmony, convey respect to the other person, and be loyal to others in the social network creates a situation in which truth is tied to social bonds and relationships. Therefore, determining which actions are right or wrong varies from one circumstance to another. Operating within this framework of different, sometimes seemingly contradictory views of a situation to create a common goal is a significant challenge. From one point of view, ethics may dictate that an honest response to a request for help may be to tell the other person that it is out of your realm of authority. From another point of view, an honest response to a request for help may be to tell the other person that you will try your best, knowing that you do not have the authority to make a change. From another point of view, an honest response is to tell the other person that you will grant the favor and then call upon another friend to provide the help, realizing that the favor may not happen in a timely manner but could still happen. From another point of view, you tell the other person that you will try your best and you find a way to make it happen. The ability to work within a framework of different, sometimes seemingly contradictory views of a situation is a significant challenge. However, the ability to accomplish tasks in this cultural environment is a strategic advantage for those people capable of working effectively within a system aiming to maintain harmony.

Words

In the Indian business environment, most professionals speak English as a second language. Most people have learned British English; some have learned American English through work or in the course of acquiring higher education, some have learned in India, some have lived and perfected their language skills abroad. Just as British and American businesspeople sometimes have communication problems because different words are used for the same thing or phrases mean different things, similar communication problems exist in India, where English is a second language, at best.

Indian businesspeople are well educated, are knowledgeable, and operate within more than one philosophical framework. As a result, they have multifaceted worldviews and often engage in abstract, theoretical discussions. Being familiar with different languages creates a facility with words and the ability to use language in a sophisticated and complicated manner. Within the requirements of maintaining respect and honor within the social structure, the ability to use words tactfully, to allow for differences, and to explore ideas is a valuable skill. As a result, it is often important to listen to what is *not* said, how something is said, the phrases used, or the way an idea is presented. Meanings are not always readily transparent—even when using the same language.

Style

The legacy of the caste system, religious philosophies, history, and disparity in wealth is still apparent in the way social protocol is used to demonstrate respect for others and their level of status. Discussion will be less direct; conversations will not proceed in a straight line. The demonstration of tact is highly valued, and social courtesy is paramount. Knowing your place in the hierarchy of the social network is essential for determining the respect due others, the appropriate degree of politeness required, and the deference due those in authority.

With this perspective, social protocol is important, fulfilling obligations is expected, favors must be granted, and trust must be earned to establish one's place in the social network. This process takes time and never ends; it is a way of life.

Logic

You are born into a certain life, and how that life is lived determines your form in the next life. The fatalism of this perspective means that there is a limit to what you can do; however, making the most out of a given circumstance is an important goal that influences your next life. A fatalistic worldview encourages acceptance and resignation toward events once all the facts are revealed and everyone understands the situation. However, there is a requirement for using argument and debate to reveal all the facts so people can see the current situation.

The more information one has, the more power one has. Lively debates aimed at examining different positions and perspectives are necessary for fully understanding the current situation. These lengthy discussions aim at a thorough understanding and will be time-consuming—time well spent according to the Indian point of view. Lively discussions, however, focus on the issues and do not become personal. As a result, no one can take offense and no one's honor is damaged.

When business deals are being negotiated and differences in opinion are not resolved or when positions are far apart, the social network becomes important. A well-respected intermediary can intervene, talk with each side, make appeals for reconciliation, and create a scenario that is acceptable to both parties. When working toward a final agreement, hierarchy has a role to play. Representatives engaged in the discussions may not be able to make concessions because the central decision maker is the one to make the final decision. Without that person's approval, the agreement cannot be made. Working through intermediaries takes time; keeping postponements for the purpose of carrying new proposals to the decision makers takes time.

Conclusion

As members of a former British colony, Indian businesspeople are familiar with the concept of rule of law and deal with a government and legal systems that are highly developed bureaucracies. At the same, the social network has its own structure, with individuals having a place in the hierarchy based upon a combination of birth, tradition, religion, education, and personal accomplishment. The systems function simultaneously, and foreign businesspeople need to navigate both.

Making contacts, earning their trust, and observing social protocol are necessary for the foreigner who is entering the social network, developing trusted partners, and conducting business. On the other hand, the foreigner must observe the regulations, policies, and procedures of the legal system. Local businesspeople are generally bicultural and able to navigate in both the formal and informal systems. That ability means that when the formal system slows down, businesspeople can approach their contacts within the social network to facilitate the process. Westerners, either unfamiliar with the process or frustrated by not being able to access either system, often consider the practice corrupt; they focus only on the bribery that is involved. However, the giving and granting of favors is how the social network functions, with or without the exchange of money.

Establishing and maintaining the system takes time; learning and using appropriate protocol takes time; incorporating social functions into business activities takes time; using indirect styles of communication takes time. However, not developing and maintaining contacts means that the only recourse an individual has is to rely upon the official system with all of its administrative complexity and bureaucracy. While it may be difficult for an outsider to understand, the Indian system does work; and the foreign businessperson wanting to succeed there must have access to the system.

CHAPTER 9

CHINA AND OVERSEAS CHINESE

Classification of Cultures Model

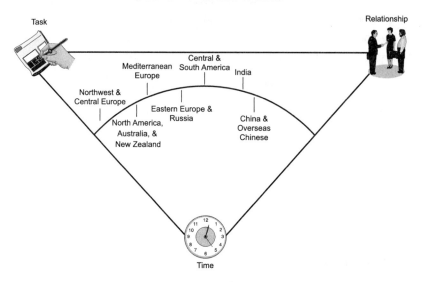

The People's Republic of China covers a vast area and is the oldest major continuing world civilization, The Middle Kingdom, with records dating back more than 3,500 years. A Confucian state ideology and common written language enabled the rulers to control this large territory and to integrate many ethnic groups and languages. After conquering China in the thirteenth century, the Mongols, nomads from north-central Asia, adopted many of the ways of the conquered Chinese, who were at a much higher level in practically every aspect of civilization. The Chinese dynastic culture continued to flourish until late in the Qing dynasty, the mid-1800s. During the nineteenth and twentieth centuries, royal family rivalries, military defeats, social strife, civil war, and foreign invasion set the stage for the creation of the PRC in 1949 under the charismatic Mao Zedong.

Fashioned after the model of the Soviet Union with strong central planning and Communist party officials controlling governmental power, China was under the control of an autocratic socialist government. Programs and policies changed over the years, but the fundamental autocratic, socialist, centrally controlled perspective remained until economic reforms were approved in 1978 and legal reforms in 1979, under the leadership of Deng Xiaoping. These changes initiated the development of a marketplace economy within the socialist government system. The economic and legal systems continued to evolve, with legal reform becoming a priority in the 1990s. By 2001, the PRC had made substantial structural changes to the extent that the country was admitted as a member of the World Trade Organization (WTO).

During tumultuous periods throughout history, many Chinese left the country and settled in new locations. As the Chinese emigrated to new locations, they adapted to the culture in their new location. However, as is the case with any ethnic or national expatriation, total assimilation usually does not occur. The local Chinese immigrants often prefer to form strong bonds with the other Chinese families in their new location and to maintain strong bonds with the family members left behind in China. While the immigrants adopt many characteristics of the new culture, many Chinese traits remain strong because of continued identification with the Chinese community. For example, the accumulation of wealth, a strong work ethic, and the ability to run a profitable business are widely regarded as characteristics of a smart businessperson who is accorded respect and face among all Chinese subcultures. In most of the overseas Chinese settlements in Southeast Asia, the Chinese often comprise 5–20 percent of the population in the new location but own the vast majority of the wealth. In many instances, during nationalistic movements or periods of tension, Chinese minorities were targeted for either expulsion or reprisal by the natives, who were resentful of "foreign" influence and/or wealth.

This chapter identifies and analyzes the common Chinese and overseas Chinese orientations toward time, task, and relationships and how they interact with structural, process, and communication concepts to impact business practices.

Structure

The role of government, rule of law, and application of hierarchy embody the rules and regulations that determine the conduct and practice of business. Because of the importance of hierarchy in the Chinese and overseas Chinese cultures, this topic will be addressed first.

Hierarchy

In China, Confucianism grew to be the dominant thought philosophy by 124 B.C. However, by 88 B.C., other philosophies, such as Buddhism and

Global Business Practices Model

Areas of World	Gov't	Law	Hier.	Privacy	Punct.	Flow	Truth	Words	Style	Logic
Northwest & Central Europe	gray	white	gray	white	white	white	white	white	white	white
North America, Australia, & NZ	white	white	white	white	white	white	white	white	white	gray
Mediterranean Europe	gray	gray	gray	gray	gray	gray	white	gray	gray	gray
Eastern Europe & Russia	gray	white	gray	gray	gray	gray	gray	gray	white	gray
South & Central America	gray	gray	black	gray	gray	gray	gray	gray	gray	gray
India	gray	gray	gray	gray	gray	gray	black	gray	gray	gray
China & Overseas Chinese	black	black	gray	black	black	black	gray	black	black	black

LEGEND

Role of Government: White = the government sets parameters and constraints to create the environment for doing business. Black = Direct involvement of government in business as a business partner.

Rule of Law: White = Reliance on systems and procedures. Black = Pragmatism or situational considerations.

Sense of Hierarchy: White = Assumption of equality. Black = Assumption of status difference.

View of Privacy: White = Business and private matters are separate. Black = Business and private matters are all part of one reality.

Punctuality: White = Fixed time. Black = Flexible or "rubber" time.

Flow of Activities: White = Time works in a linear fashion. Black = Time works in a cyclical fashion.

Truth: White = Universal truth. Black = Many truths exist at once.

Words: White = Words have explicit meanings. Black = Words have implicit meanings.

Style: White = Communication is direct and forthright. Black = Communication is indirect.

Logic: White = Formal deductive reasoning. Black = Alternative heuristic.

Taoism (Daoism), were increasing in popularity. While local variations of these belief systems existed throughout the many regions of China, contributing to conflict and unrest, development of a Confucian state and a written language served to unify the country and created the foundation for a common Chinese culture. As this foundation was modified and adapted over centuries, each version was demonstrated to be consistent with the basic teachings and assumptions of Confucianism. With the establishment of the PRC, the country became and remains officially atheist. This presents no real conflict with the many centuries of Taoism, Buddhism, and Confucianism—more philosophies than religions, all firmly ingrained as a guide for day-to-day living.

Maintaining face is a fundamental concept involving the ability to keep and enhance one's dignity, self-respect, and prestige. The basic assumptions are related to the principles of Confucianism, with its fundamental understanding of the desire to create order and harmony among vertical relationships in society. Maintaining face is essential for preserving and enhancing one's status and for increasing influence and power in society; losing face makes it difficult for an individual to operate effectively within the relationship-dominated business environment. Therefore, you must pay attention to the implications of this concept in all interactions.

The very high scores on Power Distance and Confucian Dynamism and very low scores on Individualism[1] are evidence of the current existence of this cultural perspective. These scores indicate that Chinese recognize and accept that individuals at different levels of status should have more or less power according to their position, that principles of a Confucian philosophy are the current worldview, and that there is a strong collectivist orientation to life and decision making.

This value structure translates into pragmatic rules for daily life. First, the stability of society is based upon unequal relationships among people that involve mutual, complementary obligations. Therefore, the junior person owes respect and obedience to those who are senior, and the senior person owes protection and consideration to those who are junior. Second, the family is the prototype of all social organizations, with the father being the central decision maker in the family. Therefore, the emphasis is on being a member of a family, not on being a person, as an individual. Members of the family restrain their individuality to maintain harmony within the family. Individuals contribute to family welfare as best they can, with the strong doing more than those who are not as strong. Third, virtuous behavior consists of treating others as one would like to be treated. This basic human benevolence is consistent with the reciprocal role relationships of respecting the senior person and looking after junior persons, as well as with the importance of maintaining face. Fourth, aspiring to be virtuous is a life goal. Examples of virtue as a goal include striving to acquire practical skills and education, working hard, spending money cautiously, observing moderation in all things, being patient and persevering, and retaining control of one's emotions and temper.

This set of assumptions implies that relationships among people are structured, entail obligations, require effort to maintain, and are the foundation for any other activities. Colleagues, work associates, and business partners are expected to understand and reflect this level of behavior and to respond to relationships at a much deeper level than is expected in Western countries.

---

[1] Geert Hofstede's research identified five dimensions of culture. In this chapter we will refer to Power Distance (high scores demonstrate the degree to which members of the society recognize inequalities of power), Confucian Dynamism (high scores indicate that the country values long-term commitments and respects tradition), and Individualism (high scores indicate that individual rights are paramount in that society). See www.geert-hofstede.com.

Tasks are viewed, evaluated, and implemented in terms of the relationships of the parties to the task. Maintaining the harmony of a group is important. For instance, workers in China need to feel a sense of common purpose and to work together to achieve group goals. Within these groups, members do not speak critically of each other, use titles to recognize status, and will work to complete the task well, regardless of the time it takes. Working together to complete the task is important, and competition within the group can bring the project to a standstill through the destruction of group harmony.

Stratification of society, the significance of position within society, and family-like linkages throughout society are common Chinese characteristics, in both China and overseas Chinese communities. Based upon an individual's family, background, education, and personal achievements, each individual is accorded a particular position in society. This position involves mutual dependence on other individuals, who may be family members, schoolmates, colleagues, or close friends. Success stems from, and is shared with, deceased ancestors and living network members, making family a significant factor in determining one's social position. Failure, too, is shared. Instead of being fired, an individual may be sent to work for an "uncle" in a different department to try skills in another area, which creates another opportunity for success rather than publicly identifying failure.

Helping others within this network incurs their goodwill, increases the donor's influence, and develops mutual dependence. Being able to use one's connections to marshal the necessary resources and skills to complete a task, fulfilling obligations incurred along the way, and taking responsibility to spread opportunities among network members allows one to develop, solidify, and increase social status and position.

Within many organizations, several levels of hierarchy exist, and people at each level participate in decision making as a way of involving the whole organization in the future growth of the company. Because individuals at many levels participate, decision making can take a long time, involving meetings with many different groups of people and requiring a great deal of patience. As a rule of thumb, the more important the task, the less likely that decision-making responsibility will be delegated. Therefore, one indicator of the seriousness of a discussion is the level of the person sent to the meeting.

If lower-level managers are involved in the business activities, they must have time to report back to their superiors, demonstrating their shrewdness in negotiating a good arrangement and ensuring that the agreement will enhance the face of the network. Further, involving various levels of the organization allows time for adjusting to any changes in priority or reallocation of funds, new skills, or other consequences before a decision is made. This can significantly enhance the execution of agreements because the organization's reluctance to change the status quo has been addressed during the decision-making process. When the final decision, especially if the project is important, is made at the top of the organization, as the father in a family would make the decision, execution of the implementation process is ready to begin. If the top people are involved in the discussion from the beginning, decision making can be the quickest in the world because the owner of the company has complete authority and does not manage by consensus.

Personal relationships and friendships with family members and mentors are very strong. These relationships are with specific individuals, not with companies. As a result, working networks are usually small, and a person's *guanxi* is measured by having access to and influence in many networks. *Guanxi* is an attribute one attains by demonstrating reliability, success, influence, etiquette, and reciprocity in relationships. Because industrialization in the PRC has been centrally controlled for 40 years and the country was at war for 17 years prior to Communism, the destabilization of personal relationships has not been as pervasive as in other cultures. In countries such as Australia, the EU, and the USA, systems and procedures take precedence over personal relationships. In China, systems have not taken precedence over family relationships in the business environment.

Personal loyalties can subvert the work of a large organization, with employees following the leadership of the person to whom they owe loyalty, making decisions to improve that person's status rather than making decisions that would best benefit the organization. In overseas Chinese environments, as well as in the move to a market economy in the PRC, most Chinese firms stay small in terms of number of employees and scope of product lines, continuing the tradition of small companies operating within a network of companies. The concept of giving, maintaining, and saving face is an inherent part of functioning within a network. In this web of interdependent relationships, the actions of individuals and those with whom they are associated either help solidify relationships, build relationships, or harm relationships.

Business networks function as a way of gaining access to information, opportunities, decision makers, and employees. Those networks are not necessarily based on personal connections and are more business oriented, working more as a system of contacts rather than as an emotional or formal business unit. These relationships are not with individuals who are part of one's inner circle, but are with individuals are who proven business partners. Proving to be a good business partner enhances one's *quanxi* over time.

Keeping a company small means management can be close to employees, maintain the flexibility of the organization, enable the organization to respond quickly to changes in the marketplace, and increase opportunities for more network relationships. Owners often provide capital to employees who want to set up their own businesses. This creates a group of business partners who are loyal to the individual investing in the new business, a new company with specific expertise, a debt with both financial and face implications, start-up capital, and a new business relationship in the network of everyone involved. This type of extension occurs often, creating a dynamic system of networks that is always in transition. Keeping the ever-increasing and flexible network viable is a serious and time-consuming responsibility, involving obligations of keeping in touch, doing favors, and providing appropriate responses to requests. Those individuals who are successful at fulfilling their obligations and who build up a strong "spider's web" of relationships become very powerful and influential (Montagu-Pollack, 1991).

The *spider's web* concept of management creates flexibility and speed in the marketplace. One individual's network may involve several business associates, each with different companies, in a particular industry that can be approached to fulfill a specific contract. At the same time, the individual who put the first deal together can combine a different group of business associates, each with his or her own company, to fulfill a second business deal, another group of business associates to fulfill a third deal, and so on. Constant access to current business information from a variety of sources, each with its own perspective, is a function of this ever-spreading network. Another interesting characteristic of this network arrangement is that no formal ties, contracts, or legal arrangements bind its members as a formal network, consortium, cartel, or **keiretsu** as in Japan. As a result, the system is extremely flexible, cost-effective, and responsive to the changing demands of the marketplace. Personal loyalty and responsibility to those who have been instrumental in an individual's success are not only the binding material for network relationships, but also important elements for building face and maintaining the Confucian value of respect and reverence for elders.

These factors are little appreciated or recognized in the task-oriented cultures of the West, and often overlooked by businesspeople from the more relationship-oriented regions, as well. However, network, status, centralized decision making, and flexible linkages are important elements of hierarchy that are easily identified throughout Chinese society.

Role of Government

In the PRC, the government is subordinate to the Communist party. The political and economic orientation of the government is to create a *socialist market economy* with Chinese characteristics, in which the economy is market driven but the government maintains control to ensure that policies and procedures do not conflict with socialist doctrines. While the government exercises less central control from Beijing than in the Mao-Deng eras, and on fewer issues, the government in each of the 23 provinces retains a significant degree of control over its business activities. Special economic zones generally operate with more independence from Beijing, but do control business activity within their own zone. The amount of day-to-day regulation and intervention by local and central governments continues to vary as the socialist market economy evolves.

A centrally controlled form of government is consistent with the traditional Chinese value of having power consolidated in a central place, as it was in the Dynastic era. Confucianism believes that hierarchy is the natural order of things. Using the family as an example, the father is the head of the family and makes decisions for the good of the family. In a similar fashion, the head of the party, head of the government, head of the region, head of the agency, or head of the company makes decisions for the good of everyone involved. The large bureaucracies and determination of the ultimate decision makers result in slow decision-making processes. Determining a person's rank and status in a department is important because proper protocol must be observed. Knowing the proper protocol for both formal business and formal social occasions is necessary. The visitor's credibility and face will improve if the proper seating arrangement is followed, with the most influential person being placed to the right of the most important Chinese representative. Being prepared to participate in the speech-making and give toasts at specified times during a banquet demonstrate understanding of appropriate etiquette in the local culture.

As the business environment in the PRC is in transition to a socialist market economy, businesspeople are developing some bicultural abilities. Since joining the WTO in 2001, a concerted effort has been made to increase the number of MBA programs offered within China and to increase the number of business owners and government officials being sent to training programs in Canada, the United States, and the EU. The purpose of this effort is to increase the number of government officials and business managers who understand business practices in task-oriented countries. While a task orientation is not the preferred or widely established process for doing business locally or within networks, more Chinese are able to function effectively within a task-oriented framework when necessary.

Rule of Law

Structurally, the legal system in the PRC and a number of other Southeast Asian countries in which the Chinese are very active members of the business community is not well established. As a result, the legal tradition of writing contracts to specify all the conditions of an agreement, relying on contracts to establish the expectations for future business activity, or enforcing contracts is not an important part of the East Asian traditional business process. In general, a signed contract indicates willingness to work together. Managing the details of a contract over time involves business partners with good relationships working through the difficulties of changing business conditions. Resolution of disputes, difficulties, and new issues takes place through personal relationships, not by relying on a contract that is enforced or interpreted by a court. Therefore, the relationships established between both sides at all levels of the organization need to be maintained so businesspeople can exchange information, discuss issues, and resolve problems.

Continued personal contact with Chinese partners is essential for conducting successful business transactions. If the two parties have difficulty overcoming disagreements, third parties are often asked to assist in the process. Someone who owes you a favor and to whom the other side also owes a favor can intervene and work out a compromise. In addition, someone with a higher position or more *guanxi* may be able to intercede on your behalf. If the relationship between business partners continues to strengthen and you are considered a friend, the Chinese might find ways to do extra things or make concessions that were not part of the original contract but would be beneficial given changing business circumstances. However, the obligation exists for you to respond, as a friend, in the future.

Traditionally, the agreement is the *beginning of continued negotiations*, not the culmination of discussions. An inherent characteristic of a relationship is the assumption of flexibility and willingness to work together over time to pursue joint and individual goals as business conditions change. On a daily basis, people, circumstances, markets, availability of supplies, and business environments change. A contract cannot provide for all new contingencies; therefore, a strong relationship between business partners is necessary so they can continue to work through new situations in a profitable way. The contract, or official documentation, is an outline of how the facts were seen at the time the agreement was signed, leaving room for flexibility in the implementation of a business arrangement. Therefore, requests for renegoti-ation of an agreement or a provision in the agreement are common and should not be taken as an example of bad faith or misplaced trust.

Successful Western systems tend to rely on courts to adjudicate questions found to be ambiguous after agreements have been reached. Traditionally, in European law, interpretations have been relatively limited and restricted, while common law in the British system is reasonably expansive in inter-pretation. Under the Chinese Confucian ethical system, courts are not a desirable last resort and, historically, have not been used to resolve economic conflicts between business partners. Transparent legal systems and perspec-tives have not been a part of the traditional Chinese culture. The use of courts to adjudicate civil conflict is not expected, and this recourse is not part of the current Chinese legal system.

Since the official movement to create a transparent legal system began in 1979, more than 300 laws and regulations, most of them in the economic area, have been promulgated. This established system included the creation of mediation committees, composed of informed groups of citizens who resolve about 90 percent of China's civil disputes and some minor criminal cases at no cost to the parties involved. There are currently more than 800,000 such committees in both rural and urban areas. In the 1990s, the PRC made legal reform a priority as part of the process of being admitted into the WTO. The complex system of statutes, criminal law, and code in civil, administrative, criminal, and commercial law continues to evolve. An amendment to the Constitution in 2004 provided more protection for individual human rights and for property rights. After only 25 years or so with a new and evolving civil legal system compared to thousands of years of tradition, the legal system clearly does not yet result in a business process that functions entirely according to the rule of law.

Process

While in transition to a rule of law business environment, the traditions of networks, *quanxi*, face, and respect for hierarchy remain the dominant business practices. This section examines the role of privacy, punctuality, and flow of activities in the conduct of business.

Privacy

Public and private lives are separated into the outer and inner circle. Family members, mentors, and a few long-established business partners form the inner circle. An intermediate band of that circle includes members of one's existing business network. The outer circle includes any potential business partners, anyone who has engaged in business activities not deemed "honorable" (for example, someone who had not paid his or her bills), new acquaintances, and those with whom a person has had minor business deals. Depending upon how the relationship evolves, the outsider may or may not have the opportunity to move to the intermediate band of the inner circle. Until a relationship moves to the inner circle, public and private lives are kept quite separate. Within the inner circle, the separation between public and private life is virtually nonexistent.

Entering a business network is a challenge for an outsider. Access exists through "front doors" and "back doors." Front door access is the official process, complete with all the bureaucratic guidelines. For instance, a government-sponsored trade mission may organize a trip to introduce business leaders to government, trade, and businesspeople as way to initiate business activity. Following the initial introduction, individuals attempt to learn which permits or licenses may be required for doing business, which distributors or business partners have potential, how to locate a facility, or where and how to find good employees. Depending upon the motivation and contacts of the individuals one has met, as well as the bureaucratic structure encountered, this process can be time-consuming and expensive with little apparent progress. For the process to become effective and useful, the visitor must create a relationship with the bureaucrat within the organization (business and government) who controls access to permits, joint venture approvals, partnership sanctions, or other avenues for establishing a business. Adherence to formal guidelines for protocol, a long-term perspective, and sincerity are requirements that, if met, ultimately result in a successful entry and starting point for business. The front door works; it just takes time and patience, often the characteristics missing in foreign businesspeople.

A contact with the right connections to the decision makers in a particular area can provide introductions to the decision makers, advice on how to approach the situation, or an opportunity to conduct initial discussions determining the feasibility of a particular business proposal. This assistance can decrease the amount of time required, speed up the learning process, and enhance the success of business activities. Therefore, finding someone with the right *guanxi*, developing a good relationship with that person, and using his or her assistance to enter the network can result in a starting point for business that is both more timely and efficient for the outsider.

Choosing the people with whom you do business is a critical decision. Taking the time necessary to make a good choice is an important factor in the successful completion of a project. Usually during the first several meetings, formal protocol and manners are observed by both parties and will structure elements of the discussion, such as who sits where, who begins the discussion, and what topics are appropriate.

Every Chinese businessperson has important relationship-based connections, is part of an extended network of business associates, and can assist a foreigner with important introductions. Determining which person really has access to the decision makers important to you in a particular business sector or government agency, has influence with the decision makers, and is willing to be of assistance in your endeavor is often the most important factor in transforming potential business opportunities into successful business ventures.

Therefore, it is expected that an individual's *guanxi* will be checked informally through a network before any business decisions are made. Time must be taken to learn about those individuals who offer to provide introductions, information, or potential partners. You are being checked, and potential Chinese partners assume they are being checked as well. Choosing someone to represent you within the networks of the Chinese business community is a serious decision that should be taken only after the investor has enough information to be comfortable about having this contact represent you and your company. However, access to decision makers provides only a starting point for conducting business; access does not indicate that a business deal is ensured—or even imminent.

Over time, if the personal relationship between partners continues to grow, the foreign businessperson may be invited to attend or participate in functions with members of the extended family or clan and move to the intermediate band. While acceptance into the inner circle is not likely because the visitor is not a member of the extended family and has not been a close business associate for decades, "friends" may become part of the intermediate band of business associates.

Becoming a *friend* is called **old friend** in Chinese and is a combination of business colleague and family member who supports whatever you request in expectation that you will offer a comparable favor or respond to a comparable request in the future. Hospitality to one's friends at any time is expected. Friends may be asked to make a loan to an employee in the network or to a network member's relative, to be repaid on payday. Friends assume responsibility for all members of the network along with the assumption of making decisions for the good of the network. Wealthy members of the network are expected to give generously to support friends and relatives, which not only strengthens the social relationship but also ensures economic security by creating indebtedness and loyalty on the part of those who received the gifts.

Multinational companies are expected to give funds to support community projects as a way of demonstrating their commitment to the community. This is also a way to avoid giving gifts to individuals, which often causes ethical dilemmas for the companies. Depending on the pertinent legal statutes, the donations can be tax effective. Providing financial support to individuals for doing their job or making decisions may be illegal. You need to be clear about the position of your company on this issue and make that position clear to your business partners early in the relationship.

Punctuality

The Chinese have historically described their homeland as *The Middle Kingdom*. This term reflects the way the Chinese see themselves and illustrates their different attitude toward time. By not only withstanding wars, uprisings, political challenges, and social change but also by continuing to adapt and survive, a long-term perspective and confidence in their ability to persevere provides a fundamental view of life that permeates business activity.

The Western businessperson who fails to consider these factors and tries to *cut a deal* in a time-constrained manner immediately concedes an advantage because time is not as significant a consideration from the Chinese point of view as it is to the visitor. The Chinese perspective can be a disadvantage to the visitor in this case. Knowing that Western businesspeople need to conduct business as efficiently as possible and knowing that there are deadlines and expectations for any visit, early in your visit Chinese contacts may ask when you are planning to leave. With that deadline in mind, the Chinese will plan social events to occupy your time, leaving only limited time for discussing business issues. Final resolution of these issues will be postponed until several hours before your departure, knowing that the foreigner is under great pressure to conclude a deal and that this pressure will create an advantage for the Chinese business contacts.

With the long-term mentality that comes from a culture developed over millennia, businesspeople can afford to wait for the deal that will create the most profit. Mutual success among partners and the additional face attributed to businesspeople of demonstrated acumen and wealth counts much more than delivering a contract on time.

Flow of Activities

Since Chinese businesspeople are less constrained by agreeing to business deals in a timely manner but are more constrained by accomplishing business goals profitably, the flow of business proceeds in a different manner.

The Taoist tradition perceives time as circular rather than linear. Clearly results are important to the Chinese. Therefore, as much time as is necessary to achieve those results should be taken—but nothing exists to serve as a precise beginning or ending time. As a result, the actual amount of time spent accomplishing the task is less important and more flexible than in current Western business models.

The Buddhist tradition espouses belief in a predetermined fate or destiny whereby *karma* determines what happens in this life and individual performance can influence what happens in the next life. This teaching affects the way in which individuals view their importance in decision making, their level of control over events, and the timeliness of decision making. Events will or will not occur depending upon what fate has in store, not whether a specific decision is made. Future events unfold in the future, not necessarily determined by actions in the present.

Many schemes for determining longevity, staying healthy, improving health, or learning the future are popular as a way of avoiding problems or changing one's luck. For example, *feng shui* is the ancient study of the proper alignment of objects with features of nature to ensure harmony and good fortune. By examining wind, water, and the environment, people can make decisions about an architectural design, room arrangement, or appropriate accessories to bring good luck and propitious fortune. While the future cannot be controlled and destiny is predetermined, efforts to increase good luck are common.

This general framework is an underlying set of assumptions that impact the flow of business activities. Meetings occur over time, moving along a predetermined path that can be changed with luck or good fortune, but not necessarily by individual control.

Chinese business teams often are large, with as many as ten people involved, all representing different parts of the company and different levels of authority. Identifying the leader with decision-making authority is often difficult. In addition to formal meetings and social activities, many informal meetings and social activities involving different combinations of members from the business team will occur. Since personal relationships are important, taking time for members of both groups to establish some common bonds is worth the effort. Getting to know your counterparts *and* the interpreter is essential for a smooth exchange of information as well as a growing understanding of the other side's perspective. Relying on your partner's interpreter, or one chosen by your partner for you, is not necessarily a sound strategy. Although convenient, it is not always possible to be completely confident in the interpreter who is part of the other side's network.

Within a cultural tradition emphasizing the interconnectedness of people, the environment, and the situation, Chinese businesspeople do not typically consider issues in a sequential or linear manner. Only after as much information as possible is gathered about the other side's interests and goals can the Chinese evaluate alternatives and contemplate decisions. Agreements do not happen as a matter of course throughout business discussions, but will happen at the end, when those decisions can be made with a holistic view of the situation. As a result, the timing of deadlines for decisions is an integral part of the negotiation process. Having a flexible deadline or not revealing the deadline allows participants the ability to exercise some power during negotiation, adding to face and *guanxi* of the people of influence. Immediately before a known deadline, when the other party is under a great deal of pressure to conclude a deal and time is of the essence, the Chinese will believe that the other side's best and final offer has been made and will consider an agreement or press for another concession. The Chinese will continue to press for the *best deal* until they believe it has been identified and until they have a profitable deal demonstrating their business acumen, building their face, and improving their position in the network.

Communication

Since building, maintaining, and saving face is an important factor in maintaining harmony and building *guanxi*, communication is a major factor in accomplishing these goals. Determining what to say and how to say it has important implications for creating and solidifying relationships. This section examines the communication concepts of words, truth, logic, and style within the Chinese cultural framework.

Words

Chinese is a high-context language, according to Hall (1981), meaning that the nonverbal cues provide a significant amount of meaning. The whole context, such as body language, facial expression, relationship, and hierarchy, determines the meaning of what is said. Participants must be completely conscious of not only what information is being conveyed by the content of the conversation, but also what else is being implied in the exchange. Identifying the appropriate cues and interpreting them requires attention to many details, active listening skills, observational skill, and an intense awareness and understanding of the situation and people involved. During conversations, what is *not* said is as important as, and maybe more important than, what *is* said.

The importance of giving and maintaining face is as important to the relationship as the deal itself, so all comments must be carefully considered. For instance, requesting proof may be interpreted as a sign of not believing someone's work, which is highly offensive; so requests for documentation or test results need to be made in an acceptable form. Requesting a copy of a report in an informal meeting in another context would be preferable to requesting the data immediately upon hearing the information or conclusions made based upon the information provided by the other side. Observing protocol and demonstrating respect is expected during meetings. Words used to convey ideas, ask questions, and respond to suggestions need to be carefully considered before speaking, and carefully interpreted when listening.

Because admitting to a lack of knowledge can result in a loss of face, your partner may be reluctant to reveal any ignorance. Admission of ignorance will be avoided, so any questions about whether the other side understands something will be answered in the affirmative. On the other hand, assuming a lack of information by making a presentation on an elementary level in a condescending manner is insulting. Presenting information and instructions in an interactive manner enables you to observe your partner's level of understanding or expertise without asking direct questions.

A deal has not been reached until the top person has agreed. Often, an agreement is made because a deadline is reached or because one side is trying to accommodate the other side. Saying *yes* does not always mean a commitment to the details of the agreement; in some cases, saying *yes* might merely signal that the other side desires to please you in order to continue the relationship and to keep the negotiation process alive.

Identifying specific meanings of words provides one level of understanding. However, that meaning needs to be reinterpreted in terms of the context, the people, the relationships, the topics, the immediacy of the situation, and what was left out of the discussion.

Truth

The philosophical orientation of monotheistic religious traditions regarding a universal truth does not exist in Chinese culture with a philosophical tradition stressing harmony in hierarchical situations and pragmatism. Chinese participants in business do not expect one perspective to be true. Without a set of universal principles of right and wrong, each situation must be evaluated in its own circumstance. Therefore, a problem solved in a certain way in one situation may not be solved in the same manner in another similar situation involving other individuals and different relationships.

One of the fundamental beliefs consistent across Confucianism, Buddhism, and Taoism is that no one human being has the truth. Different views of a situation, different perceptions, and different philosophies can and do all exist at the same time, inconsistencies and discrepancies notwithstanding. This causes individuals to accept different interpretations of the truth or to see alternatives that often elude linear thinkers. Ethics and truth are tied to the situation, the relationships involved, and one's position in the hierarchy. Determination of which actions are right or wrong varies from one situation to another. Operating within this framework of different, sometimes seemingly contradictory, views of a situation to create a common goal is a significant challenge. The ability to accomplish tasks in this cultural context, being aware of these kinds of differences, is a strategic advantage to the foreign businessperson.

Logic

As the relationship between potential business partners is being developed and the stage is being set for conducting business, a substantial amount of time will be spent establishing parameters, constraints, and direction. Chinese business partners most often use a win-lose approach in which the initial request is high and may be reduced later. Determining the parameters of the business discussions is a negotiation in itself.

Adopting an agenda is a serious discussion that determines which subjects will or will not be discussed. An attempt will be made to keep topics off the agenda if one side does not want to discuss them or to concede anything in this specific area. Putting a topic on the agenda implies a type of concession—that the topic is one that needs resolution—or may be perceived as signaling an area that will be discussed with an intent to change positions to make an agreement.

As topics, their importance, and their relevance to the underlying issue are discussed, Chinese participants often use hypothetical examples or historical trends to move the focus from the status quo to the future. In the process, the Chinese propose principles when describing these trends or examples and attempt to establish them as agreed-upon perspectives, which, in turn, become *de facto* rules for conducting business. In addition, judgments often are presented in a way that establishes them as a fact. For example, a Chinese negotiator might present the following reasoning:

> Company A and Company B from Country Z had agreed to build a new factory each year in Wu Han. In 1988 and 1989, the promise was not kept, and neither company built new factories for two years. Unreliability is a characteristic of Country Z. Since the promises could be broken by Company A and Company B, we know that all parties from Country Z can break promises when doing business in China. So I know you will understand when we decide to change our delivery schedule.

This comment uses behavior of other companies from your country to establish an accepted principle without regard for specific circumstances. Agreeing with the statement that the two companies did not keep their promise without a discussion or the addition of qualifying statements establishes a presumption that the basic principle of breaking promises is all right. Further discussion will proceed from that accepted premise uncontested, and may be used to preempt counterarguments later in the discussion.

If the conversation begins to include historical examples of trends from which basic principles are being extracted, participants need to consider these ideas very carefully before deciding to accept them. If accepted, they will form a foundation to which other arguments will be anchored.

Conversely, when visitors try to establish principles, the Chinese response may be that they do not "want to waste time on empty argument," thereby resisting the creation of principles proposed by the visitor. Therefore, the visiting businesspeople must be prepared to work through this discount and to establish principles from which specific contracts can be written. Doing so often requires multiple meetings, conferences among team members, discussions with the home office, and agreement on the limits to which the team is prepared to concede. Being patient and keeping the end in mind are paramount in meeting such objections.

A traditional method of persuasion used by the Chinese is "shaming," which has been used by parents as a primary sanction to control their children and train them to exhibit desired behavior. If children are shamed into doing the right thing, they are often grateful because they know they are performing appropriate behaviors that help them save face and develop *guanxi* in later situations.

In business, several specific tactics can be used to shame the other side. For instance, explanations can be denounced as insufficient by calling the expertise of the other side into question or by finding and exploiting logical contradictions in the other side's presentation. Personal criticism is also a tactic for shaming the other side; sometimes the other side will be put on the defensive by making individual faults and mistakes an issue. Any of these tactics will increase the tension because, if the accusations are true, you will lose face and have to work to build more. The reason for creating this situation is the belief that in defending a position, the other side will reveal more agenda items, interests, and goals that might otherwise remain hidden. Obtaining additional information is perceived as facilitating the negotiation. Shaming or criticizing the other side to reveal more information is one influence strategy used by the Chinese to shift the nature of the discussion and to elicit concessions from the other side.

In the event you are subjected to this influence tactic, simply go back to the assertiveness techniques commonly used and successfully deployed over the past generation—for example, restating your original position clearly, deflecting personal barbs by objectively clarifying the statements, or diluting the criticism with active listening. Another response to shaming is to recast or reinterpret an event in light of principles that were established earlier, making the situation appear to be an example of normal procedures, or to negotiate a new approach because of the problems created by past actions.

Criticizing the other side also can increase tensions and create a great risk for a loss of face that damages the relationship. Responses to criticism often include an attempt to expose a problem of the other side, a threat to expose something about the other side, a shift of responsibility for creating the rift in the negotiations, or creation of a symbolic response that does not affect the substance of discussions.

When the Chinese are considering whether to do business with foreign companies, criteria for decision making include evaluating the reputation of the other company; the amount of service or support that will be provided; and, of course, the price. Typically, Chinese businesspeople know the value of money and are concerned about how long money will *sleep,* or be tied up in a nonearning capacity, such as the length of time inventory is in a warehouse. Decisions to cut costs to a minimum are common, meaning that the cheaper approach is generally chosen and that the Chinese will pay as little as possible for services or workers.

Through the informal network, markets, companies, products, services, and competitive prices will have been researched and the other side will have at least a general idea, if not specific knowledge, of your product's or service's price. If an initial offer is too high, the suspicion arises that one side is trying to take advantage of the other; if a substantial cut is made from an initial high offer, the other side might think you are trying to steal from them; if you offer a discount price, that price becomes the benchmark for all subsequent negotiations. Some of the younger Chinese businesspeople are more aggressive, more profit-oriented, and less face-conscious than the older generation. More of today's businesspeople and government officials are also receiving MBAs and training in Western countries and are able to conduct business with a wide repertoire of skills.

Making concessions and maintaining face is a delicate balancing act. On the one hand, making a gesture of goodwill and being willing to make concessions is important for maintaining good relationships. On the other hand, maintaining strength and power in the negotiation is essential for making the best deal. Comments conveying the sentiment of the "certainty of finding a solution" or being "absolutely certain that the problems will be solved" indicate flexibility and interest in making concessions to achieve a successful solution. By conveying the belief that this attitude should be taken by both sides, no weakness is revealed and no one loses face.

Typically, the first concessions are likely to be the most generous, tapering to a few minor concessions as the process continues. Once the other side has made a concession, the typical Chinese response is to acknowledge the other side's flexibility or concessions as "a certain progress" and to push for more concessions. The push will continue until no more concessions are forthcoming or the deadline has been reached. There is generally a great unwillingness by the Chinese to make concessions and lose face.

Another tactic is giving an indication of rejection without saying *no* and waiting to see if the other side sees the problem and makes a concession. If so, that person wins respect not only for being able to understand the situation, but also for resolving the impasse. High context cultures have expectations that implied needs will be met without explicit discussion. Participants may continue talking indirectly and ambiguously until areas of agreement can be found. If they cannot be found, a go-between might be used because directly pursuing a disagreement would destroy the harmony between the two sides.

As discussions continue, both sides understand who is the winner and who is the loser; however, the loser, if Chinese, must be able to save face. The winner needs to make concessions at the end so the loser can save face; the winner should not bring up the fact of winning in later conversations. Since everyone knows who won, talking about it results in a more serious loss of face to the other side. If the loser is not able to save face, this offense may cause a return to formal etiquette or may be serious enough to render the loser unable to do business with the other side in the future. While the orientation toward making deals is win-lose, the final result must be carefully orchestrated so that the loser can maintain face and continue to be a willing business partner in the future, when opportunity and advantage, defined by the circumstances at the time, result in another discussion about doing business together.

Style

In general, the process of bargaining is seen as enjoyable, so more time is spent on this activity. In a Confucian culture, maintaining harmony throughout this process is an important goal. As a result, the style of communication is extremely important. First, respect due other individuals must be demonstrated at all times. For instance, confrontation is not desirable. Using a tone of voice that conveys respect to the other individual is appropriate; emotions must be controlled; arguing with those at lower levels is not desirable; boasting about one's own accomplishments is inappropriate. Protecting and extending face to others has major implications both for what is said and what is left unsaid during conversations. Care must be taken to "give face" or to say things in a way that enhances the image of the other person; doing that will "extend the face" of the person speaking; each person takes care to protect his or her face by saying things in a way that promotes harmony within the group.

Second, face encompasses the reciprocal relationship aspects of respect and deference and is meaningful only in relation to others. Therefore, developing a relationship with someone includes reciprocity in obligations and creates a set of expectations regarding future behavior. Superiors must be respected and shown deference, while those of lower status must be protected by deeds as well as in conversation. Understanding this approach to business conversations and behavior allows one to understand better what is said and, importantly, not said during meetings.

Third, the individual's network of relationships is critical to success, influence, and power. One's face can be influenced by the actions of other individuals in the network. Within the hierarchy of an organization or network, an individual's face can be enhanced or reduced by the actions of those who report to that person. For instance, much time is spent on conferences with the business team and its superior before permission is given to enter an agreement because a bad agreement can bring a loss of face to one's superior. The amount of time spent on this process is not important;

taking time to develop a good agreement that gives face to the individuals involved and to their boss is critical. Proceeding carefully and making wise decisions is important for the whole network because loss of face by one person influences loss of face for the individual, his or her family, business associates, and all members in the network of relationships.

Face reflects the approval of the community and, therefore, is of far greater value than material wealth. If others in the community do not treat a person with deference or convey face upon an individual, that person finds it extremely difficult to work within the community. Those who contribute to a loss of face are isolated from the network, relationships are weakened or broken, and those individuals must work their way back into the network on a personal level with the individual who was offended. Obtaining, maintaining, and increasing face makes it possible for an individual to do business. The social contacts are more important than specifications, price, or a specific academic degree when conducting business.

Respect always must be earned, and doing so takes time. Displaying a sincere interest in the local Chinese culture is one valuable approach to establishing a relationship. Demonstrating some knowledge of local culture is helpful. However, do not fall into the trap of the amateur and try to establish yourself as an expert in a subject about which you have only a surface knowledge. Instead, be humble regarding your own knowledge and ask questions to show an interest in learning more about the culture. Be willing to visit local companies and be sensitive to the pride that the Chinese have in their accomplishments, but do not make praiseworthy comments that might sound condescending. This kind of *polite talk*, exchanging pleasantries and giving face, can last for several meetings and involve much circumlocution. Whether subsequent meetings continue with the same level of formality or become increasingly more flexible and less formal is one way of measuring whether the relationship is improving. While you are getting to know this potential business partner, the Chinese likely will be checking on you through their network of contacts.

Many of these initial meetings are part of a social occasion, such as a banquet. The seating arrangement at a banquet is an important part of the protocol. For instance, the most important foreigner is seated to the right of the most important Chinese, followed by a clear order of the hierarchy around the table. While the social occasion is used to demonstrate hospitality and respect, important business issues are sometimes discussed after several meetings of this type have occurred. Much of the conversation entails giving face to the other members who are present. Participants who not only digest the food but also the conversation can develop a better understanding of the other side's point of view and identify possible areas of agreement or potential ways of resolving difficulties.

Gift giving is also an important element in establishing relationships. Determining the proper value of a gift is critical because giving an item that is too valuable may cause the person receiving the gift to lose face or create an expectation that difficult favors will be asked. Different occasions require gifts of different values, strangers do not usually give gifts, and gifts are usually given for a reason. Therefore, during the early stages of a relationship, moderately priced gifts are most appropriate and given to demonstrate hospitality—to thank a host for dinner, for a banquet, or for taking time to meet with you—without establishing any expectations for future favors. A modest gift demonstrates hospitality and good manners. An expensive gift might be construed as a bribe, which is illegal in some countries and intrusive in the business relationship when done inappropriately. In some countries, an expensive gift creates an uncomfortable situation because one side now feels obliged to do something in return for the favor, and the relationship is off balance. For many Westerners, the gifts received are expected to become company or government property and are not kept by individuals. Make sure you know your organization's expectations prior to accepting any gifts from potential partners.

By establishing relationships with business partners, an individual can build upon the *guanxi* inherent in family relationships to develop his or her own reputation and status within the business community. As *guanxi* increases, an individual has access to a greater number of businesses, more diverse levels and areas of expertise, more positions within the bureaucracy, and more knowledge of business affairs and opportunities. Developing *guanxi* or standing within the business network establishes an individual's reputation as an honorable businessperson, and that reputation, in turn, can open doors for future business opportunities.

Business discussions take place anytime participants meet, whether formally or informally. An assumption that is made regarding potential business partners is that each party comes with a specific agenda, which may be hidden, so time should be spent trying to identify and understand the other side's agenda. Doing so may be a challenge, depending upon the other side's willingness to reveal agenda items. One common strategy used by the Chinese is to encourage the other side to talk first about concerns, issues, and ideas while reserving any comments. By so doing, the Chinese can keep their agenda hidden while trying to determine the interests of the other side. Understanding what is important and of concern to the other side is important because opportunities arise from every situation. With a realistic and pragmatic view of the situation, the Chinese will respond to opportunities as they emerge. However, the Chinese orientation is to keep at least part of their agenda hidden. First, the high context language does not encourage an elaboration of intentions and expectations. Second, complete candor regarding intentions and objectives reduces opportunities for flexibility later in the process. The preferred approach by the Chinese is to elicit as much information from the other side as possible without revealing too much of their own.

Conclusion

Devoting time to the creation and maintenance of relationships is a critical factor for success in the PRC and the overseas Chinese communities. These networks form the foundation of business activity—from identifying opportunities, to obtaining funding, to evaluating potential business partners, to implementing business deals. Conversational tact and appropriate concession strategies are necessary communication tools; managing face, increasing *guanxi*, and obtaining a profit are underlying themes to all business activities.

The process begins with formal business and social meetings, during which protocol must be observed. During this time, the potential Chinese partner is using network contacts to determine your experience, status, authority, and company's position. Over time, meetings may become less formal and more information will be solicited and, perhaps, shared. After doing a number of business projects together successfully, you may become a "friend," which entails obligations and responsibilities. As a friend, a foreigner will likely be called upon to offer assistance in business and personal matters. As a friend, the foreigner is also expected to make requests for favors. In this way, the relationship will continue to build and strengthen.

A growing number of businesspeople in the PRC received MBAs in North America, Australia, or Europe; are participating in MBA programs in China; or are involved in training programs in North America or Europe. These people are being trained to be bicultural and have increasing facility in adapting to Western business practices. However, since basic values and acceptable behaviors are created in childhood and generally do not change unless a person is faced with life-threatening, traumatic events, decision making still revolves around traditional processes.

As the legal and market systems evolve and function with more predictability, businesspeople may put more of their faith in the systems. Today different parts of the PRC are in different stages of transition. Overseas Chinese operate within the structure of systems and the rule of law of the country in which they operate and live, as well as within the traditional Chinese social network. Even when the potential Chinese business partner speaks English as a second language, has an MBA, and understands Western business systems, it is incumbent upon the foreign businessperson to assume that the traditional system is in place. There is still much information that is transmitted throughout the business network, and the foreign businessperson is well advised to honor the tradition, create a place within the system, and use it to gather information. China is a complex country in which to do business, and success will demand a great deal of attention and sensitivity to the Chinese way of doing business.

CHAPTER 10

JAPAN AND SOUTH KOREA

Classification of Cultures Model

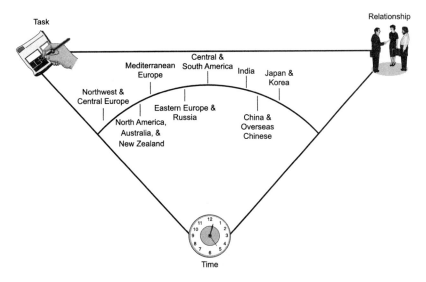

Although they have had distinctly different historical development, both Japan and Korea share some fundamental characteristics and will be grouped together for this discussion. The sophisticated businessperson will make distinctions between these two cultures apparent during the conduct of business, while noting the similarities privately.

As an island culture, Japan remains essentially homogeneous. Characteristics of an island culture are the strong sense of self-identity as a country, the desire to maintain the country's independence, and a belief in maintaining the common good. The ethnic population is 99 percent Japanese. Creation of a unique culture, shared by the whole population, was reinforced when Japan isolated itself from foreign influence for more than two centuries, from 1636 to 1854. While the Japanese culture was confirmed and reinforced during this period, the attitude toward outside influences had not changed from earlier centuries: Study the new information and technology, choose to accept some principles, and incorporate them into existing beliefs and value systems, making the changes completely in a Japanese fashion.

With a developing industrial sector in the nineteenth and twentieth centuries, the lack of natural resources or raw materials as an island nation created a strong incentive to develop linkages with other geographic locations having the missing resources. These relationships are the primary vehicles by which new ideas, theories, and philosophies are introduced into the country. Through the centuries, foreign influence has waxed and waned. However, the Japanese have always modified foreign management practices, such as Deming's principles of quality, and incorporated them with Japanese beliefs, such as *kaizen*, which is a belief in creating improvement by making small changes over time and thereby creating a unique Japanese set of business practices.

A fundamental belief among Japanese is that change is inevitable and natural. The Japanese have been able to maintain their identity while continuing to adapt throughout history. Faced with new beliefs, such as Buddhism or Catholicism, the Japanese accept and incorporate what is valuable for the industrial and economic sectors as they remain constant to their philosophical, spiritual, and artistic heritage. As a result, the Japanese culture is much like a stereo component system, with many separate pieces comprising a finely tuned and coherent whole. The separate components are completely interdependent and each relies on the other to get the desired result. Further, as new ideas or practices are discovered and adapted, they seem to accumulate one upon the other, with each one as a distinct but interdependent part of the whole. While some beliefs appear to be contradictory, they coexist as part of the larger Japanese culture.

This orientation to specific, continuous change in the for-profit area is consistent with an agrarian perspective toward time that views individual events as parts of a recurring cycle. Events are not viewed as discrete activities, but as part of a larger whole. Completion of tasks is viewed as part of the overall objective and can be executed only by people in an ever-changing environment. Since the linkages of events, tasks, and objectives occur through people, relationships are of high importance and must be developed prior to conducting business. Cycles of events and individual tasks work through people, so time must be taken to understand the people with whom you will work and to work within the cycle of change.

Korea, historically termed the "Hermit Kingdom" as a result of its resistance to foreign influence, is a peninsula locked into land contact with the rest of East Asia. Korea has managed to retain a distinct identity while completely dwarfed, in a historical sense, by China to its west. As a result, Korea has homogeneity similar to that of an island culture, including one dominant ethnic group with a small minority of about 20,000 ethnic Chinese.

While under Chinese rule, the peninsula had relative independence because of its location and pragmatic approach to the payment of tribute to and diplomacy with the emperor in Beijing. With declining Chinese power and a weakened domestic posture at the end of the nineteenth century, Korea was open to Western and Japanese encroachment. In 1910, Japan began a 35-year period of imperial rule over Korea, trying to supplant the Korean language and culture and mirroring a historical nightmare of the Japanese invasion of Korea in the sixteenth century. This level of historical animosity and hostility between the two countries is never far from the consciousness of Koreans, particularly the older generation, the carrier of tradition. However, most restrictions on Japanese movies, popular music, and fashion have been lifted, with younger Koreans now eagerly following Japanese pop culture.

While having been influenced by both the Chinese and Japanese cultures, an important Korean attitude is *han*, which means the ability to survive. Other groups may come and go, some new ideas may be forced on the

Global Business Practices Model

Areas of World	Gov't	Law	Hier.	Privacy	Punct.	Flow	Truth	Words	Style	Logic
Northwest & Central Europe	▨		▨							
North America, Australia, & NZ										▨
Mediterranean Europe	▨		▨		▨	▨			▨	
Eastern Europe & Russia	▨		▨		▨					▨
South & Central America	▨		■	▨	▨					
India	▨		▨	▨	▨		■			▨
China & Overseas Chinese	■	▨	▨	▨	■	■		▨	▨	▨
Japan & Korea	▨	▨	■	▨		▨	▨	▨	■	▨

LEGEND

Role of Government: White = the government sets parameters and constraints to create the environment for doing business. Black = Direct involvement of government in business as a business partner.

Rule of Law: White = Reliance on systems and procedures. Black = Pragmatism or situational considerations.

Sense of Hierarchy: White = Assumption of equality. Black = Assumption of status difference.

View of Privacy: White = Business and private matters are separate. Black = Business and private matters are all part of one reality.

Punctuality: White = Fixed time. Black = Flexible or "rubber" time.

Flow of Activities: White = Time works in a linear fashion. Black = Time works in a cyclical fashion.

Truth: White = Universal truth. Black = Many truths exist at once.

Words: White = Words have explicit meanings. Black = Words have implicit meanings.

Style: White = Communication is direct and forthright. Black = Communication is indirect.

Logic: White = Formal deductive reasoning. Black = Alternative heuristic.

people, some ideas may be incorporated, some ideas will be thrown off as soon as possible, but through it all, Koreans will endure and remain Korean.

Both Japanese and South Korean business cultures are a unique blend of Asian characteristics, Western influences, island culture or isolation perspectives, and Buddhist values. Since their orientation toward time, task, and relationships is unique among the Asian cultures, so, too, is their approach to business practice. This chapter will examine the elements of structure, process, and communication that influence the unique business cultures of Japan and South Korea.

Structure

While Buddhist, Taoist, Shinto, and Confucian philosophies influence the role of hierarchy, as they do in Chinese and overseas Chinese cultures, the resulting configuration in Japan and South Korea is distinctly different from the Chinese *spider web* configuration. The role of government and rule of law will also be discussed in this section.

Hierarchy

The most common religions in Japan are Shinto and Buddhist (84 percent), with a small group designated as "other" (16 percent). In South Korea, 46 percent of the population has no religious affiliation, with 26 percent identifying themselves as Christian, 26 percent as Buddhist, only 1 percent as Confucian, and 1 percent as other. The significantly higher scores on Power Distance and Confucian Dynamism factors, along with the significantly lower scores on Individualism,[1] demonstrate the importance of Buddhist, Taoist, Confucian, and Shinto influences on the sense of hierarchy in Japan. While almost half of Koreans currently have no religious affiliation, the Japanese and Chinese philosophies of hierarchy, similar in Shinto, Buddhist, Taoist, and Confucian traditions, have had significant impact on cultural evolution in South Korea. This philosophy of a paternalistic hierarchy translates into autocratic hierarchies within both government and business organizations. While the structure of organizations has many similarities between the countries, the decision-making processes in Japan and South Korea differ and will be discussed in the

---

[1] Geert Hofstede's research identified five dimensions of culture. In this chapter, high Power Distance scores demonstrate the degree to which members of the society recognize inequalities of power, high Confucian Dynamism scores indicate the extent to which the country values long-term commitments and respects tradition. High Individualism scores indicate that individual rights are important in that society. See www.geert-hofstede.com.

section on process. Similarities between the countries include the belief that society is based upon unequal relationships among people that involve mutual, complementary obligations.

The concept of the individual is not as important in Japan as is the relationship with family, friends, and colleagues; so the Japanese will often de-emphasize their individual work while emphasizing the contribution of others to the group's results. The individual contribution to a group is tempered with harmony with all members because the group itself has its own identity and works as one. In this respect, the Japanese are reflecting the Asian and Buddhist philosophy of attributing good fortune to the efforts of others, recognizing that the sum of the whole group, in this case, is greater than the individual parts. Having a sense of obligation to the efforts of others reinforces the group perspective and results in the Japanese concept of mutual dependence and concern for the opinion of others. Interdependence is a fundamental element of the Japanese and Korean cultures and permeates business and personal relationships at all levels of an organization as well as between companies. Thus, the personal relationship leads to corporate relationships that can withstand tough times in the marketplace.

As a result, networks are a fundamental element of doing business in Japan and South Korea. Not only the particular network to which one belongs, but also one's *position* within that network constrains and structures the type of relationships that exist and can be developed with other individuals. Based upon one's family, background, education, and personal achievements, each individual is accorded a particular position within society, involving mutual dependence with other individuals who may be family members, schoolmates, colleagues, or close friends. Success stems from and is shared with deceased ancestors and living network members, making family a significant factor in determining one's social position. Failure, too, is shared. Instead of being fired, an individual may be given a *window seat*, meaning that this individual will be given work to do but will no longer be a central part of decision making. Being able to use one's connections to marshal the necessary resources and skills to complete a task, fulfilling obligations incurred along the way, and taking responsibility to spread opportunities among network members enables one to develop, solidify, and increase social status and position.

The visitor must establish relationships with network members before it is possible to do business. This process can be time-consuming and requires a great deal of patience, beginning with small projects used to initiate the relationship and building to larger projects over a period of time. As an individual meets or exceeds expectations on each project, the partner's confidence in that individual's ability to successfully and appropriately conduct business grows. A decision to enter into a relationship with another company through another individual is not taken lightly because of the resulting obligations.

The sense of inner and outer circles exists at several levels and is fundamental to the types of relationships that can be established. To fully understand the Japanese character, one must have a "Japanese ear," possible only if you are Japanese and brought up with Japanese values, beliefs, and philosophies. A strong belief among the Japanese is that foreigners, *gaijin*, can never understand the Japanese heart. The *gaijin*, literally, is the person outside the Japanese clan or ethnic group. This homogeneous inner circle of the Japanese permits effective communication among members of the clan using a high context language.

The insularity of both the Japanese island culture and the South Korean peninsular culture allows much meaning to be understood without verbal communication and for nonverbal communication to convey a great deal of meaning. The Japanese and South Koreans will allow a foreigner to participate only to the extent that they see it being to their benefit. Many non-Japanese become disillusioned with this dynamic and withdraw from relationships in frustration.

On a business level, networks also involve an inner and outer set of relationships based on a system of favors, duty, and obligations, referred to as *giri* and *on*. Over time, interaction between networks increases based upon requests for favors, granting of favors, and making efforts to know and understand one another. To penetrate a network successfully, two routes with some likelihood of success are possible. One is to use the official route, contacting organizations like one's home country's Department of Commerce or equivalent, the Japanese External Trade Organization (JETRO), individual prefecture or government offices in Japan, official trade missions, or trade associations. Individuals from these organizations can facilitate introductions to appropriate representatives who can identify businesspeople with potential interest in your service or product. They may be able to make introductions and/or arrange meetings. Thus, the process of identifying and evaluating networks can begin.

A second alternative is to use consultants or friends of friends to identify appropriate businesses, social events, trade shows, or other business activities that can be vehicles for obtaining introductions to businesspeople with influence. Meeting the right people and successfully establishing a strong initial relationship with them can facilitate access to the existing network and identification of business opportunities. Introductions are not casually made because making an introduction is also a recommendation or endorsement of that individual. The success or failure of the recommended person reflects upon the person who made the introduction, with face and respect accruing to those who know both partners well enough to see the mutual benefit of the introduction. Maintaining harmony among relationships is important in Japan and Korea.

People have responsibility for one another within their business network and will pass along their evaluation of a person's reputation. Having your good reputation endorsed by an introduction to the right people is critical for success. On the one hand, the complex government structure, rules, and demanding levels of quality make it appear that everything is impossible. On the other hand, anything is possible depending upon whom you know and how you approach them.

The structure and process of business relationships in Japan and South Korea is distinctly different from the Chinese approach. The Chinese *spider web* approach results in a loose structure that is ambiguous and dynamic. In nineteenth-century Japan, businesses were organized as a **zaibatsu**, which were family-controlled banking and industrial groups that pooled resources, created interdependent directorships, coordinated among companies, and had close ties with political parties. They helped finance strategic enterprises in Japan, Taiwan, and Korea. After World War II, the *zaibatsu* were officially broken up but reemerged in the 1950s and 1960s as *keiretsu*. Each *keiretsu* is a group of companies that can pool resources and works together in competition against other *keiretsu*. Within each *keiretsu*, the suppliers, banks, manufacturers, and distributors share information about customers, the industry, the environment, and their own companies. The competition for market share and profits among *keiretsu* is intense. Membership is long standing, and very few companies do business with more than one *keiretsu*.

In South Korea, family-owned enterprises have long been a major part of the economy. During the 1960s, the *chaebol*, modeled after the *zaibatsu* of Japan, were created as state-corporate alliances under the leadership of Park Chung Hee. The most significant difference between the two was that the *zaibatsu* were organized around a bank and the *chaebol* were forbidden from owning a bank. The government nationalized the banks of South Korea and was able to channel capital to industries deemed necessary for achieving national objectives. Many of the *chaebol* became indebted to independent banks as well as state banks and were unable to repay their debts during the Asian currency crisis. The most spectacular collapse was that of the Daewoo Group in mid-1999 with $80 billion in unpaid debt. As in the case of most situations across the globe involving a great deal of available money in good times, investigations have exposed widespread corruption in the past that continues at this time.

The major difference from the Chinese approach is that the *keiretsu* and *chaebol* require formal, stable linkages between companies. Companies belong to only one formal arrangement, making the choice of a network even more important because changing networks does not happen easily or often in either Japan or South Korea.

Role of Government

South Korea is a democratic republic with power shared between the president and the legislature. Japan is a constitutional monarchy with a parliamentary government. Both countries are democratic, but democracy is not one generally agreed-upon form of government. In the Western world, democratic ideals emphasize a separation between government and business. However, democracy in Japan, South Korea, and the other Asian countries involves an interdependent role between government and business.

The *chaebol* in South Korea involve close relationships between government agencies and family-owned companies. This relationship spurred phenomenal growth in South Korea, with the government determining what industries were necessary for growth. Being a part of the nation's economic development strategy enabled the government to provide bank funding, tax relief, and preferential treatment for specific industries and companies. In some cases, the relationships involved corruption resulting in the collapse of some *chaebol*. Current efforts to reform corrupt practices have met with limited success, and investigations into fraudulent accounting and bribery continue.

In Japan, the Ministry of International Trade and Industry (MITI) was created in 1949 to serve as an architect of industrial policy, an arbiter on industrial problems and disputes, and a regulator for both industry and trade. A major objective was to strengthen the country's industrial base. While MITI did not have the authority to manage industry along the lines of a centrally planned economy, it did provide industries with administrative guidance and direction, both formal and informal, on modernization, technology, investments in new plants and equipment, and domestic and foreign competition. As industry became stronger, MITI's policies also changed. During the 1980s, the ministry helped to craft a number of measures aimed at opening and promoting specific markets, including the creation of an import promotion office within the ministry. The close relationship between MITI and industry allows the ministry to play a role in fostering more open markets, but conflict remains between the desire to open markets and the need to promote new and growth industries. The Japanese government also has a major regulatory role. For example, the government's efforts to keep society safe from products of other lands results in the blockage or prohibition of products from other countries.

Both countries are democracies. The orientation toward the role of government in business activities is best described as a willing partnership between government and business, with emphasis on growth and the creation of new jobs and markets for the countries. The government in South Korea has maintained very close ties with business, although it is in the process of promoting more independent management and adherence to standards throughout the business community. The government in Japan is to provide advice, encouragement, and support for exporting and importing activities. Both countries continue the process of modifying the relationship between government and business, adhering to the belief in continuous change as part of life. At this time, however, it is important for the foreign businessperson to continue to recognize the interdependence between the political and economic agenda in these countries and develop a strategy for managing this aspect of the relationship.

Rule of Law

The legal system in Japan is modeled after the European civil law system, but it also has been influenced by the common law system. The South Korean legal system is a combination of civil and common law influenced by Chinese classical thought. With constitutions created after World War II establishing these legal systems, the rule of law has a very short history in comparison with the traditional cultures in these countries. As a result, the rule of law is not the foundational philosophy in Japan or Korea that it is in Western countries and must be understood in terms of its position as one more layer interacting with the traditional, relationship-based culture.

As in other Asian cultures, the essence of doing business is not how binding the words of a contract are in a court of law, but in how binding the obligations of a relationship are over time. Sincere effort must be made to ensure the vitality of the relationship, both immediately after an agreement is reached and over time.

Difficulties, disagreements, and differences of opinion will occur—circumstances and conditions never remain the same, and change is expected. Taking time to get to know potential business partners is important because you will work with them for a long time. If the relationship is strong, if there is a good understanding of one another, if there is a common overall view of the joint project, then problems arising from new information, changed circumstances, or uncontrollable events can be resolved in a mutually satisfactory manner. However, if the relationship is not strong, if there is little understanding of the other side, or if the project is perceived differently, then resolving problems will be extremely difficult.

Contracts are taken very seriously as an agreement between parties to establish a working relationship. This is constant throughout the Asian countries. In general, the words in the document are a framework, not a specific definition of what is expected, as is the case in most Western countries. Because circumstances outside the control of either party, such as a change in the value of one country's currency, problems with transportation, or employee problems, are unpredictable, a contract cannot cover every contingency. Therefore, the objective of a contract is to establish a relationship that can and will adapt to changing circumstances.

The contract establishes a legal relationship and identifies the direction to be taken in a joint project. On the one hand, the weaker partner cannot argue and bicker over the terms of the contract in the same way that a son cannot come back and argue once his father makes a decision. However, the concepts of *giri* and *on* create a condition whereby the father figure, the stronger of the partners, monitors the situation and is willing to modify the decision if circumstances change and another decision is in the weaker member's best interest.

Therefore, a contract can be considered a *minimal deal* that can be broadened and modified as conditions change. The concept of changed circumstances, *jijo henko*, means that the details are always subject to renegotiation. While circumstances may change, necessitating a change in the specifics of the contract, the broad outline of the contract and the strong relationship of the two parties enable both sides to adjust, adapt, and continue working toward their mutual goal. However, it is the relationship rather than the contract that ensures success.

Nonetheless, contracts are taken very seriously because the relationship established by the contract entails both a moral and a legal obligation. The parties have agreed to work together; therefore, they now have an obligation, *on*, to be responsible for one another, *giri*, and to work for each other to ensure the success of the joint project, *kan*. The assumption is that whatever difficulties arise because of changed circumstances can and will be worked on together because of the strong relationship. If it is not possible to work out the disagreement and a third party, such as a legal authority or government agency, must be consulted, the relationship is thought to have failed. Because the relationship is the sustaining part of the working arrangement, the Japanese, in particular, take time to consider the other party, to evaluate the other party's strengths and weaknesses, and to assess the other party's reputation as a *good* business partner. Knowing the specific details of a particular business arrangement is not as critical as knowing whether one can depend upon the other person in times of difficulty. If a long-term relationship is in place, the written agreement is a formality that can be the basis of expanded opportunity as circumstances evolve over the course of a long-term relationship between individuals and organizations.

Restructuring of the *chaebols* in South Korea has caused a shift in the influence of both the government and the legal system. Japan's political system is managing a course through a turbulent period, facing demands to restructure the banking system and create more transparency in business practices. Neither one of these countries has a Western style rule of law and will not have one in the foreseeable future, if ever. As a result, the businessperson seeking to do business successfully in either Japan or South Korea needs to manage the constraints of the WTO legal system, the current laws in the country, the laws of his or her company's home country, his or her company's policies, and the local relationships.

Process

The unique approach to business organizations, as well as the mixture of Western and Asian influences in the government and legal systems, creates a unique process for doing business in Japan and South Korea. This section examines the impact of the role of privacy, punctuality, and flow of events on business practice.

Privacy

While the emphasis on developing personal relationships is extremely high in Japan, sharing personal information is not very common, even after years of working together as colleagues. With a strong and well-protected inner circle, personal information is not usually revealed to anyone outside that inner circle. Being sensitive to feelings that are only implicitly revealed during conversation is a necessary and highly valued skilled in relationships. However, having to express feelings is viewed as a breakdown in the high context language system. Maintaining *wa*, the sense of harmony and mutual interdependence, is important. Sharing private information is not.

In South Korea, **kibun**, or inner feelings, need to be kept in good order because to damage *kibun* may cut off a relationship and create an enemy. If someone has damaged your *kibun*, or feelings, you would not do business with that person, even if that person were unaware of having done something wrong. To Koreans, harmonious personal relationships respect the feelings of the other person. However, personal information is not shared with others who are not part of the inner circle.

Visitors need to invest time learning when to discuss specific business topics, when to discuss social topics, and what social topics are acceptable. In addition, being able to participate in these conversations in a way that maintains harmony and does not offend the person with whom you are trying to establish a relationship will enhance your credibility and face.

Punctuality

As Japan and South Korea went through amazing economic growth from the 1970s through the mid-1990s, infrastructure developed a level of sophistication enabling public transportation systems to run on time. The ability to depend upon transportation systems created the expectation for goods to arrive on time. The combination of reliable transportation systems, need for frequent deliveries by small retail outlets, and Deming's teachings about variability and reliability led to the development of and reliance on just-in-time delivery systems.

These efficient systems also correspond with the expectation for people to arrive on time. Because of this highly efficient system, business expectations are that activities begin and end on time. In Japan, banquets are scheduled to start at a specific time and end at a specific time. While the events do not start and end with the same precision of the train system, the variation is within small limits. A toast will mark the beginning of the event, and a cheer will mark the end of the event. To enhance your good standing in the network, you need to arrive on time and leave at the proper time.

In general, both countries are punctual in a Western sense in that business processes involving technology are expected to use time efficiently. Similarly, business events take place at scheduled times, with a minor grace period for automobile traffic. However, the number of events scheduled per day or week and the pace of those events do not follow the Western sense of time. The events happen according to a different rhythm.

Flow of Events

The flow of events follows an agrarian sense of time, emphasizing the cyclical flow of activities rather than the efficiency of the industrial revolution. As such, events are not viewed as discrete activities, but as parts of a whole. Therefore, time has a longer-term focus, with individuals and events always viewed as part of a larger dynamic. As a result, task completion is viewed as part of the overall objective and can be executed only by people in an ever-changing environment. Since the linkages of events, tasks, and objectives occur through people, relationships are of very high importance and must be developed prior to conducting business. Cycles of events and individual tasks work through people, so time must be taken to understand the people with whom you will work and to work within the cycle of change.

Interdependence evolves over the course of many events or activities. For example, giving time for a meeting creates *on*, or indebtedness, which a person carries until the favor is returned, thereby creating a new obligation. *Giri* is a sense of duty to repay indebtedness. A gift may be offered to thank another person for spending time meeting with you, which then creates indebtedness to the person giving you the gift. The sense of doing and returning favors for someone, *on* and *giri*, is part of the foundation for the *attitude of reciprocity*, which is a basic assumption for strong, long-term relationships between people and companies. Over time, people and companies develop close, interdependent working relationships based upon a shared history of learning how reliable, loyal, and dependable the others are. In this way, a good personal connection develops, called **naniwabushi**, a term that encompasses several levels of relationship, reciprocity, language use, and interdependence.

To settle on a recommendation, agreement, or course of action, many informal meetings and conversations are held to propose an idea, lay the groundwork, find out what objections exist, resolve differences, and obtain commitment to the idea before it is ever formally proposed. Informally, between people who have good relationships, proposals are tested and agreements created before formal meetings take place. This process takes place throughout the organization and across functions. It requires considerable time and effort, frequent contact, and continued presence for success.

Both Japan and Korea have high context languages, as well as a belief in the importance of maintaining harmony in relationships. It is not surprising that this process proceeds in an ambiguous fashion amid a stream of information, many tangential conversations, and postponements that often lead to more meetings. Subordinates are asked to gather more information, requests are made for reworked proposals, and suggestions are offered as a way of moving beyond the proposal being discussed. Breaks in the discussions are taken often so that more information can be gathered and members of the team can confer with one another and with their superiors, developing consensus after the new information is understood. This process, while somewhat confusing and seemingly redundant, results in good decisions, with a great deal of consensus.

However, decisions cannot be changed easily when new ideas are suggested as possible concessions or compromise during a formal business meeting. The *ringi* process of decision making requires that everyone participating in the decision must share in making the decision, and consensus is necessary. Therefore, any proposed concessions or compromises must be taken back to the group in a private session, where they will be discussed and agreed upon before the team members can make any commitments at a formal meeting of both parties. As a result, the process can be extremely slow and may even be used as a defensive tactic to delay the process.

Concessions and agreements are made at the end of the process just before the signing deadline. When all the issues, proposals, and concessions have been presented, discussed, and understood and when compromises have revealed all the concessions that the other side is likely to make, the Japanese side will come to an agreement—if an agreement is to be made. Generally decisions are made at the end all at once, not sequentially during the course of discussion.

While the meetings may start on time, there is no pressure to make decisions until all the issues are examined thoroughly by the company's internal team and explored in both formal and informal conversations with members of the other side's business team. Given the high-context language and need for consensus within the organization, the number and pacing of meetings follows a cyclical rather than efficiency path. As much time as is necessary will be taken for meetings until both sides are comfortable with the agreement. Then a formal meeting will be scheduled to mark the agreement, sign the document, and solidify the relationship.

Communication

Words, concepts of truth, logic, and style create a distinctive communication process that is challenging for outsiders. This section examines the role of these concepts in the communication process.

Words

Japan, as an island culture, and peninsular South Korea, with its tradition of maintaining its identity even when a tributary state to a more powerful neighbor, each with basically only one ethnic group in the country, have great homogeneity within their culture and their language. As a result of the shared heritage of accidental and deliberate isolation, people in island cultures or self-contained cultures generally have a "group mind" that is understood and subscribed to by most, if not all, of the people. Outlooks on life, perspectives on the world, and strategies for success generally are widely understood and strongly held by members of these cultures. So strong is this group perspective that those who have lived and worked outside the country for a time and return home are often viewed as *tainted*. For example, children graduating from non-Japanese high schools usually are not admitted directly into Japanese universities. Many go to universities run by non-Japanese organizations or attend special schools preparing for tests that will demonstrate their ability to function in a Japanese university. Isolation becomes desirable as a way of preserving the *group mind* and often evolves into a distinctly ethnocentric perspective toward the rest of the world.

Both Korean and Japanese are high context languages, meaning that the words themselves do not convey precise meanings. With a *group mind*, members can rely upon their strong common cultural heritage to interpret imprecise words with appropriate nonverbal elements so that shared understanding results. For example, there are so many nonverbal ways to indicate disagreement that the word *no* is not really necessary. Therefore, *only insiders* can really understand the Japanese language. The belief that a *gaijin* can never be an insider is virtually universal; as a result, a level of identification and understanding exists among the Japanese that may never occur between the Japanese and non-Japanese.

Formal and ritualized forms of behavior and language, recognized by all Japanese participants as appropriate, are used to establish and maintain relationships. During initial visits, conversation usually revolves around social topics such as sports events, general economic circumstances, a person's hobbies, very general information about families, and general activities. Several Japanese *lubricant expressions* can be used to facilitate interactions, establish interdependency, and create harmony. Examples of how to use these expressions include expressing an understanding of how the other side is feeling, showing due consideration by hesitating before responding (*so desu ne*—"well, let's see"), delaying commitment or avoiding saying *no* while helping the other side save face by saying "we'll think about it" in response to the other side's proposal, and using appropriate rhetorical expressions during ceremonial occasions, or using *tracking* expressions such as *hai* or *so desu ka* while the other side is talking.

Learning when and where to use these expressions appropriately is necessary for building relationships in Japan and Korea. These techniques demonstrate the outsider's interest in the other side, willingness to give the other side's interests high priority, and an effort at understanding the other side's perspective. Overt expressions of anger, frustration, or displeasure are detrimental to a relationship, especially in an early stage of relationship development, and need to be avoided.

Communication is often used indirectly in these high context cultures. For instance, one side might begin talking about its company and concerns modestly, with hesitation and apparent apologies, not stating wishes immediately or directly, even while knowing the other side values size, growth, competence, and achievement. Because of the high context languages, much information is communicated through silence, glances, or seemingly cryptic comments. So, to be a good communicator, a foreigner in Japan or Korea must learn to understand the nuances of the conversation; try to discern the inner thoughts of the other side; and be sensitive to the interaction of feelings and content, sometimes described as *belly talk*. Learning to interpret spoken and unspoken information is a necessary skill for being able to gather all the information that is being conveyed during these meetings. It is important to *read the feelings*, **ishin-denshin**, of the participants in the meeting. Both active listening and careful, unobtrusive evaluation of the body language of the speakers will give the visitor a sense of what is being said and not said during sessions. The successful person does business quietly, not by boasting about individual accomplishments, but by modestly presenting competency and developing the capacity to understand three to four times as much Japanese or Korean as can be spoken. This is a skill seldom seen in Western businesspeople, who rely almost exclusively on interpreters.

This process usually involves several meetings over the course of weeks or months, but enough time will be taken by the Japanese to understand every point, evaluate the other side, and test the strength of the relationship and sincerity of the other side prior to entering into agreements. Typically, the Japanese are more vigorous at seeking information from the non-Japanese than they will be about providing it. Often, a direct request from a foreigner will elicit an indirect reply. Therefore, discussions generally follow a more subdued tone, with each side trying to please the other.

Wording of contracts is also a challenge for a Western businessperson. With words that have many meanings, crafting a contract or agreement to specify who will do what tasks within a specific time frame and where it will be done is a challenging task. Willingness to sign the contract means that the Japanese or South Korean businessperson wants to do business with you. However, the details of the contract will often remain somewhat ambiguous. The real power of enforcement comes not from the courts, but from the honor of the people involved. Therefore, taking time to get to know your potential business partners well before doing business is a valuable investment of time.

Truth

One of the fundamental beliefs consistent among Confucianism, Buddhism, Taoism, and Shintoism is that no one human being has the truth. Different views of a situation, different perceptions, and different philosophies can and do all exist at the same time. Another characteristic of these worldviews is a highly pragmatic approach to issues. Each situation is different, so it is important to determine what will and will not work in a specific situation. Expecting one rule, guideline, or decision to fit all circumstances is unrealistic. Truth, too, is tied to the social bonds that exist in a given situation. Therefore, determination of what is right or wrong often varies from one circumstance to another.

For example, in Japan, there are two words for truth, *tatamae* and *honne*. *Tatamae* is public truth or public standing—the information that will be conveyed to outsiders at formal meetings and reveals the company's formal position. *Honne*, on the other hand, is private truth revealed, in part, *only* to someone in the inner circle. Over time, if a foreign businessperson becomes part of an intermediate circle of accepted business associates, more individual feelings may be revealed. However, this will not happen during a formal meeting with members of both business teams present.

If you and the Japanese businessperson have developed a good connection, you may be asked to attend a social event. Outside the office, with no other official connection present, the Japanese businessperson may reveal more information about the company's position, issues, concerns, or needs. However, this information will be conveyed from the perspective of someone who uses a high context language. You will need to be observant of nonverbal communication, aware of the relationship between the two of you, and listen for what is not said. You will be given more insight into the other side's position but will still know only one part of the whole. In addition, this information should not be referred to directly during any public meetings—it is just understood that you both know you have the information.

Just because the Japanese or South Korean businessperson uses British or American English does not mean that the conversation or agreement will be more specific or concrete. English is being used to convey ambiguous words that take on meaning from the situation and relationship. The meaning of the English word does not represent the whole picture. The fact that the meaning is somehow *not true* is really not the point. Time, experience, and successful joint activities are necessary for understanding business partners. Honorable businesspeople keep their word, meaning that they honor the intent of the agreement. The path to integrity is through harmony rather than truth.

Logic

The decision-making process winds its way through a series of activities that are both task and relationship oriented. In this section of the chapter, we use Japanese terms and phrases to illustrate the way business is typically conducted. There are many similarities with the processes used in Korea, which will not be repeated here.

The formal opening process usually includes a broad introduction, **naniwabushi**, to establish good terms and personal relationships; it has three parts: **kikkake, seme,** and **urei**. Westerners often become frustrated at having to spend so much time on seemingly irrelevant information and matters of form. However, the information presented serves a necessary purpose to the Japanese and must be followed with great care.

Overt, direct bargaining strategies usually have no effect and can even be met by withdrawal from the negotiation process in an attempt to avoid confrontation. One area that remains constant throughout all business meetings is continued evaluation of the other side's trustworthiness and reliability while working to maintain a good relationship. Individuals from each side are likely to meet outside of formal meetings to test suggestions and to exchange possible solutions indirectly, always avoiding a direct *no* or loss of face.

The Japanese, and even more so the Koreans, who rigidly adhere to hierarchy, typically are not persuaded by the logical construction of an argument or by the verbal skills of the other side. Rather, they are influenced by the status and age of the other side's representative, age and reputation of the other side's company, and/or an intuitive feeling that a particular decision is more appropriate for the situation. The goal is to develop a *heart-to-heart* understanding with the other side that includes an agreement of intentions on broad issues rather than on details. The logical argument must include an understanding of social circumstances in the relationships and feelings as well as facts and reasoning.

Generally, the buyer is in a superior position and tends to choose or structure the general framework of the agreement. However, keeping in mind the concept of *amae*, or indulgent dependency, the buyer has the responsibility of considering the needs of the seller and not taking advantage of the seller. In addition, the stronger side makes concessions to the weaker side so the weaker side will *win*, thereby saving face and enabling both parties to be in a position to do business together in the future. Remember, all relationships are long term. Fortune and advantage may change, but respectful relations will be the vehicle by which both parties continue to interact, regardless of which party is superior at any point in time. In like manner, the importance of relationships and the need to save face or enhance good feeling, **kibun**, foster a win-win approach to conducting business in South Korea.

However, coming to an agreement does not happen easily. Discussions over price and terms are very common. In South Korea, the opening price is usually high so that a good deal can still be made after agreeing to significant concessions. If the other side's position is not acceptable, *no* will be stated in a variety of indirect ways without actually saying *no* to avoid hurting the other person's feelings or damaging the relationship.

Style

Over time, the foreign businessperson learns about the situation; the other company, products, or services; and the individuals involved during several meetings, beginning with general issues and moving to more specific issues in due time. The process begins formally with an **aisatsu**, or formal greeting. The circumstances, relationship of the people involved, importance of the matter at hand, and location of the meeting influence not only what is said, but also what is not said. The senior person from one company makes an *aisatsu* greeting to his or her equal from the other company, who then responds in a manner appropriate to his or her rank and status.

One of the cultural characteristics that enable the Japanese and Koreans to coordinate interpretations while using a high context language is that rituals, **kata**, or correct behaviors are an integral part of life. Depending upon the people involved, their individual status, their relationship, the event, the purpose of the conversation, and the location, certain behaviors are prescribed, expected, and implicitly evaluated. For example, the difficulty of learning the appropriate bowing behavior stems from variations according to status, position, purpose of conversation, relationship, and company's status. Learning to bow is not difficult. Learning to bow at the appropriate angle with the appropriate deference for different occasions and individuals is quite difficult; but, luckily for the foreign businessperson, there is a great deal of latitude given for trying to do it correctly.

Getting access to the network is only the first step; knowing how to work effectively within the network is the next step. Within a Japanese organization, work groups are very common and have a sense of themselves and their mutual interdependence and good relationships, referred to as the *wa* of the group. This harmonious balance must not be disturbed by arguing directly in public over issues. Generally, decisions are made by groups at various levels throughout the organization arriving at consensus. The typical Japanese business team represents multiple disciplines and/or levels from the organization. Areas of responsibility and functional representation may be ambiguous, so the team members serve multiple functions, facilitating both the negotiating process with the other side and the decision-making process within the company. The team usually does not have the authority to make decisions but will submit its recommendations to top management for final approval. As a result, determining who the members of the business team are, their status within the company, their areas of expertise, and their power is a very important step in understanding the Japanese team with whom you will be working. While the team process may differ slightly in Korean organizations, the requirement of submitting decisions to top management for final approval is the same.

During preliminary meetings, much time is spent gathering information from the other side. One way to avoid taking large risks is to have as much information as possible before making a decision. Therefore, a great deal of time is spent trying to determine what the other side wants and what agreements the other side would find acceptable. This process also allows each side to get to know the other side better, to build a stronger relationship between the companies, and to better understand the other organization.

Consensus within the business team and between the team and top management is necessary for an agreement. However, that does not preclude disagreement among the members of the team. In fact, conflict among members of the team may be very strong as they argue among themselves for different positions. However, this conflict usually is not revealed during the formal meetings and so may not be obvious to the other side. This is another reason why personal relationships between subordinates on both teams are essential for making progress if an impasse develops.

Recognizing and effectively dealing with controversy and disagreement are essential for a successful business relationship. Assuming a *take-charge* role to identify, isolate, and address each issue involving a difference of opinion is, predictably, not successful. Generally, each side delivers a presentation regarding its position and proposal, taking time to answer the other side's questions in some detail, allowing the other side an opportunity to react and draw its own conclusions. As information is presented in blocks, each side takes time to assimilate the information before reacting to it. A quick response is neither expected nor accepted. In both countries, a more intuitive than explicit approach is often successfully used, with each side filling in the necessary details. This approach has been described as follows: "I start my sentence, and you finish it." In fact, verbally supplying all the details for the other side may be perceived as an insult because, by doing so, you have not allowed the other side to participate and interpret the meaning of the conversation for itself. Rather, it is more appropriate to let the other side fill in its own details and draw its own conclusions. If clarification is needed, more sessions will be scheduled to draw out the specifics.

Both sides will not always agree with one another and will not always be prepared to make a decision on every issue mentioned during the presentations. However, Japanese and Koreans rarely say *no*. Statements such as "We note your point," "We lack the authority to make a decision on this issue," or "Because of a tight schedule, we cannot conclude all of our discussion at this time" indicate that the other side wants time to confer on the issue and is not prepared to respond.

Both sides must strive to develop a method of handling disagreements that permits harmony, *wa*, to be maintained. Informal meetings or conversations at social events between similar ranking members of the teams often take place outside the formal sessions. At this time, disagreements can be addressed, conflicting points of view can be exchanged, and essential criteria for reaching conclusions or disagreements can be established. Concentrating attacks on the other party's weak points is not an effective tactic, because it is obvious to everyone involved that this is a weak area. Focusing more attention on the weakness will harm the other side's face, which ultimately will be detrimental to the company-to-company relationship and might sour the entire process.

In some cases, an intermediary or third party is used to ask rude or difficult questions that might harm the relationship if asked directly. By using an outside person, no one is embarrassed or loses face, and the relationship can be maintained. The intervention of a third party requires that both sides have some kind of relationship with the third party. This is a normal part of a Japanese or Korean approach to a delicate or potentially embarrassing situation, useful because it enables one side to change not in response to a direct counterpart, but in response to someone not participating in the negotiation so neither side will lose face and partners can continue as equals in the negotiation.

The goal is to continue discussing ideas, proposals, opportunities, and concerns while working to develop *kan*, an inward understanding to which all parties agree. Direct confrontation and overtly persuasive tactics are inappropriate and used only as a last resort because they can result in a loss of face. However, issues can be pursued by lower-level representatives outside the formal meetings or through the intercession of a common friend as a third-party intermediary. This is particularly effective when one position has evolved or develops to one of less-than-equal stature and developing or continuing a long-term relationship remains important.

In Japan and Korea, there are many opportunities to formally and jointly show your support for your partner; for example, anniversaries of important events such as the date of initial agreements, launches of new products, or official company or government meetings. Each can be observed together. With histories of ritual and custom, protocol demands that specific behaviors be used, certain kinds of gifts be given, and formal declarations be made at these events. Attending to the protocol requirements is an important part of nurturing a relationship.

Having members of the project team visit each other's facilities to report on progress, discuss new issues, or present new information is another way to nurture the relationship, learn about potential difficulties early, and stimulate the flow of information between partners. It is inappropriate *not* to visit at least annually. Make sure you schedule such events well in advance to allow your Japanese or South Korean host time to plan both business and social activities to expose you to a broader circle of the partner's network. Developing, nurturing, and maintaining a strong relationship takes time and effort; however, without each side expending the effort, business ventures in Japan or South Korea are not likely to be successful.

One major difference, reflecting the decreased emphasis on Shintoism and Buddhism in South Korea, relates to the concept of harmony. While maintaining harmony within a group is extremely important and while relationships between government and business have helped fuel economic development in South Korea, there is a long history of dissension, protest, and disagreement between groups. These disagreements are more vocal and direct in South Korea than in Japan. However, relationships within a group and within the group of companies working together are very strong and need to be maintained.

Conclusion

The Japanese and South Korean orientations to time, task, and relationship are unique. Scheduled activities must be punctual and complete, per the schedule. At the same time, the larger view of making things happen and preparing for business is not time driven. Setting direction, establishing new businesses, creating opportunities, or exploiting advantage can take as much time as is needed to generate performance in accordance with Japanese and

South Korean standards and the necessary level of comfort. The least important parts of the process to the Japanese and South Koreans are critical elements for Westerners, which creates a distinctly different business process.

Relationships are essential elements of doing business. Formal networks exist among groups of companies based upon long-standing working arrangements and personal relationships. Therefore, penetrating an existing network can be extremely difficult for an outsider. Contacts and introductions can enable you to meet someone who is part of a strong network. If you are able to develop a good relationship with that person, you may well be invited to meet a second, more important person in the network. After the network has been evaluated and found to be strong, and once introductions are made so that you can meet the people of influence and access, several meetings will usually occur so you can determine whether or not your estimation is correct and you can get your organization into a position to be considered as a potential partner by a network member.

When you are developing personal relationships in Japan and South Korea, several items need to be emphasized: a number of meetings will occur before any business is discussed, the relationship will be based on reciprocity, saving and maintaining face is essential at all levels all the time, the Japanese or South Korean team will ask for a great deal of information, the Japanese or South Korean team will be reluctant to supply a great deal of information, and an attempt to determine the other side's interests will be based both on explicit data as well as implicit information and may be carried by third parties known to both sides.

Most of the discussion of difficult issues takes place outside the formal meetings. At formal meetings, the protocol is to be polite and follow a specific pattern. The Japanese or South Korean team members will not be prepared to respond to new information or proposals until the decision-making group has reached a consensus, outside the formal meeting, regarding the new proposal.

Agreements are important because a relationship with the intention to do business together is established. The specific words and details of the agreement usually are not the most critical element, because the circumstances, conditions, and environment of the marketplace change, and, therefore, companies will need to change along with them. The relationship carries obligations and a sense of moral duty for the business partner, which is the most important part of the contract. This obligation includes maintaining relationships and harmony as a critical component of the success of the business endeavor. If the relationships are not working, everything is impossible; if the relationships are working, anything is possible.

CHAPTER 11

MIDDLE EAST

Classification of Cultures Model

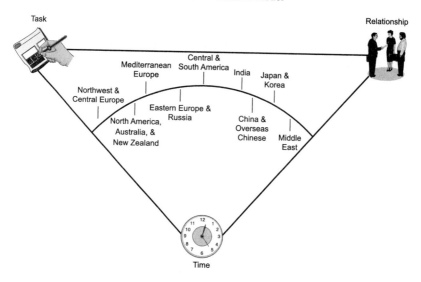

By 200 B.C., the Romans had already established what a German cartographer in the late 1800s termed the "Silk Road." The route brought the exotic spices and products of the "East" to Rome. While the Romans were not the primary traders, the opportunity for great wealth created a merchant economy that was incorporated by the more ancient cultures of the Arabs, Persians, and Greeks along the route. Since this natural trading route was developed on the basis of trade and exchange, the intermingling of ideas and goods was easily accepted and became a norm in the region.

The term *Middle East* is a leftover of European suzerainty as this area was midway between the major European Powers and East Asia, the focal point of European interest since the *Age of Discovery* initiated by the Portuguese in the late 1400s. Throughout the history of this region, which saw the genesis of Judaism, Christianity, and Islam, conquerors and rulers as diverse as the Hittites, Egyptians, Israelites, Assyrians, Babylonians, Persians, Greeks, Romans, Arabs, Muslims, Crusaders, Mameluks, Ottoman Turks, French,

Germans, and British made their way through this area, conquering, ruling, living, and participating in the development of the culture in this region.

The result of this activity in the Middle East is a dizzying combination of ethnic groups, religious affiliations, and political orientation. In many of the countries, such as Saudi Arabia, Israel, or Iran, there is no distinction between the religious state and the government, which makes the practice of governing and conducting business distinctly different from the political model currently followed in the majority of countries, which segments the religious from the secular world. In addition, not all inhabitants of Israel are Jewish; some Arabs in Israel are Muslim and some are Christian, a situation that has yet to be reconciled in that country. The Arab ethnic group and Islamic religion, however, dominate the population of the Middle East and have had the most significant effect on how business is conducted in this area.

For several thousand years, the empires of this region tolerated and accepted distinct ethnicities as part of the way of life, creating broader, adaptive thinking processes, which led to remarkable accomplishments in all aspects of culture as well as in the conduct of business. It is a twentieth-century legacy to identify and eliminate entire ethnic populations and to be totally intolerant of previously tolerated religious beliefs within national boundaries. At the end of World War II, Israel was created as a new country for the Jewish population that had survived the Holocaust. The indigenous Palestinian population faced the choice of living in a Jewish religious-based country or moving to a different country, which created an ongoing political and religious struggle. External wars and internal civil strife have routinely occurred from Morocco to Afghanistan during the post–World War II era after colonial rule ended and national entities emerged. The struggles continue today.

In ancient history, Judaism was founded in the Middle East and continued with a position of religious and political strength through the Roman Imperial era. Christianity traces its roots to this area, as does Islam. In post-Roman times, Islam developed in the Arabian Peninsula and spread throughout the region in a few generations. It continues to define the culture of the entire region and will be the dominant religious and political factor in the foreseeable future. While Islam is identified with the Arabs of the Middle East, not all members of Islam are Arabs and not all members live in the Middle East. In fact, only a quarter of the global Muslim population is Arab. Islam dominates the Middle East for several reasons: The religion originated in Arabia; the holiest places of the religion are there; the seat of the religion remained there even during the proselytizing period of A.D. 850–1200; the Arab population retained the philosophical leadership of the religion; and the **Qur'an**, the holy book of Islam, was not allowed to be translated into local languages, remaining only in Arabic. In Islam, it is the revealed word of God, not subject to interpretation. It is the literal truth and can be recited verbatim by many devout Muslims.

To state that Islam is the governing influence of religious kingdoms and of the secular states of the Middle East, without ever looking at the basic tenets of the religion, does not give the foreign traveler the needed knowledge to conduct business successfully. To understand the behaviors of the inhabitants of this region, then, it is necessary to understand at least the basic precepts of Islam. Like other monotheistic religions, Islam provides a prescribed set of behaviors that are used by believers to guide their actions. Like the Ten Commandments of Judaism, Islam has its Five Pillars: (1) profession of faith, **shahada**, which is simply the sincere statement of the belief that "There is no god but Allah and Muhammad is his Prophet"; (2) ritual prayer five times a day, **salah**; (3) almsgiving, **zakah**, to be used primarily for the poor; (4) fasting, **sawm**, during the ninth month of the Islamic calendar, **Ramadan**; and (5) pilgrimage to the holy place once in a lifetime, **hajj**. While there are many sects, each having a different interpretation of Islam, all Islamic believers adhere to the Five Pillars of faith and are influenced by them in their interactions with others. Islam continues to be a vigorous and dynamic religion that pervades virtually every facet of business and social behavior. It must be understood and respected for business to be successful in this part of the world.

In this region, work does not have the same intrinsic value as it does in other parts of the world. Accomplishing tasks is not a consuming drive, and people work at a more leisurely pace, with greater emphasis on interpersonal relationships. Therefore, the emphasis on timely task completion is less in this area of the world than in the industrialized nations. As a result, businesspeople from outside the region need to exercise a great deal of patience when doing business in the Middle East. Plans and decisions will be made, but there is less belief in one's personal ability to change events or to make things happen when Allah has already determined whether these events will come to pass.

Middle Easterners, like most people, are proud of their long and distinguished cultural heritage—from the glories of the ancient Egyptian civilization to the distinguished Arab civilization to the Caliphate, including their mathematical and scientific achievements, Arabic language, architectural developments, art, and poetry. Many aspects of the modern Middle

Eastern lifestyle have their origins in ancient traditions. For example, the Bedouin nomadic lifestyle has influenced the current emphasis on hospitality and generosity. In nomadic communities, any visitor was accepted into one's home and offered hospitality for up to three days primarily because of the harsh traveling environment and the difficulties common to all people in an arid climate. Today this spirit of generosity and hospitality to visitors continues, and the primary responsibility of any host is that time is expected to be devoted to the social aspects of making a visitor comfortable. Therefore, as a habitual behavior, spending time being courteous is a highly valued and respected activity, vital to conducting business. It is incumbent upon the visitor to be as gracious accepting and appreciating the offered courtesy of the host as it is for the host to be gracious in making the offer.

Another key value, common to all from this region, is a strong sense of justice, which is based on *Shari'ah*, the Islamic law derived from the *Qur'an*. Middle Easterners are morally outraged by historical events that have harmed their people or their countries or by any individual person's behavior that goes against their sense of justice. This sense of outrage will be communicated. If an appropriate apology is not forthcoming, the person committing the offense may then be considered an enemy.

The Islamic belief in predetermination is also a fundamental religious doctrine that has significant influence on business practices and is different from the generally understood Christian or Chinese *work ethic*. The fundamental belief is that as Supreme Being, Allah has humanity's destiny in his hands, that all actions are predetermined, and that individual choice affects what will happen to individuals only marginally. Therefore, their lives are in Allah's hands. The phrases **inshallah**, "if Allah wills it," and **bukra inshallah**, "tomorrow if Allah wills," are often heard in planning or decision-making discussions. As a result, the emphasis placed on long-range planning or working to manage future activities or empowerment, common in current Western management theory, is not widely practiced in this region. However, it is being tolerated more as the interchange between the industrial nations and the oil-producing nations continues to increase.

In recent years, the Middle East has gone, and is still going, through profound changes as the countries evolve from an agricultural or seminomadic tribal basis to an industrial economic base. Middle Eastern countries are facing the task of blending religious beliefs that form the basis of their culture with forms of government and economic policies influenced mainly by Western philosophies, just as the PRC and the countries of Eastern Europe are doing.

Traditionally, business and introductions have been done through third parties and, in many instances, still are. At the same time that traditional methods are preferred, new methods are being introduced in many places. In Saudi Arabia, for example, instead of going through Muslim middlemen to identify suppliers or manufacturers, some companies are now issuing *Requests for Proposals* (RFPs), allowing any company from anywhere in the world to bid. However, even though Western business practices may be adopted in specific circumstances, cultural traditions continue to be strong and tend to be modified or adapted in light of changing circumstances rather than abandoned entirely. It is a common mistake to think that "modern" or "Western" practices of doing business are followed just because a specific event or activity is recognizable to the Western businessperson. Assuming a whole business dynamic, including its assumptions, from one specific activity or event sets the foreigner up for a surprise when resulting behaviors are not what was

Global Business Practices Model

Areas of World	Gov't	Law	Hier.	Privacy	Punct.	Flow	Truth	Words	Style	Logic
Northwest & Central Europe										
North America, Australia, & NZ										
Mediterranean Europe										
Eastern Europe & Russia										
South & Central America										
India										
China & Overseas Chinese										
Japan & Korea										
Middle East										

LEGEND

Role of Government: White = the government sets parameters and constraints to create the environment for doing business. Black = Direct involvement of government in business as a business partner.

Rule of Law: White = Reliance on systems and procedures. Black = Pragmatism or situational considerations.

Sense of Hierarchy: White = Assumption of equality. Black = Assumption of status difference.

View of Privacy: White = Business and private matters are separate. Black = Business and private matters are all part of one reality.

Punctuality: White = Fixed time. Black = Flexible or "rubber" time.

Flow of Activities: White = Time works in a linear fashion. Black = Time works in a cyclical fashion.

Truth: White = Universal truth. Black = Many truths exist at once.

Words: White = Words have explicit meanings. Black = Words have implicit meanings.

Style: White = Communication is direct and forthright. Black = Communication is indirect.

Logic: White = Formal deductive reasoning. Black = Alternative heuristic.

expected from someone operating from that specific set of business assumptions. Cultures change at a glacial pace, adapting by necessity but remaining consistent and coherent to those who are acculturated within the cultures.

The rest of this chapter will examine the elements of structure, process, and communication as they affect business practices in the Middle East.

Structure

The sense of hierarchy, role of government, and rule of law combine to structure the practice of business. This section will discuss each of these elements.

Hierarchy

While personal relationships are strong in Eastern Europe, Latin America, China, Japan, and South Korea, these relationships are relatively wide ranging, including family members, clan members, tribe members, network members, or even close friends. A significant difference in the Middle East is that the family and extended family is the fundamental social unit throughout society and the dominant force in every relationship. Individuals are known by their family and its reputation. Loyalty and duty to the family are greater than any other social obligation, and all social relations are tied, directly or indirectly, to the family. Nothing will be accomplished without connections and relationships with the family who has influence over or involvement with the particular product, activity, or service that the foreigner is representing.

Furthermore, the Middle East is classified as a "top-man" culture (Hall, 1980), which means that decision making is centralized with the titular head of the organization, which is also consistent with Power Distance scores in the region.[1] In Islam, there is no intermediary between Allah and humans; likewise, no intermediary comes between the sheik, the traditional local leader, and the peasants. Within families, there is no intermediary or screening role between family members and the top man. People come to deal directly with the top man. It appears chaotic, but there is an orderly process followed in the protocol of getting the family head's attention. In all cases, everyone pays deference to the head of the family. Not only does the top man make the important decisions brought to him by anyone in the family, but also his authority is never challenged.

---

[1] Geert Hofstede's research identified five dimensions of culture. High scores on Power Distance demonstrate the degree to which members of the society recognize inequalities of power. See www.geert-hofstede.com.

Given the importance of family and the consequent social obligation to be loyal to the family, the responsibility to care for family members is also taken seriously. What is routinely referred to as nepotism in other countries, with law and ethics steadfastly opposing any *hint* of the practice, is considered an honorable obligation to many traditional Arabs. For instance, in Lebanon, an applicant for a position brought his uncle to a job interview and sat quietly while his more distinguished uncle did all the talking during the interview. Local partners expect to give business to their subsidiaries or shipping lines, often owned by those related either directly or through marriage.

Business decisions usually are made by the top man in the family, who controls the distribution chain, manufacturing facility, or retail outlet necessary for the success of a product. In virtually every location, either by law or local practice, a foreign firm must have a local partner or sponsor as the interface to work through local legal and cultural situations, work with local suppliers and trade channels, intervene in national government relations, make introductions, provide advice, and accumulate and interpret local information. Once a partner, an agent, or a consultant has been selected, do not expect the person to take care of all the work for a foreign partner or to engage in physical work. Doing hard physical work is not a part of the culture and is an inappropriate expectation for someone of high status. Since labor is very inexpensive, it is easy to hire people to perform that work. Expecting a partner to arrange furniture in a new office or stock shelves in a store is unrealistic and would usually be considered insulting. Locals do not expect their foreign partner to do this type of work, either.

Developing contacts; understanding the power structure between and among families and tribes; and investigating potential business partners, consultants, or agents all take time. Once a partner, a consultant, or an agent is chosen, a good relationship must be established with that person and the network to begin the process of gaining access to the family that is most influential in a particular business.

Networks work through personal relationships; without personal relationships, access to families and the top man is not possible. Developing sincere, personal relationships with the people who can provide access to the families and the networks and developing personal relationships with family members who can influence or make decisions affecting the business are the most important business activities. If this stage is not successfully managed, it is very unlikely that business will ever transact. A caution to this idea: If your product is the only one available in the market, you may have some initial success on a familiar time and task basis. However, this success will last only until a suitable local replacement is available. Technology can be duplicated or purchased quickly. Service can be duplicated easily once it is shown to be profitable. Relationships cannot be purchased or duplicated. If a foreigner is competing against people who have already worked on building a relationship, he or she is working with a disadvantage before starting.

Only blood relatives are members of the inner circle. Membership in an intermediate circle brings identification with that particular family. Foreigners are not allowed into the inner circle of the family simply because they are not blood relatives; however, they may be accepted into an intermediate layer adjacent to the inner circle. Being identified as having an association with a particular family determines a person's social status and network of connections. However, the social pressure and obligations resulting from this identification are significant. While individuals are valued and primary in Islam, the demands of conformity within the hierarchical and authoritarian Middle Eastern structure are high, requiring adherence to norms for appropriate behavior that are established within each family specifically and society in general. The result is honor, social prestige, a secure place in society, and family obligations. For instance, bosses are expected to assist with their employees' (many of whom are relatives), personal problems, sickness, debts, or other individual problems. Providing financial, social, or psychological assistance to family members is expected and encouraged. Within this social structure, going outside of secular rules or business practices is viewed as a responsible person's effort to help a brother in need and, therefore, not considered unethical, as it is by Western standards, as long as the behavior does not conflict with the higher moral authority of the religion practiced in the community. It is not uncommon for a business owner to pay for the funeral expenses of a worker's father or to share in the costs of the wedding of a worker's daughter even when the worker is not related by blood.

According to Islam, dignity, personal honor, and family honor are high values and very important to believers. Everyone needs to conform to the family's norms of behavior to maintain individual respect and status and to avoid bringing shame or disrespect to the individual and to the family. Failure to conform brings shame not only to the family, but also to the clan, tribe, and country. The degree of shame depends upon the level of the dissonant behavior.

Becoming accepted as a business partner in a family network is a significant event that usually occurs neither quickly nor easily, but only after much scrutiny, many conversations, and the successful handling of minor activities.

Participating in the network entails a set of obligations involving both business and personal activities. Taking time to learn the environment, situation, and expectations that are involved is extremely important and is always time well spent. Learning the language, even a rudimentary attempt, and understanding and respecting the rituals of the religion will demonstrate a level of sincerity that will be greatly valued.

Role of Government

A distinctive feature of countries in the Middle East is the relationship among religion, tribes, and government. Forms of government differ, such as a monarchy in Saudi Arabia, or a constitutional monarchy as in Jordan and Kuwait, or a theocratic republic in Iran, or a republic as in Egypt, or a parliamentary democracy as in Israel, or a federation as in the United Arab Emirates. However, the influence and presence of local tribes and religion are part of all of these governments, resulting in conflict, tension, and uneasy coalitions. Each of these countries faces the challenge of creating a role for itself in today's interdependent world and must develop coordinated activities in the midst of strong ethnic and religious differences and traditions. Developing a position of strength, individual identity, and interdependency consistent with religious beliefs respectful of tribal differences is very new and represents a transition for all countries in this region.

Since there is no separation between secular and religious activities in most of the Middle Eastern countries, religious holidays and functions are a formal part of the world of business. For instance, Muslims need to pray five times during the day and will stop what they are doing to pray at the specified times. In addition, business meetings and activities are severely curtailed during Ramadan, the ninth month of the Arab calendar, much like the Christmas holidays or year-end celebrations disrupt the flow of business in other parts of the world.

The foreign businessperson faces the challenge of being aware of tribal differences, understanding the fundamentals of the prevailing religious beliefs, and respecting differences that occur in this region. Some of the differences have a long history involving offended honor and past injustices that continue today, all of which influence governmental decisions. Since the government plays a major role in the conduct of business in most of these countries, success requires understanding the local reality of each country's government and its involvement in business activities. In countries that use religion as the legal foundation of their systems, doing business is difficult for businesspeople from countries that rely on constitutions or tort law to establish precedent and predict business outcomes. It is essential to get good advice, either from consultants, agents, or friends or from *middlemen*, who thrive in a culture in which words are not always the definitive response.

Rule of Law

Some countries, such as Iran and Saudi Arabia, use a legal system based on Islam; other countries use a combination of legal systems. For instance, Jordan uses a combination of principles from Islam and French code for its legal system. Israel uses common law with principles of Judaism, Christianity, and Islam to create its legal system. Yemen's legal system is based upon principles from Islamic, Turkish, English, and tribal law. Just as the government incorporates religious tenets in the political system, so the legal system either incorporates or is based entirely upon religious tenets. Every country, including Israel, includes some aspects of Islam in its legal code.

Part of that tradition and the shared cultural values is that, in the Middle East, the unofficial pressure of sanctions from the family for not observing appropriate business behavior is stronger than any contract. If a family member has a business arrangement with another family member, nonpayment of a loan is not an option but has little to do with a written agreement. Since failure to pay back a loan brings shame on both the individual and the family, causing the individual to be ostracized and the family to have a bad name until honor can be restored, a written agreement does not provide more incentive to pay back the loan than the social norms do.

In general, however, preparing a contract is useful because it is a commonly understood starting point for continued business activity. Remembering that many Middle Eastern countries have no separation between the religious and the secular, in neither law nor government, assumptions about typical legal principles, such as liability, may not hold and contracts must be written to comply with religious law and principles. For instance, a taxi driver is an employee of the taxi company, so the employer, the taxi company, is liable if an accident occurs. According to Islamic law, insurance is considered the same as gambling because it is Allah's will that if something happens, one's destiny is to recover from it. Therefore, insurance is illegal in many Middle Eastern countries. However, insurance is a very successful product; it needs to be called something different, and the contracts need to be written very carefully. Although Islamic law prohibits taking interest on loans, "administrative fees" are appropriate and can be collected. Each situation is viewed as a unique event, and decisions in one circumstance do not have to be consistent with any other decision or circumstance. For those accustomed to precedent and interpretation, initial business dealings in this region can be confusing and frustrating. Recognize that, in the end, the system works; it is up to the foreigner to learn how and with what degree of freedom business can be accomplished.

As circumstances change, everyday realities of doing business must accommodate those changes. Local officials have been known to make agreements to save face, even though they have no authority to enforce the contract to which they agreed. As technology changes and as the countries become more industrialized and have greater interaction with representatives of other regions, the business environment will continue its dynamic evolution. At present, signed contracts are not considered the conclusion of a business deal and do not necessarily establish expectations of specific activities being completed in a particular way, by a certain date at a specific cost.

Preparing a contract and getting agreement, however, does clarify many issues, provides some parameters within which both sides will operate, and signifies an intention to work together. Signing the contract is the beginning of a close working relationship, not the culmination of a process. It represents the symbolic ties individuals have agreed to and the anticipation of continued good relations.

Along with the signed agreement comes the obligation to maintain relationships. As in any family-like relationship, maintenance of the relationships must be attended to during the course of the year, both during formal and informal activities. Personal contact is required on a periodic basis at all levels in the organization. Having people at different levels visit their counterparts allows information to be gathered formally and informally at the operational, functional, administrative, and executive levels of the organization. Keeping the lines of communication open and maintaining regular contact allows changing circumstances to become known early, which is critical for managing the implementation of a contract in a continually changing business environment.

Process

The separation between public and private lives is related to where, when, and how long business activities occur or what is appropriate for discussion during business exchanges. In addition, the sense of punctuality and the flow of activities over time affect the practice of business. This section examines all three issues.

Privacy

In the Middle East, the process of building relationships has a different style and rhythm than in other regions, where personal lives are segmented from professional lives and, at the end of establishing sincere personal relationships, people know more about each other than they do in other regions. The style of decision making, form of logic, communication style, and view of time are distinct to the Middle East. Social events involving business meetings take place in a Middle Eastern format. With the historical traditions in the Middle East, life in a harsh climate, and the difficulty of travel, the first emphasis is likely to be on hospitality for the visitor.

Once invited into the local partner's private office, greetings will be elaborate and formal, including an exchange of business cards and informal questions about travel, accommodations, and comfort. Tea, coffee, and light refreshments almost always are offered as a sign of hospitality and cordiality. As a guest, a visitor is expected to partake of something; to refuse is to refuse a host's offer of friendship. Pleasantries will be exchanged, but avoid asking personal questions. Alcohol is not permitted in most countries and is never offered to a foreigner by a host.

Direct questions about people's wives, politics, religion, or other people in the room are not appropriate. As a good business practice, avoid the use of humor or off-color words or phrases, which are never appropriate in a business context and especially inappropriate in a cross-cultural one. Generosity is important, and almost all individuals wish to avoid the reputation of being *stingy*. Therefore, a host will offer as much as, and the best, he can. In any event, the visitor is obligated to return the hospitality offered when the situation changes and the guest is the host.

The top man generally prefers to meet with one person rather than with a committee when doing business. Relationships are between individuals, not organizations, and getting to know an individual very well is an important part of the process of deciding whether to do business with that person. However, the preference for meeting with an individual does not necessarily mean that the meeting will be a private one, between two people in an office, with the door closed. The public and professional lives of Middle Easterners are not private; only their personal lives are private. Therefore, a business meeting usually takes place in a room that can accommodate a group of people. The door to the room is left open, several other people may also be present for their individual meetings, visitors come and go during the meeting, and phone calls are taken.

The distinction between inner and outer circle also relates to a difference between business behavior and public behavior. The emphasis on dignity, respect, and proper behavior refers to situations involving personal contact. Public situations such as waiting in line for a taxi, having a clerk wait on you, or getting a car serviced are considered to involve *impersonal* contact; therefore, a different set of behaviors applies. In these impersonal situations, the sense of individuality is dominant and everyone looks out for themselves. Whoever is able to jostle to the front will be helped first, or whoever demands attention will receive it. Therefore, as a norm, queuing is not typically followed at any public activity. The distinction between personal and impersonal situations is important to note for determining appropriate behavior in specific situations.

Punctuality

Time comes and time goes by, but time is not under the control of individuals. In agrarian societies, each season has its own set of required activities based upon predictable cycles of rain or heat. In nomadic societies, movement occurs because of access to food and water, not a specific schedule. In Islamic cultures believing in predetermination, no person can change the course that Allah has set in motion. Therefore, punctuality is viewed in a completely different context. While the intention is always to follow a set of activities that are consistent with the precepts of Islam, no individual has control over the journey. Knowing that circumstances vary and conditions change, a sequence of events may not take place when planned or in the same order. However, whatever circumstances change or whatever challenges occur, they were preordained to happen and are your responsibility to manage as best you can along the new direction your path is taking. Within this context, punctuality is not a major concern.

In meetings, the top man always has multiple demands on his time. Any relatives who have requests, even during a business appointment, will take precedence over business activities. Meetings need to be scheduled to avoid prayer times. As a result, it is not unusual for a visitor to have to wait before being allowed in for a meeting or before continuing previous discussions. In addition, multiple interruptions will occur during a private meeting. The amount of waiting time depends upon what other situations are happening at the same time and how important your issue is in relation to the other situations. Punctuality is unpredictable at best. Impatience on the part of the foreign guest will be ignored, so any physical expressions of displeasure at being kept waiting are fruitless and a sign of insensitivity.

Flow of Activities

Relationships with people are considered so important throughout the Arabic cultures that courtesy and hospitality are more important than the effective use of time. In addition, the Islamic nations have a strong belief in predetermination, which means that there is little one can do to influence the will of Allah. The emphasis on accomplishing tasks is not a habit that is learned early in one's life. Therefore, the process of establishing relationships and being involved in normal business activities receives more emphasis than the goal of arriving at a signed contract. Business activities move through stages at a distinctive pace.

Choosing the best local person to be your partner or sponsor and choosing the firm and/or family to work with is a critical decision. An incorrect choice will be a constant problem and ultimately harmful to long-term business results. Therefore, taking the time to investigate potential local partners, rather than relying on first impressions or limited information, must be the decision that has the top priority. As a foreign visitor, you can begin by investigating the person's and the company's reputation with other foreign banks and companies with whom you do business. If possible, determine the potential partner's length of association with the person or firm, the demonstrated growth of the company, market growth, and talent of the individual in the marketplace. Asking additional questions of sources and other companies with whom your potential partner does business can determine the company's financial reputation and reveal whether it pays its bills regularly or is unreasonably late. Examining the reputation, growth, and success of any independent operations the person operates aside from the specific business of interest to you will also reveal useful information. Look beyond the appearance of the office and the ways conversation and hospitality with the person are conducted. Spending the time to conduct this investigation thoroughly is essential to making an informed choice. Informal channels, or **bazaari**, are extremely important in the process of doing business. Therefore, it is absolutely necessary to invest the time to investigate how potential partners work and determine who is really well connected and capable of providing what an organization needs to work productively in this culture.

While getting to know the family members of the potential partner, a series of social meetings will occur without any business being discussed. The purpose of the first meeting is only to get acquainted and will not usually adhere to a fixed agenda. An ancient Arab proverb says, "Haste comes from the devil." Therefore, any demonstration of impatience is completely unacceptable and will keep a foreigner from attaining entry into the network or meeting objectives. Business activities proceed at a different pace in the Middle East than in Western countries. Rather than trying to speed up the process, the foreigner is best served by understanding why it proceeds more slowly, by developing insights into the process of doing business, and by taking the time necessary to evaluate the situation and people accurately. Be patient and use time wisely by gathering information and choosing partners carefully. Remain flexible, sincere, and interested; and be ready to move forward at the locals' pace.

This meeting process may continue for a period of days or as several meetings over months and is considered normal, important business activity. The objective of this process is to learn as much as possible about the foreigner or nonblood relation while determining whether to do business with that person. It is not reasonable to assume that continued social courtesies indicate that a deal or contract will be signed as a result of participating in the process. Being allowed to move from the outer circle of an individual's network to membership in an intermediary level or identification with the inner family circle is a significant step that entails rights and obligations. This kind of position is not offered to everyone. Being offered tea at several meetings does not necessarily mean you are moving to an intermediary level. Bedouin tradition, which influences the entire Middle East in this respect, dictates that up to three days' hospitality be offered to any traveler. It is unthinkable to someone from this region to be inhospitable to a guest. Hospitality, however, does not imply a desire to begin a long-term personal or business relationship.

The pace and structure of meetings remains flexible, even when using a prepared agenda, because of the many interruptions. Family matters always receive a higher priority than business and will be attended to first. Therefore, business conversations may well be interrupted for family matters requiring the top man's attention. Business matters will be handled in good time depending upon how well connected you are, how you respond to offered hospitality, how well you demonstrate patience, and how important your business concern is to the top man.

Communication

With the influence of religion on the government and legal structure and the influence of Bedouin traditions on hospitality, attributes of these characteristics have an impact on the communication process, which is highly sensitive to cultural nuances. While many languages are spoken throughout the Middle East, Arabic is common to all as either a major language or an underlying influence. This section discusses the impact of the perception of truth, words, logic, and style on communication.

Truth

Arabic is a high context language (Hall, 1981), meaning that the words are interpreted by taking nonverbal cues, relationships, and circumstances into account. Direct, straightforward responses to questions should not be expected. Statements are designed to maintain harmony, to give no offense, and to reveal little. Islam is a monotheistic religion that believes in universal truth; however, maintaining harmony within one's inner circle is paramount. Each family guards its honor jealously and responds to attacks on it. As a result, information needs to be communicated in a way that respects the other side's honor. Protecting one's honor from attack is important.

The fear of bringing shame to one's family is so severe and the motivation to avoid it at all costs so strong that an initial response is to hide one's shame. An ancient Arab proverb holds that "a concealed sin is two-thirds forgiven." In response to the question, "How are things?" a typical response of *mastur al-hal*, roughly translated as "we're all right," literally means "we are not exposed to hunger, illness, or anything bad because we are under the cover of God." If a hidden shame or dishonor is exposed, it typically must be avenged because honor must be restored at all costs.

This kind of socialized norm results in difficult situations with foreigners who give an affront after having been brought into one's circle of family and network of friends. The dilemma is whether to shun the foreigner, the severest type of punishment, which would effectively end the work relationship, or to wait for an apology and make-up behaviors the foreigner may not recognize are needed. Foreigners need to demonstrate sensitivity to local norms and have a circle of friends, sometimes termed "cultural informants," who can coach and mentor them to succeed. Humor is especially difficult to use properly. Even when locals are making fun of themselves, agreeing with them will likely cause offense.

In public meetings, one can say all kinds of things because the environment and occasion will be taken into account as words are interpreted and associates will keep destructive actions from occurring unless a question of honor is involved. The role of the outside person is to talk with both parties, offer ideas for resolving differences, get each side's reactions, modify proposals, solicit reactions again, and continue this process until differences are resolved.

Words

Words alone are inadequate to understand the nuances of meaning in a high context culture as is found throughout this region. Participants must be able to relate the words, actions, body language, and implications to the problem-solving equation. During meetings, Middle Easterners carefully observe the foreigner's reactions to topics, issues, and events to learn about the foreigner. The languages in this region are high context, so observation of the environment, situation, and people is practiced routinely to fully comprehend what is being communicated. Therefore, all nonverbal communication is important and becomes a significant part of the personal quality of relationships. People will likely sit or stand close, within 6–8 inches, as a normal practice. This close proximity is to show courtesy and to be able to touch the person with whom one is talking. In addition, a host can more easily look directly at a visitor to demonstrate attention and can evaluate reactions by watching the pupils of the visitor's eyes.

Setting the goals and strategic direction, delegating authority for staffing, and providing money for the activity makes it possible for work to be done. However, it is essential to provide frequent periodic checks not only to see how things are progressing but also to adjust plans and schedules according to what is really happening. Words remain ambiguous, as in other high context language cultures, and cannot be relied upon to specify who does want, when, and where.

Logic

Being allowed to meet with the top man or being offered repeated social courtesies does not indicate that a contract will be offered or that a deal will be signed. The meeting will not be private between two people; there will be many people talking about different issues. This is consistent with the dominant nonlinear approach to relationships and problem solving that is exhibited in the logical pattern of circular thinking.

Linear patterns of logic or arguments based on precedent do not carry much weight in persuading people in this region. Each new situation is perceived as a unique event presented to both sides to influence the outcome to the best of their abilities, given that the outcome is part of Allah's plan. Established guidelines for decision making or procedures for handling particular situations do not exist. The circumstance, events, and people involved in each situation must be examined, put into the proper context, and a decision made for that particular situation.

The form of reasoning and pattern of communication are circular or looping. As a meeting begins, refreshments will be offered, reference will be made to the last meeting, some conversation may occur about the current trip, the topic of this meeting may be identified, then the conversation may return to something that pertains to one of the people met on the previous trip, refreshments may be offered again, a comment may be made about some construction that has occurred in the city or plant, one or several people may leave the meeting to pray, then a comment may be made about the visitor's home city, then a short discussion may take place regarding the topic of today's meeting, then a reference to how something from that conversation applies to a cousin of someone the visitor had met earlier may be discussed, then a conversation about dinner plans for the evening may take place, then a reference may be made to the importance of today's meeting, and so on. Eventually, refreshments may be offered again and the time for another meeting will be arranged. Meanwhile, many interruptions have occurred. The foreigner must be patient and proactive, participating in the communication process to demonstrate sincerity and to build relations. Oblique references to the task will occur and be built upon over an extended period of time.

As references are made to the topic at hand and as the bargaining occurs, tactics are likely to be distributive, or win–lose. Bargaining is an integral part of life in the Middle East and occurs everywhere, all the time. The conversation always loops back to the topic at hand, with the intention of getting the best deal possible for your own side. The initial advantage a foreign product or service may have by being the only one available will last only until someone with a strong relationship has a comparable product or service. When the initial advantage erodes, the foreign businessperson will have to defend rather than expand his or her position. Maximizing profit tends to be secondary to the Middle Easterners compared to developing and maintaining good personal relationships among friends and in one's network. Being able to successfully build personal relationships is fundamental to establishing the Middle Easterners' confidence in a partner.

Several meetings usually are required before decisions are made. Between the formal meetings, informal meetings between staff members occur and often are even more important than the ritual meetings with the top man. During the informal meetings, staff members can clarify thorny issues, explore creative alternatives, evaluate the resoluteness of the other side's position, and gather additional information as to likely outcomes. Since the information gathered at the informal meetings is transmitted to the top man on the local side, he is knowledgeable at the next formal meeting, can offer acceptable alternatives, knows how far he can push the other side, and will not risk offending the other side while continuing to bargain for a better deal.

Often, social contacts between parties are more significant than technical specifications and price, but bargaining continues to be an important part of the process at all times. Given the distributive orientation and tradition of bargaining, making concessions is also part of the process. On the one hand, Middle Easterners usually ask for a price higher than the one they expect to agree upon at the end. Remembering that the Middle East is a high context language area, the asking price also conveys an implicit message, so there are many levels of meaning when asking a high price. For instance, the top man could suggest a price that is an "insult" price, a "go away" price, a "don't bother me" price, or an "I don't want to sell" price, which could convey the idea that either "I'm willing but not too enthusiastic about selling" or "I'd like to sell but am not very eager to sell, but you're a close friend, so I'll consider it."

The offer has meaning beyond its substance, and all the possible meanings must be considered part of the offer, and all of the possible meanings must be considered part of the process of doing business. A local partner, agent, or consultant can offer a very helpful perspective and useful insight at this time. Having taken the time to choose this person wisely is certainly an asset during the process because having a reliable resource to interpret what the conversation means will be extremely useful to the foreign businessperson. Let interpreters use the local language to get the intent of issues among the native speakers. After these discussions, a simple *yes* or *no* may be stated and the foreigner need not be suspicious, merely accepting of the outcome.

However, if an Arab is insulted during these discussions and the appropriate apology is not offered, the emotion of hurt turns to anger and the Arab may move into a "spite" response. At this point, the Arab will do anything to avenge his honor without regard for the consequences, and it is highly unlikely that anyone can intervene successfully until the matter takes its course. Learning the formalities of appropriate behavior, offering symbolic apologies for public slights, and working with an informed local partner or consultant are critical for avoiding this situation.

Offering symbolic apologies for public slights and refraining from insulting comments does not mean that one cannot engage in tough bargaining. Being able to bargain hard is a desirable and respected trait. The goal for businesspeople is to be clever enough to present a pleasant, sociable image while still being able to get a good deal without offending the other side.

Style

Several other characteristics associated with the people of this region have their origins in the Bedouin culture: restlessness, mobility, gallantry, courage, patience, and endurance. Given these historical cultural traits, widely shared and admired by members of the government and business community, today's description of Middle Easterners as emotional, sentimental, warm, hospitable, friendly, and courteous is not surprising. What is surprising to many from the West is the manifestation of these traits. Visiting foreigners often think Middle Easterners are angry because they use many physical gestures and speak loudly in an animated manner. Speaking loudly is a characteristic of someone who is emotionally engaged in a conversation, but emotion is not necessarily anger. These emotional displays frequently are misinterpreted by people who are trained to portray a neutral demeanor.

Since Middle Easterners are sincerely concerned about an individual's personal well-being and truly want to get to know people on a personal basis, their communication style is very personal. For example, people try to physically break down barriers by standing very close to other people during conversations, about 6–8 inches, using a lot of direct eye contact, and having physical contact, for example, by resting a hand on the other person's knee or arm. Sometimes foreigners simply warrant a stare from a local person.

Once a local partner, consultant, or agent has obtained an initial appointment for you with the top man, appropriate social behavior is essential. Some countries require more formality than others, but generally, several social meetings will take place that require formal social behavior, including such things as simple as accepting the beverages offered in hospitality, patiently participating in one of several meetings taking place with the top man generally at the same time, being interrupted frequently by telephone calls or messages for the top man, or having to wait while other visitors are welcomed. This process is likely to occur several times without any business being discussed.

Business activities proceed at a very different pace in the Middle East than elsewhere in the developed economies. Rather than trying to speed up the process, the foreigner is best served by understanding why it proceeds more slowly, by developing insights into the process of doing business, and by taking the time necessary to evaluate the situation and people accurately.

In addition to the primary business partner, other family members are due visible respect by nonblood relations. Any rude, frank, or blunt comments about family or tribe members or about locals in general are not appropriate and are considered an affront to that person's dignity. Criticizing someone in public or showing condescension to anyone is extremely bad form, because this is an affront to an individual's self-respect and dignity. A comment such as "How could you make that mistake again? I just explained that yesterday" is too strong in this context. Even the computer's "bleep," which calls attention to an individual's mistake to anyone within hearing range, is offensive. One company responded by taking the "bleep" out of the program so mistakes would not be publicly identified. Individuals are easily slighted and hurt, and these slights to one's dignity and self-respect are considered a serious affront that can result in someone losing respect and/or status. The person who engaged in inappropriate social behavior by making the slight may also lose the respect of others in the network, may end up excluded from the network, and/or may be labeled an enemy or infidel, depending upon the severity of the slight.

If, after several formal and informal meetings, disagreements continue unresolved, third-party outsiders, respected by both sides, are usually asked to intervene. When parties have irreconcilable starting positions, a respected third-party mediator may be effective, as evidenced by the role of former U.S. President Jimmy Carter in drafting the Middle East Accords between Egypt and Israel in 1979.

Conclusion

Although differences among the Middle Eastern countries are many and significant, the predominance of the Arab and Islamic cultures determines the orientation to time, task, and relationships. Family is the highest priority, and a foreigner should expect that time will always be taken to attend to family matters first. People are identified by the family they are part of, and business networks are established along family lines. If appropriate relationships are not established with a family that controls access to materials, distribution, or retail outlets for your product or service, no business will happen. Therefore, taking time to develop access to the family network is a critical business activity. While the pattern of emphasis in the Middle East is similar to that of other relationship-oriented cultures, the crucial nature of family relationships is significantly more important.

Just as Middle Eastern businesspeople will take time to get to know a visitor, a foreign businessperson needs to take time to evaluate potential partners, agents, or consultants to determine whether they are the best resource for his or her purposes. Developing these relationships depends upon your ability to adapt to the business structure in the Middle East, the timing of business meetings, and whether you display appropriate social skills. Having a reliable local resource person is an indispensable asset for acquiring this knowledge. Decision making is centralized and, once the proper connections are established, access to the decision maker is possible and the process of building a relationship with that person begins. If the relationship-building process goes well and the foreigner is accepted into the intermediate layer of the circle of contacts, you assume obligations and responsibilities to assist other family members regarding business or personal problems in addition to your personal obligations to the head of the family.

Tasks are approached in terms of the belief in predestination; those things that Allah wills to happen will happen. Therefore, planning for the future and managing future activities are not normally high-priority activities. As a result, the pace of business is more present oriented and less hurried than in many other areas of the world.

While relationships are a significant part of the business process, bargaining is also a major part of life in the Middle East. To effectively participate in the bargaining process, learning how to interpret words in relation to the nonverbal actions and environmental elements of the situation is extremely important in this high context language region. The logic is circular rather than linear; the assumptions of business activity are different; the meaning and assumptions of issues to address in a contract are unique to the Middle East, where many countries do not separate religion and business; and contracts are more a sign of intent and not as important as personal obligations.

Since family and religious obligations are more important than business activity in many countries, this region has its own distinctive pace for conducting business. Building and maintaining relationships are critical activities requiring a great deal of time. Hospitality, appropriate social behaviors, and patience with the pace of business are valued traits. Demonstrating respect for other people in business situations, using good social skills, performing required social obligations well, behaving as a responsible member of the family, and bargaining hard for a better deal without offending the other people are important and respected skills for success in the Middle East.

CHAPTER 12

AFRICA

Classification of Cultures Model

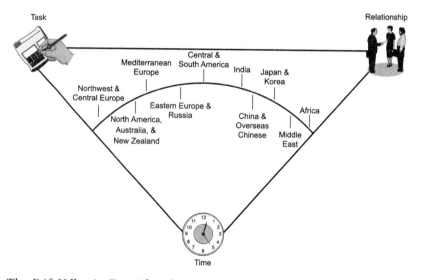

The Rift Valley in East Africa has provided an almost unbroken history of the earliest development and evolution of humans. It is now accepted as the earliest identified location for what we call the human species. Aside from the ancient Egyptian culture of the Nile Valley, one of the most highly developed and lasting empires in history, the remainder of the African continent has not produced enduring influences on the rest of the world. The lack of developed transportation and communication systems; the persistent record of elections resulting in governments with no pretense of honesty, existing simply to enrich the rulers for as long as possible; the colonial residue of the dominance by minorities throughout the sub-Saharan continent; warring factions in the commodity-rich regions; and the absence of basic health and social services for the growing population have all contributed to the persistent low level of development in the countries.

The African population has broad diversity, with many tribes, languages, beliefs, and ethnicities. Since crossing the desert or navigating the rain forests was extremely hazardous, many of the tribes remained confined to local areas, which kept them relatively isolated from one another.

The Romans crossed the Mediterranean Sea, bringing their cultural influence to North Africa. In an effort to find the Silk Route by sea, many European countries landed on and colonized locations along the coasts of Africa. From the sixteenth century to the mid-twentieth century, the Portuguese, Belgians, French, Dutch, Germans, Italians, Spanish, and British developed colonies throughout Africa, which became the basis for the current political map. When the majority of the colonial powers were preparing to exit the continent in 1956, the per capita income of sub-Saharan Africa was about the same as that of Southeast Asia. Since that time, per capital income has remained approximately the same in Africa, while the per capita income in Southeast Asian countries such as Singapore and Taiwan has risen to a much higher level.

When colonizers claimed or conquered new territory, they established an administrative system in that country. The indigenous people were not usually welcomed by the colonials into the governmental arrangement or elite circles of society. Operating within the governmental, educational, and social systems created by the colonial power, members of the local population learned to adapt to this overlaid culture just to survive and, in many cases, to do business successfully.

The large number of tribes in Africa and the number of foreign countries influencing different tribes results in a diverse cultural milieu. Unlike Australia, New Zealand, North America, and South America, the colonizing countries did not push aside the natives as they claimed the new land for their home country. In some cases, dual cultures exist between the colonizers and local tribes, as in India. Some Africans are bicultural, having been educated in the former colonial power's educational system. The overwhelming majority, however, live primarily within one culture. Like India, there is no unifying language. Unlike India, where over 80 percent of the population consider themselves Hindu, the majority of Africans do not follow a common religion. Unlike India, colonized as a single geographic region by the British, different regions of Africa were colonized by different countries whose methodology and approach to the population and its needs varied considerably.

With no unifying leadership, language, tribe, religion, or colonial influence, there is no single "African" culture. The foreign businessperson needs to become familiar with the characteristics of the country being visited, including the languages, the tribes, and the colonial influence. The local cultures, which have continued, are based upon pastoral, agricultural, nomadic, hunting, and trading traditions. The local traditions in a country colonized primarily by Arabs, with a large number of local residents who currently practice Islam, are very different from the local traditions in a country colonized by France or one colonized by the Portuguese or the British. However, there is a major unifying force throughout the continent that does impact business practices in a similar way. The continued existence of a tribal culture in countries that are, for the most part, not yet industrialized results in an approach to business that has similarities among all of the countries. Even those countries that have modernized, such as Egypt and South Africa, have a two-tiered economy with the majority of the population, generally rural, maintaining their traditions and ways of doing business.

This chapter explores the general cultural characteristics of the native African population that influence the conduct of business. To more fully understand the business practices in each country, you will find it useful to

Global Business Practices Model

Areas of World	Gov't	Law	Hier.	Privacy	Punct.	Flow	Truth	Words	Style	Logic
Northwest & Central Europe	gray	white	gray	white	white	white	white	white	white	white
North America, Australia, & NZ	white	white	white	white	white	white	white	white	white	gray
Mediterranean Europe	gray	white	gray	gray	white	gray	white	white	gray	white
Eastern Europe & Russia	gray	gray	gray	white	gray	gray	gray	gray	white	gray
South & Central America	gray	gray	black	gray	gray	black	gray	gray	gray	gray
India	gray	gray	black	gray	white	gray	black	gray	gray	gray
China & Overseas Chinese	black	gray	gray	black	black	black	black	black	black	black
Japan & Korea	black	gray	black	black	white	black	black	black	black	black
Middle East	black	gray	black	black	black	black	black	black	black	black
Africa	black	gray	black	black	black	black	black	black	black	black

LEGEND

Role of Government: White = the government sets parameters and constraints to create the environment for doing business. Black = Direct involvement of government in business as a business partner.

Rule of Law: White = Reliance on systems and procedures. Black = Pragmatism or situational considerations.

Sense of Hierarchy: White = Assumption of equality. Black = Assumption of status difference.

View of Privacy: White = Business and private matters are separate. Black = Business and private matters are all part of one reality.

Punctuality: White = Fixed time. Black = Flexible or "rubber" time.

Flow of Activities: White = Time works in a linear fashion. Black = Time works in a cyclical fashion.

Truth: White = Universal truth. Black = Many truths exist at once.

Words: White = Words have explicit meanings. Black = Words have implicit meanings.

Style: White = Communication is direct and forthright. Black = Communication is indirect.

Logic: White = Formal deductive reasoning. Black = Alternative heuristic.

examine the history of the country to determine which colonizers, which tribes, which religions, and which languages have had the strongest influences in that country. Another notable characteristic that is common throughout Africa is that people in the urban areas conduct business differently than in the rural, more traditional areas. This chapter discusses the structure, process, and communication used in business activities, primarily from sub-Saharan Africa to South Africa. For North Africa, refer to the business practices of the Middle East. In certain cases such as South Africa, the culture of the colonizing country may have to be studied to more appropriately understand the dominant business practices.

Structure

The tradition of hierarchy mixes with the government and legal systems to create the structure for the practice of business. Most of the countries are independent or protectorates with their own form of government. In general, the African countries are in a period of transition, much like Eastern Europe and some Southeast Asian countries, trying to establish stable government and legal systems.

Hierarchy

Tribal networks are the fundamental structure for doing business in Africa, thereby making relationships the cornerstone of any business activity. The family and tribe are the basic units of society in Africa. The scores for Power Distance and Individualism[1] in Hofstede's system for East Africa and West Africa support the importance of hierarchy and the group orientation of individuals. The families and tribes provide emotional, financial, and spiritual security, as well as a sense of self. This unit forms a strong *inner circle* to which outsiders are very seldom admitted. In Kenya, the inner circle relationship is called **uthoni**. Over time, you may move from the position of *outsider* to an intermediate location of *trusted friend*; but very seldom will an *outsider* ever become part of the *inner circle*.

Within the family and tribe, one's **position** within the network constrains and structures the type of relationships that exists and can be developed with other individuals. The tribes bestow each individual member with a place in the social structure for both identity and reference. In addition, they establish

---

[1] Geert Hofstede's research identified five dimensions of culture. High Power Distance scores demonstrate the degree to which members of the society recognize inequalities of power. High Individualism scores indicate that individual rights are paramount in that society. See www.geert-hofstede.com.

guidelines for acceptable behavior. In these countries, except for those that are primarily Muslim or Christian, the tribal regulations also hold moral connotations. As a result, members of the tribe are closely bound and strangers are not made to feel very welcome. Anyone who violates the norms of behavior for the tribe can be cast out of the inner circle.

Only those who demonstrate that they can and will conform to the established norms and behaviors of the group are considered for entry into the intermediate circle. The ability to behave in ways appropriate to one's status and to preserve harmony, even at an individual's expense, is a basic virtue. Maintaining your honor is also essential for preserving and enhancing your status within the tribe and for increasing influence and power in society. Therefore, understanding how these social networks operate and learning how to develop relationships with members of the network are essential activities for successful business transactions. Business, while influenced on the surface by European traditions, actually transfers the social behaviors and norms from the tribal societies into the workplace.

The tribe, therefore, is very powerful. Decisions are made at the top by the "big man," the leader who has influence, can facilitate activities, is trusted by all of the tribal members, grants favors, and has the highest status within the network. In many African countries, the tribal hierarchy determines who gets a particular job. When someone moves to the city to take a job for higher pay, that person has an obligation to share his or her income with family and relations back in the village. Initially, the purpose of contacts is to learn about the culture, the networks, the decision-making process, and the formal business practices to determine which networks or channels are most appropriate for your product or service. A great deal of time and effort needs to be spent evaluating the individual with whom you are considering doing business by determining whether the individual actually has access to the people promised, how much influence the individual has within the tribe, who the *actual* contacts are, what their style of doing business is, and their reputation as businesspeople.

Determining the position of your contact within the tribe, the influence of the tribe within the government, and how influence is shared between the tribe and the government is an important assessment for conducting business successfully. Taking time to be sure you feel comfortable with your assessment is time well spent.

Role of Government

Virtually all of the African countries are independent. Most have established their own forms of government, often borrowing many of the governmental principles from the colonial country. However, most also have introduced their own beliefs, customs, and traditions to create a true hybrid system. The legacy is that the members of the indigenous population, at least in the first few generations after independence, are somewhat bicultural; they know how to do business within the cultural constraints of their native culture, and they know how to do business within the cultural constraints of the former colonial country. As such, these people are extremely flexible and adaptable.

Most of the African countries are republics, parliamentary republics, or constitutional democracies. A few, like Libya, are dictatorships; and a few, like Morocco, are constitutional monarchies. In general, the European colonials greatly influenced the system of government. However, just because the form of government is a parliamentary republic or constitutional democracy does not mean that the systems are stable, reliable, and work independently. The tribal traditions of hierarchy, favors, and protecting one's network are interwoven into all forms of government. Depending upon where a country is in the transition from tribal rule to the institutionalization of government, the system of government is more or less reliable. For the foreign businessperson, the results of elections are more significant in Africa than elsewhere in the world. If the contacts with whom you conduct business and their network are voted out and a new tribe gains power, business may cease abruptly. The development of networks and influence is more critical in Africa than is typically understood by businesspeople.

Rule of Law

As each country created its form of independent government, a legal system was also created. Given the cultural diversity, there are also different legal systems throughout the African countries. Depending upon the colonizing country, the legal systems of some African countries are based upon the French, Roman, Dutch, British, Islamic, Portuguese, Spanish, or Anglo systems of law. However, most countries created a system that blends several of the previously mentioned forms of law with local tribal law or customary law. As a result, the legal systems differ from country to country, none are a clear application of one system, all have local traditions intertwined, and the systems continue to evolve.

Personal relationships need to be developed first because they provide the foundation for stable extended business relationships. As a friend, you will likely be called upon to offer assistance in business and personal matters. Your ability to honor your word is, however, an important factor in maintaining your place and increasing status within the local business network. Written contracts are not as important as they are in task-oriented countries.

Since the future is uncertain and unforeseeable, the terms of a contract will need to be adjusted as circumstances change. Surely, the other side, as a friend and valued partner in business, will be accommodating to requests for assistance. Furthermore, the legal systems vary in structure, stability, standing, and enforcement abilities. As a result, the standing of legal contracts can be questionable and must be investigated carefully before creating a contract. This is best done through either your formal government representative at a consulate, an international attorney with a good network in Africa, or a trusted local contact.

Like other countries in which personal connections are important, "facilitation payments," "dash," incentives," or bribes are often used to provide access to decision makers. However, these services and/or payments may be illegal depending upon the country in which the activity takes place, the country where the participants or companies are headquartered, or the country in which the individuals involved live and work. Therefore, determining the laws and regulations of the country in which your company is based, the country of your citizenship, and the country in which you will be doing business is absolutely essential before engaging in any of these activities. Further, the foreigner's socialized values and judgments of the intentions of the participants simply do not apply as long as no legal prohibitions are violated.

There is an exception to personal relationships being first. If the foreign business has a clearly superior product or service or a unique position in the market—for example, it is the sole supplier to the market—it may be able to forgo personal relationships, at least initially. In such a case, you may be able to enter the market through an invitation of either a network member or the government. However, if an imitator comes from a local network or is connected to the network via personal relationship, the foreign business market position is in jeopardy.

The common thread among the African countries is that they either do not yet have well-established legal, financial, or governmental institutions to support their economies or are in the process of developing them. In either case, the systems cannot be relied upon to function reliably with effective legal enforcement.

Process

How, where, and when business takes place differs between task-oriented and relationship-oriented countries. This section addresses how the division between public and private life, punctuality, and the flow of activities affect the process of conducting business.

Privacy

As in other relationship-oriented countries, the difference between membership in the outer circle and inner circle is an important distinguishing factor. Within the inner circle, there is little difference between private and public lives. The division between private and public lives is significant with members of the outer circle. However, members of the outer circle need to develop an appropriate personal connection if they are to move to the intermediate circle and become a preferred business partner. The process involves making a *personalized* connection, but that does not mean "personal" or *casual*.

Conversations during initial meetings may be spent on small talk, but personal topics should be avoided. Talking about family members, politics, holidays, or personal hobbies may be too personal until a relationship has been established. Talking about the countryside, traditions, or cuisine may be a good way to demonstrate your interest in and respect for the local culture. Progression to a more informal style of interaction takes place very slowly and only if the foreigner is accepted. The foreign businessperson must resist the urge to conduct business too quickly. A show of impatience may cause the opportunity for doing business to be lost.

Continued adherence to local protocol, interest in the local business environment, and reliable performance on initial projects may result in a change of position to the intermediate circle. Over time, if the personal relationship continues to grow, the foreign businessperson may be invited to attend or participate in functions with members of the extended family or tribe. In Africa, self-restraint in expression is more highly valued than self-expression. As a result, private life is kept to oneself outside of the inner circle. Too much personal independence might result in being shunned by an African's home group, which would cause loss of economic and social support in the important segments of an individual's life.

Maintaining relationships among network members is important. Agreeing to be a *friend* in this business environment involves being accepted into the intermediate circle and entails reciprocal obligations. A *friend* is called *elder* or *younger brother* in East Africa, and *home boy* in West Africa, which is a combination of business colleague, lifelong friend, younger brother, older brother, or someone who supports a request in expectation that you will offer a comparable favor or respond to a comparable request in the future. Once accepted as a friend in Africa, someone from the network can drop in at any time to visit another friend at home. Formal invitations are not common, but hospitality to one's friends at any time is expected. Friends may be asked to extend the time of a payment without any penalty. A manager may be asked to make a loan to an employee from the local network or to a relation of network members, to be repaid on payday. For a *friend* or *brother,* responsibility for all members of the network or tribe and the well-being of the network or tribe is assumed and required.

Wealthy members of the network or tribe are expected to give generously to support friends and relatives, which not only strengthens the social relationship but also ensures economic security by creating indebtedness and loyalty on the part of those who received the gifts. Multinational or global companies are expected to give funds to support community projects as a way of demonstrating their commitment to the community. These donations are also a way to avoid giving gifts to individuals, which often causes ethical dilemmas for the companies, and may be an effective tax choice depending upon the legal status of the action.

Punctuality

Task completion is, at most, of equal importance to the relationship and not viewed as the only criterion for evaluating success. Time is clearly flexible, with different criteria being used to determine which activities are deemed more important, thereby deserving more time, whether time is a critical constraint for task completion, and how much time should be spent on various activities. Significant ties to a local community are characterized by the development of personal relationships, distrust of outsiders, and an orientation to accomplishing tasks by working through networks.

Time is generally viewed as flexible and unlimited. Terms such as *African time, jam karat,* or *rubber time* convey the idea that time is abundant, a limitless pool that stretches into the future. So, of course, time can always be taken for important activities, such as attending to family or friends. With this attitude prevalent, it is not surprising that people who are in a hurry, rushing to accomplish a task quickly, are often viewed with suspicion, making it difficult to build trust. In countries with an agrarian or nomadic tradition, the flow of time has more relation to the completion of activities than to the specific time on a schedule.

Flow of Time

A combination of Muslim, Christian, and animism beliefs affects the orientation toward time, creating a view of time as flexible, cyclical, and abundant.

Therefore, in Africa, deadlines for completed tasks and *efficiency* are not valued the same way they are in task-oriented cultures. Accomplishing tasks in the most efficient and effective manner is not a criterion for evaluating success. After all, these tasks are only one part of life and will be accomplished in their own time. Tasks that fit within the blueprint of life will be accomplished in their own good time, but only if harmony within the tribe is maintained.

Because strangers are not welcome and decision making is often centralized within the tribe or government, using a consultant, agent, friend, or middleperson to introduce you to members of a tribe is often the most effective way of gaining access to the people who wield power. If chosen carefully and if effective personal relationships are established, these contacts may even become mentors or allies as you continue to work in the country providing valuable advice and knowledge about business practices and methods. While a preliminary introduction may be made by letter, the foreign businessperson will need to meet personally with the tribal, business, and government representatives. Mentioning that you know other members of the tribe or their relatives can facilitate your acceptance into the group.

Providing introductions is, at times, an opportunity for network members to earn additional income or favors. However, these services and/or payments may be illegal; and company lawyers should be consulted before proceeding to engage in this activity. Introductions, alone, do not guarantee business. Once initial introductions have been made, time must be spent developing a relationship with key individuals in the tribe to establish a personal connection, to allow time to be evaluated, and to move closer to the inner circle, which has the power to decide whether there is a chance to do business.

Establishing credibility and rapport must be done in person and will be time-consuming. For example, one manager trying to enter the market in an African country made four trips to the potential partner and visited with the owner, having tea, coffee, dinners, and light entertainment. The manager's boss, back in the home country, kept asking how things were going; the manager replied that everything was going great but gave the boss no details. On the fifth trip, the visiting businessperson, in conversation with the local owner, introduced the possibility of a joint venture, and, after normal negotiations over subsequent visits, the deal was made. This particular manager knew that spending time with the owner, drinking tea and lemonade, and visiting the owner's compound for dinner were necessary for developing trust and the comfort necessary to do business. If time is not spent earning trust and comfort, business opportunities either will never arise or a deal will never come to fruition.

In Africa, the visiting patterns can be quite complex. During an initial meeting with tribal representatives, the visitor, the *outsider*, might be seated in the middle of a circle of 10 to 30 "big men" for conversation with all of them to create a sense of brotherhood or **uthoni** (Fadiman, 1989). Each guest, including the *outside man*, incurs the obligation to continue to build *uthoni* by visiting each member of the group and the host. In addition, the *outside man* will extend the hospitality of his house to any male member of the group that chooses to drop in at any time. By taking time to get to know one another, evaluate one another, learn the local customs, and determine whether the other person is honorable, the network is making a decision as to whether business should be conducted with this person. If the personal evaluation is negative, meetings never will progress beyond this preliminary stage. If the decision is positive, business subjects will be mentioned tentatively in general terms.

Communication

During these meetings, the use of words, perception of truth, forms of logic, and style of communication affect the formation and maintenance of relationships as well as the conduct of business. This section will address each of these topics.

Words

The number of different languages in Africa is overwhelming. For example, Nigeria and Zaire **each** have more than 250 different languages and dialects. These languages are not in Hall's (1981) classification system; however, given the cultural similarities with other agrarian and nomadic societies as well as the importance of relationships, we can assume that the local languages are high context, meaning that relationships are significant arbiters of meaning. Developing a relationship is fundamental to any interaction, business or social. Knowing the status and the relative importance of an individual as well as the network of influence to which a person belongs determines, in part, how the words are to be interpreted.

Meaning is derived from the conversation, tone, atmosphere, body language, facial expressions, gestures, feelings, and general willingness of the parties to come to a good understanding. Participants must be completely conscious of not only what information is being conveyed by the content of the conversation, but also what else is being communicated. Identifying the appropriate cues and interpreting them requires attention to many details, active listening skills, observational skill, and an intense awareness and understanding of the situation and people involved.

Whether local businesspeople use a low context language, such as English or Dutch, or converse through a translator using their local language, the high context environment is most important. People work to develop their intuition, are socialized to read others' actions and body language, use their developed intuition to understand the situation, and make their decisions accordingly. Therefore, discussions generally follow a more subdued tone, with each side trying to please the other.

Truth

Enhancing one's status, protecting the tribe, and maintaining harmony are primary goals. Local businesspeople learn to use language in tactful, ambiguous, and clever ways to present a point of view. Presenting a position or responding to a question in a way that does not offend is highly valued.

Being honorable and adhering to the norms of the tribe are critical behaviors for success. Delivering on promises, providing useful information, and using influence in judicial ways enhances an individual's reputation. Not being able to deliver what was promised, providing information that cannot be trusted, or using influence in inappropriate ways result in an individual losing status. Having other tribe members trust what one says is critical for good standing.

However, that same norm does not necessarily apply across tribal lines. The Islamic and Christian religions, which believe in a universal truth, have significant numbers of members in some African countries. However, conversing in ways that maintain harmony and protect one's tribe and family are more important than adhering to an abstract universal truth.

The foreign businessperson cannot accept what is said at face value. Rather, investing the time to get to know the people involved, checking the information provided, and making small business deals first are a good strategy. Over time, as you receive useful information from a particular source, develop a personal connection with a person, and successfully conclude some small projects, you move into the intermediate circle and then have an obligation to make decisions that protect the tribe. At this point, the foreign businessperson needs to check with company headquarters regarding the legality and ethics of misconstruing information or providing favors for the tribe.

Logic

Local businesspeople have traditional, local religious beliefs in nature worship or animism, accept many gods, and often believe in reincarnation. The strong affinity with nature leads to a cyclical worldview in which everything has a season and there is an appropriate time for everything. In addition, a fatalist belief inhibits people from taking control and actively trying to change events. Never underestimate the pragmatism of business partners when their interests are at stake.

The fatalist perspective also encourages acceptance, tolerance, and resignation toward events. Once the facts are revealed, everyone knows what the situation is and, since there is little reason to try to change fate and very little experience in taking initiative, people accept the situation as they see it. Therefore, the party with more information has more power. Because everyone outside of the tribe is considered an outsider and competitor, information is not readily shared because competition between tribes is intense.

Precedents often are used to describe or understand situations, but precedents cannot be used to predict decisions. Given the importance of relationships and situations, an assumption that similar problems will be solved in the same way as in the past is not valid. Decisions usually are arrived at in a roundabout way, using a circular kind of reasoning and polite conversation, often over extended periods.

Since bargaining is a tradition in the marketplace and in the countries with a strong trading tradition, distributive or high-pressure tactics are common during business discussions. Participants can be competitive, confrontational, uncompromising, and inflexible. However, confrontational words should be avoided to keep the exchange from becoming combative, perhaps resulting in your potential partner's walking away from the exchange. Relationships and being part of or accepted by the tribe are still the most important part of the process as both sides work toward an agreement. In Kenya, traditionally, initial concessions are low and increase in size over time. In South Africa, concessions are made begrudgingly at the end, only after everything else has failed to work. In Nigeria, agreements are reached slowly through compromise.

Hierarchy within the tribe is important. The local business representatives might be unable to make concessions because final agreements must be made by the tribal leader or company president or approved by the *big man* in the network. If so, businesspeople report back to the decision makers, who will take counsel and then make a decision. The process continues in this manner until issues are resolved, either by one side making a concession or compromise that is acceptable to everyone or by having a go-between propose concessions or compromises that are agreeable to both sides.

Style

Variation in style exists across African countries depending upon how well the locals adapted to the colonial culture, the educational level of the tribal leaders, the primary religious influence, whether the location was on a trading route, whether the local tribes were nomads or farmers, and how well the different tribes within a country get along. Hospitality, respect for those in the inner circle, suspicion of outsiders, and a long process of developing personal connections are important common characteristics of style.

Respect for other individuals and their status in the tribe is demonstrated by following an established protocol for social exchanges. For each position or level of status, there are specific rules of behavior to demonstrate respect, such as using titles or appropriate forms of address when speaking to someone, accepting offers of food and drink, or choosing appropriate topics for social conversation. Formally demonstrating respect for someone's status in the tribe or network is a fundamental element of appropriate behavior for developing personal connections. If appropriate formalities are not observed, the intermediate circle will never open for you. Taking time to be introduced, to get to know the local businesspeople, to let the local businesspeople know you, and to demonstrate your ability to function within the tribe takes place over a number of meetings in a paced manner.

Business exchanges are not always quiet or submissive. For instance, the Nigerian people love language and are likely to talk and argue vigorously. Nevertheless, decisions are based upon intuition, experience, and emotion as well as the age and experience of the person who is talking. Generally, coercion is not an effective tactic in any of these countries. Respect for the other person needs to be displayed even when disagreeing vigorously.

Conclusion

Entering the tribal network inside the government and in the business community is the most important and difficult first step for outsiders. Taking time to meet and build a relationship with people who can introduce you to decision makers is essential, followed by the process of building a relationship with the decision makers. If trust is established over time, you may be accepted into the intermediate circle as a *friend*, which entails obligations and responsibilities.

During this process, both sides have been evaluating the other, determining whether the other side is a reputable business partner, and deciding whether to do business with the other side. If the decision about the individual is positive, the business process continues. The purpose of this process is to explore issues, find possible areas of agreement, and/or discover possible weaknesses in the other side. The process tends to be circular and indirect, placing the emphasis on exploration rather than persuasion. Concessions are important but are not easily accomplished. The importance of demonstrating respect precludes direct personal confrontation on areas of disagreement. However, lively discussions expressing disagreement on issues are valued in some countries. If the disagreement cannot be resolved, an outside third party known to both sides may act as a go-between. In some instances, concessions are expected from the wealthier side or the side with the best position. Often, the concessions are made at the last minute, when everything else has failed.

Relationships are most important, and government and legal structures are not well established throughout Africa. Therefore, written contracts are not always perceived as important or reliable. As the situation and environment changes, friends, who are in constant contact with one another, will adapt the agreement to work around changing circumstances. Learning to know potential business partners well is not a waste of time on seemingly inconsequential social activities, but an important investment in evaluating business opportunities and in expanding existing business.

CHAPTER 13

WHAT IS ADAPTATION?

You are a product of a specific culture, with the appropriate behaviors and values of your formative period. While still a child, you were taught what to do, what not to do, what was polite, what was impolite, how to approach the truth, what beliefs and assumptions to value, how important family is, how to treat other people, and how to value task completion. Family, religion, community, and peers influence the value system that each person adopts as a child, and modification occurs via the educational process and company norms. Although a member of several cultural groups, such as country, region, locality, ethnic group, religion, and family, your experience and personal perspective create a unique manifestation of culture. The visiting businessperson must remember that while an overarching cultural classification is a good place to begin, it is *only* a place to begin. In each situation, the visitor needs to understand the local businesspeople as individuals and learn their approach to business and decision making.

To avoid offending the local businessperson, thereby precluding an opportunity to do business, the foreign visitor needs to identify appropriate behavior and styles of communication, understand how decisions are made, and adapt appropriately. This is common advice and usually the end of the discussion. However, that advice means that everyone inherently understands how to adapt. In reality, a wide range of adaptive behaviors are possible, but there are some parameters to remember. Straying too far on the side of "going native" or assuming that all businesspeople are the same usually results in offending your partner, demonstrating a lack of sincerity, and diminishing the possibility of successful business.

"Going native" is not adaptation. First, unless you were raised in a particular culture or lived as part of that culture for many years, you really don't know all the nuances of language, belief systems, and attitudes that influence behavior. Try explaining the excitement of a particular event to someone from a distinctly different cultural group. For instance, explaining the excitement that people in the midwestern or northeastern United States have for Groundhog Day to someone from Indonesia is quite a challenge. Without understanding all of the assumptions and nuances, you are not really a native.

Second, trying to demonstrate your ability to fit in when you really do not presents a false front. The locals might think you are making fun of them because when you don't act exactly like a member of the culture, you create the impression of parodying the culture and your sincerity is called into question. Your attempt at being native only raises suspicion and distrust, keeping you in the "outsider" circle.

Assuming adaptation is not necessary is also mistake, with one exception. If the product or service you provide is the only one available, adaptation is not necessary because the other side's need for the product overrides any personal issues. However, if there are comparable products or services available on the market, adaptation is necessary for success. Cultural values are the foundation for decision making and creating expectations regarding the practice of business. Without understanding the other side's decision-making process or respecting the expectations for business activity, you demonstrate an affront to your potential partner by assuming your approach to doing business is the only way.

Within these two ends of the continuum, the amount of adaptation required in a particular business situation and the degree of adaptation that one individual can make vary. The more competition there is for your product or service, the more adaptation is necessary. The more flexibility an individual's personality allows, the more comfortable the variety of adaptive behaviors will be. The more stressful the situation, the more a person reverts to his or her core beliefs and is less likely to adapt.

For those who are required to travel for a few days to another area of the world for meetings, equipment or technology repair work, conferences, or fieldwork, learning about that area of the world and behaviors that are polite is important. For those who will be visiting another area of the world for a short stay (for example, two weeks to six months) for training, sales, or research, learning the pace of business activities, a few words and phrases of the local language, something about the major religions, appropriate business behavior, learning style, and decision-making process is necessary. For those who will be living in another part of the world for an extended time (for example, a year or more), learning survival skills in the language; mastering a rudimentary understanding of the major religions, the role of networks, the role of private versus public lives, decision-making processes, values, and use of time; and finding a mentor are valuable steps in the adaptation process.

The rest of this chapter examines adaptation related to a number of issues that need to be considered when doing business in other parts of the world. If the country you are going to visit is on either side of your home culture on the Classification of Cultures Model, adaptation is easier because there is more overlap between the cultural groups. However, no two groups are identical, so adaptation is still necessary for both personal and professional success.

Language

Being fluent in the language of the country you are visiting or moving to is ideal, but not always possible. A minimal level of adaptation is to learn a few polite phrases to demonstrate your respect and desire to adapt. Making the effort to move outside of your comfort zone and attempt the local language demonstrates flexibility. This is generally sufficient for those traveling to another country for a few days or a short-term visit. For those planning an extended stay or those representing the company in a major negotiation, this level of adaptation is not sufficient, especially in relationship-oriented cultures.

If you will be living in country for an extended period, you need to learn enough of the local language to navigate around the city, manage daily tasks, and participate in local events. At the very least, you need to learn polite phrases and a minimal acquaintance with common phrases, requests, and responses. In addition, you need to have a fluent, native speaker on your staff with whom you develop a strong relationship and work with closely. This person needs to attend meetings, do necessary translations, and, most important, debrief you after meetings on any side conversations and interpretations of nonverbal cues. In those cultures in which relationships are important, you will be participating in social events in which your counterpart is getting to know you as a person. You may want to be learning about your "new friend" as well as be using all the aids available. If you cannot use the native language for social conversations, you are at a disadvantage in getting to know the other person.

When it comes to finalizing a draft of the contract, a native speaker must be involved, especially in countries with high context languages, even if the contract is being drafted in your language. The words in the contract need to be evaluated either in a precise manner, which requires the advice of someone who is a native and understands local idioms, or in terms of context, which requires a native who is familiar with the significance of nonverbal cues.

While you are not always required or able to learn the local language, you can learn some polite phrases and demonstrate respect. The longer you are in the country, the more of the local language you should be able to use. However, doing business requires getting to know individuals and drafting contracts. In these situations, you need the advice of someone who is a native speaker whether or not you speak the local language.

Team Composition

As in most business situations, the size of the team is determined by the client or customer. If your business partner expects a private meeting with one individual, your team would be best suited to meet that expectation and have one member. An exception might be that when you are visiting a country a long distance away, either in actual miles or in position on the Classification of Cultures Model, two people would be appropriate. While each person may experience information overload, having two sets of eyes and ears to observe and listen will obtain more information to evaluate and report.

In those countries in which hierarchy is important, the team composition needs to include members from different levels of the home company. Determining the purpose of the meeting is the first step. Depending upon whether the visit is to explore ideas, to repair a manufacturing problem, to conduct training, or to make a regularly scheduled annual visit, you will also need to identify the functional expertise required. Functional expertise needs to be balanced with level and status in the organization so that the match between teams is roughly equivalent. The next decision is choosing which levels of hierarchy from your company will be involved in the business transactions. Determining the highest level of hierarchy from the other side will dictate the level of hierarchy needed to represent your organization. Determining the importance and/or significance of the meeting is the third step. If the meeting has great importance, either officially—for example, signing documents—or symbolically—for example, the opening of the joint venture office—someone from the top ranks and preferably the CEO or president of the company needs to head the team.

Depending upon the importance of formality and protocol in the country you are visiting, the importance of collective behavior in that culture, and the role of hierarchy, you need to determine who will most likely represent the other side, what activities will be involved or topics will be discussed, how much time will be involved, and what decision-making processes will be used. With this knowledge, you can then determine the number of people representing what functions with what expertise who need to be members of your team.

Team Selection

Knowing which people with what levels of status and what areas of expertise need to be included in the team is the first step. Selecting the most appropriate people to be members of the team is the next step. Simply being at the appropriate level in the hierarchy and having previously demonstrated technical expertise and strong business skills in your home country are not sufficient credentials in and of themselves. Current technical expertise, appropriate status within the organization, and the demonstrated ability to work effectively in the country being visited are all criteria for selection. Identifying the possible candidates with the required technical expertise and status is relatively straightforward. Determining which of those people will work best in the country being visited has at least equal importance but is a difficult challenge.

If an individual is very successful in a home country requiring adherence to procedures and policies and emphasizing task completion within a specified time period but is not comfortable with ambiguity, success as a member of the team going to a country with a polychronic orientation to time or using a high context language has a predictably low outcome. On the other hand, if an individual functions very well in an ambiguous, "flexible time" environment, success in a task-oriented country that requires adherence to policies and procedures within specified time periods is not likely.

If an individual has demonstrated flexibility at home, has expressed an interest in overseas assignments, is willing to learn about the culture of the country, and is willing to acquire some language skill, assigning that person as a team member, not leader, is a good idea. As the person demonstrates competence in cultures close to that of the home country and continues to demonstrate flexibility in adapting to cultures that are different, more responsibility for the team can be assigned to that individual. Not everyone has a flexible personality or is willing to adopt new behaviors or communication styles. In that case, being a member of the team to provide technical expertise is still possible, but responsibility for conducting business should be limited in scope, and assigning that individual to countries most similar to the home country will result in more success, both for the individual and for the company.

Preparation at Home

Once the team members have been chosen, preparation for the trip should begin. First, team members need an overview of the culture in that area of the world, like that provided in the previous chapters. This learning is a good foundation for creating a sense of a region and creating very broad expectations. Second, learning about the country's history, ethnic groups, religions, art, cuisine, and politics provides more depth to the understanding of that country, remembering that the longer the in-country stay will be, the more knowledge team members need to have. Third, developing some familiarity with the language is always useful. Polite phrases are appropriate if the team's stay will be short. Some conversational ability is especially useful in relationship-oriented countries or for longer stays in the host country.

In addition to learning about the country to be visited, preparation needs to include discussions of the team's structure, decision-making authority, the roles of each member, and company policy regarding activities that could be considered unethical or illegal in either country. Team members need to know their roles, whether as a provider of technical expertise, social facilitator, observer, decision maker, or formal leader. Prior to departing, the team needs clarity on the handling of anticipated issues—for example, which questions individual team members handle on their own and report back to the team or which questions individual team members bring back to the team for a decision. If this is not clearly determined before leaving the home country, it is relatively easy for the other side to create divisions among the team and play one person against another. If everyone is clear about his or her role before leaving and regular team meetings are held while in-country to share information, report on activities, and share interpretations, then the team can present a united and professional front.

Another item for preparation at home is to share an expectation of what is likely to occur during the trip; this includes more than the itinerary. The team members need an expectation of what formal activities will take place, how they are expected to function during those activities, what information activities are likely to take place, how they are expected to function during those activities, whether there is free time, what expectations the team leader has for how to spend free time, what protocol needs to be observed, what behaviors are appropriate or inappropriate, and what topics of conversation are appropriate or inappropriate. Upon completion of this level of preparation, the individual or team is ready to embark on the trip.

Orientation in Country

Depending on how far the team travels, either in terms of cultural distance or geographical distance or time, members need time to reorient themselves to the country being visited. Arriving two or three days before meetings begin is essential for a first trip; arriving one or two days before meetings begin is necessary when traveling transoceanically. Arriving just in time to attend a meeting and leaving immediately after a meeting is acceptable only when you have a strong established relationship with someone who is comfortable with a stronger task/time orientation, or when distance is not an issue.

When arriving in the country, orientation for the initial visit includes developing a sense of location: Where is the hotel? What transportation modes are available? Where will the meetings take place? How long does it take to get to the meetings? Where are needed services such as restaurants, travel agencies, or banks located? In addition, those visiting for the first time need to adjust their expectations of culture, cuisine, art, and language to the reality of being in the country. Arriving early provides time to visit a local museum to learn about the area, people, or public artifacts of importance to the local population. Taking a bus tour of the area or city provides an overview of the layout of important landmarks. Reading a local newspaper, if in your language or if you understand the local language, provides a sense of major current events. Browsing in stores or going to restaurants in different areas of the city provides an intuitive feel for the people, pace of life, and local interests.

The more familiar you are with the local country, the shorter this orientation phase can be. However, depending upon the distance traveled, it is essential to allow for the opportunity to manage jet lag. If you are fatigued to the point of falling asleep during meetings, you will have difficulty responding to questions coherently, much less taking in all the contextual clues and listening for what is *not* said. The more experience you have with international travel, the better you will know how much time you need to function at your best.

Always take the local culture into consideration. If you are traveling to a country that is relationship-oriented, you need to provide for social time before beginning business. Either the other side needs to get to know you, wants to demonstrate their pride in local architecture, art, cuisine, and accomplishments, or likely wants time to reconnect on a personal level. Without these kinds of nontask-related activities, the local businesspeople cannot function well and your insistence on doing business first will only result in frustration for both sides.

Meetings in the Host Country

Once your team is in the host country, the meetings, training sessions, research, or service calls begin. Depending upon the time orientation in that country, the schedule may or may not have been changed while you traveled, may or may not be adhered to, or the team organizer may be asked to meet with the local organizer to review and *update* the schedule. Just because you scheduled meetings and confirmed the times before leaving does not mean everything will occur as scheduled.

Depending upon the country, you may be expected to attend a social event first; to have a formal opening meeting, which is in many cases a ritual with no expectation of substantive discussion; or to engage in serious negotiation shortly into the first meeting. If the first meeting is not what you expected, what then? How do you respond? Your ability to adapt is immediately being put to the test. Have you given the team organizer the authority to change the schedule, or do those decisions need to be approved by or coordinated with the team leader? Have you left important documents at the hotel because you were not expecting a substantive discussion? Is your team visibly surprised and confused by the change in plans? Requesting a short break is entirely appropriate so your team members can collect themselves, determine which plan of action is being followed, and return to the meeting organized and prepared.

The local team organizer may be asking for your departure to arrange for transportation back to the airport. Are you leaving within 24 hours? If not, the other side does not need that information yet. However, you need to respond in a way that does not offend and enables the other side to save face. Having prepared for this possibility, your team organizer may indicate that your team would like to travel to a nearby shrine, museum, church, or site of local significance at the completion of business. A time for completion of business can be agreed upon and you can accept the local organizer's assistance or advice for planning the outing. However, both sides know that your departure is flexible and you do not expect the business decisions to be constrained by time.

Preparation also needs to include planning for informal meetings. In relationship-oriented cultures, official conversations in formal meetings are often guarded and must be interpreted in light of which people are in attendance, the status of those individuals, and other contextual characteristics. In hierarchical countries, team members will be paired with members of the local company of like status and/or expertise. In social settings, information about concerns, issues, concessions, and constraints may be shared. Remember that the other side is trying to obtain similar information from you. Effective team members have demonstrated their ability to reveal information that facilitates the discussion without compromising your team's approach, to ask questions appropriately, to listen to what the other side reveals, and to observe contextual clues. At the end of the evening or before meetings begin the next day, team members need to share what they have learned and use the information to shape the formal discussions for the day.

The timing, pacing, and flow of business meetings have different require-ments with each cultural group. Your ability to understand the differences and respect the pace demonstrates your sensitivity and ability to work effec-tively in that country. Demonstrating impatience and anger at the slow process, changes in plans, or inability of the other side to come to a decision at the table reflects badly and raises doubts about your ability to function effectively and on whether you and your home corporation are worthy of an introduction to any superiors in the organization.

Determining how the other side uses meetings when making decisions results in a better use of meeting time. In those cultures requiring consensus for decisions or having the person at the top of the organization make the decision, new ideas proposed during a meeting cannot be decided at that meeting. If the individuals participating in the meeting do not have the authority to make decisions or if a group consensus is required, new ideas can be proposed, discussed, explored, and debated but cannot be approved or denied. After a break allowing the other team to meet or the leader to check with the top person in the organization or for decisions makers in the com-pany to make a group decision, the team can return with the ability to make a decision about the new idea. However, if the idea or proposal is modified, another adjournment is necessary. Knowing the decision-making style of the other side helps your team understand the need for frequent adjournments and the inability of the other side to make quick decisions.

Communication Style

Sometimes you will be expected to have credible facts and figures available to support your claims; sometimes you will be expected to demonstrate past ex-perience with other respected companies; sometimes you will be expected to demonstrate your honor and credibility; sometimes you will be required to demonstrate your or the company's expertise; sometimes you will be required to demonstrate appropriate etiquette; sometimes you will be required to demonstrate your facility with language; sometimes you will be expected to demonstrate your ability to allow others to save face; sometimes you will be expected to demonstrate respect; sometimes you will be required to do several of these things. Adaptation is possible when you have a repertoire of skills available and know when it is appropriate to use which skills.

If you have one communication style that is effective in your home coun-try and use that style everywhere, you are not likely to be successful in other cultures. We have mentioned several times that differences exist within countries and success depends upon identifying the local reality. If that is necessary within a country, then using only one style when moving to another area of the country or dealing with another cultural group is not a formula for success. What is the reality in the location where you are doing business? Are you going to be asked specific questions requiring immediate, factual responses with documentation? If so, you need to be prepared. Are you going to be expected to engage in abstract discussions of ideas? Are you ready to establish main principles based on the proposals that will be evaluated at the next meeting? Are you expected to refrain from any substantive business discussions at a particular meeting? Do you know what information to provide when participating in a meeting at which competitors are present? Being prepared with the appropriate information for discussions with members of a particular cultural group is critical for success.

Being able to change communication strategies from direct to indirect styles is a skill that takes time to develop. If you are from a cultural group that expects to ask questions and receive frank, honest responses and you are doing business in a country that uses indirect communication aimed at creating and maintaining harmony, or vice versa, business meetings may be frustrating for both parties. From your perspective, your intent is simply to be efficient, get to the point, get the information on the table, address the issues, and move along. As the discussion proceeds, the other side continues with oblique, ambiguous responses that require a lot of work to interpret. You feel as though you are in the position of having to solve a puzzle or riddle. Your counterpart may feel as though he or she has been insulted. Both sides are frustrated, and the conversation goes nowhere.

For someone in a low context, nonhierarchical cultural group, developing facility at indirect communication requires a great deal of effort and concentration and the ability to resist saying, "Can't we just get to the point?" For someone in a high-context, hierarchical cultural group, presenting an idea in a direct manner requires the ability to engage in rude behavior that has the possibility of disrupting the harmony—a very great risk. Learning to recognize an indirect pattern of communication enables you to better interpret what the other side is saying and take into account all the contextual cues.

Follow-Up Activities

Once an agreement is made, either orally or in writing, successful adaptation requires knowing how to manage the agreement. When doing business in countries with stable systems that adhere to the rule of law, completion of an agreement identifies who will do what, within what time frame, to what set of requirements, and with what penalties for nonperformance. Follow-up activities do not involve more than checking on the status of projects, asking straightforward questions, and accepting responses at face value. If difficulties are identified early, participants can often find a way to satisfy the terms of the contract, even if modified slightly. Businesspeople are perceived as being professional and good business partners if they consistently manage projects according to the details specified in the agreement.

When conducting business in countries in transition with unstable government and/or legal systems, where transparency and rule of law are not accepted norms, or where professional and credible business behavior is not associated with delivering the details of an agreement as specified, follow-up activities are very different. In many of these countries, languages are high context, so if you send an e-mail or a fax asking if the project is on time, you will receive a reply saying that it is. However, interpret that response in light of the context in which since you are the buyer—offending you is not an option and maintaining harmony is important. It is entirely predictable that the response will be that the project is on time. However, does that response mean the project is really on time? Of course not. It means that the other side understands that you want to hear that it is on time. Asking direct questions results in yes answers that do not necessarily mean yes in many cases.

In these situations, you are not likely to learn the actual status of a project in an e-mail or a fax. On-site observation, informal discussions, and indirect questions are the best tools for eliciting the information you need. Depending upon the information needed, you can identify the member of your team who has a relationship with the person from the other team who is likely to have the required information, and you can send that person to visit. Taking announced and unannounced tours of the facility, observing activity during working hours, and asking informal questions in a tactful manner will reveal the information you need. Depending upon the nature of the assistance required or the authority the visitor has, discussions can be held to offer training programs, purchase new equipment, introduce new processes, or provide assistance with delivery as a way of solving problems without mentioning the problem; instead this is seen more as making a suggestion, as a method of continuous improvement, or as a goodwill offering from a *friend*.

For those businesspeople acculturated to operating in time/task cultures, these types of activities are often viewed as a waste of time and needless expenditure of money. However, relying upon simple affirmatives to e-mail and fax inquiries will turn out to be a bigger waste of time and money when the orders are late or of inferior quality. Learning the skills necessary for managing contracts is critical in those areas in which legal systems are not stable and in which you cannot rely upon the enforcement of contracts.

Conclusion

The concept of equifinality holds that there are many equal ways to reach a final goal. The importance of that concept in the context of global business practices is that the assumption that your culture's way of doing business is the only successful method is simply irrelevant. There is more than one way to successfully conduct business that is ethical and legal. In fact, when doing business around the world, there is no one set of business practices that work equally well everywhere. When outside of the home country, visiting businesspeople need to adapt to be successful.

The purpose of this book is to provide a framework for practicing business in a global environment. The Classification of Cultures Model identifies major cultural groups that are distinctly different from one another but share major similarities among the countries within that group. The model provides a place to begin when analyzing similarities and differences across groups. When conducting business in other countries, the role of government in relation to business activities, the type of legal system, and the reliability of enforcement are important factors when determining the structure of business practices. In those countries with reliable, stable government and legal systems, business practices are understood to be more transparent and predictable. In those countries that do not yet have reliable, stable government and legal systems, the informal hierarchy provides structure for the social system that is just as, if not more, important for understanding the practice of business. Only those admitted to an intermediate or inner circle are trusted business partners. In some countries, an outsider will never be admitted to the inner circle but can enter an intermediate circle of proven business associates. Entry into either of these circles entails rights and obligations that are as binding as any written contract. Understanding the operation of government, legal systems, and network hierarchies is essential for understanding the structure that business practices follow in a particular culture.

The Classification of Cultures Model demonstrates how cultural groups use time differently. While everyone has the same number of hours in the day, time is used in different ways for the process of doing business. Cultural groups on the left-hand side of the model view time as linear, sequential, and segmentable. Professional business behavior is associated with efficiency and the ability to accomplish tasks within specified time periods. Cultural groups on the right-hand side of the model view time as polychronic and cyclical, meaning that more than one activity can take place at the same time and that there is always more time. Professional business behavior is associated with the ability to multitask, to identify tasks with the highest priority whether they are personal or business related, and to take the time to complete the task well. Thus, the flow of business activities differs. Depending upon how a particular cultural group separates its personal life from its business life determines when it is appropriate to discuss what topics. Learning to navigate business processes that operate on different time schedules and to identify appropriate topics of conversation for each part of the process are skills for adapting successfully when conducting business in other cultures.

Since languages, philosophies, and religions involve different belief systems, communication operates in different ways across cultural groups. Depending upon whether members of a cultural group believe in a universal truth or believe creating harmony is necessary, they view truth from a different perspective. Knowing the viewpoint of the people with whom you do business is critical for correctly interpreting what they tell you. Some languages are high context, requiring knowledge of the relationship between speakers and interpretation of all nonverbal cues for understanding, and some are low context, indicating that the words have specific meanings relatively independent of the speakers and the context. Depending upon the philosophical tradition of the cultural group, forms of logic may be inductive, deductive, or cyclical depending upon factual data, one's honor, reputation, or expertise as evidence. Arguments, requests, and responses can be presented in direct or indirect style depending upon the cultural imperative in a specific region of the world.

Each business meeting is a unique event. Depending upon the organizations involved, organizational relationships, individuals, individual relationships, market, product, and circumstances of the parties, the demands, objectives, strategies, and conduct of each meeting will differ. By utilizing the perspectives presented in this book, you can more readily prepare for these meetings with a greater repertoire of skills. Your ability to use these skills and adapt to the conditions of each specific business meeting will determine your success. The models and discussions presented in this book provide the springboard for your adaptation. Much success to you all!

REFERENCES

Abegglan, James C. and George Stalk, Jr. (1995), *Kaisha: The Japanese Corporation*. New York: Basic Books.

Adler, Nancy J. and John L. Graham (1989), "Cross-Cultural Interaction: The International Comparison Fallacy?" *Journal of International Business Studies* (Fall), pp. 515–37.

Agarwal, Sanjeev (1993), "Influence of Formalization on Role Stress, Organizational Commitment, and Work Alienation of Salespersons: A Cross-National Comparative Study," *Journal of International Business Studies* (Fourth Quarter), pp. 715–39.

Albaum, Gerald (1967), "Exploring Interaction in a Marketing Situation," *Journal of Marketing Research*, Vol. 4 (May), pp. 168–72.

Alexander, Joe F., Patrick L. Schul, and Emin Babakus (1991), "Analyzing Interpersonal Communications in Industrial Marketing Negotiations," *Journal of Academy of Marketing Science*, Vol. 19, No. 2, pp. 129–39.

Alghanim, Kutayba (1976), "How to Do Business in the Middle East," *Management Review* (August), pp. 19–28.

Anderson, James C., Hakan Hakansson, and Jan Johanson (1994), "Dyadic Business Relationships Within a Business Network Context," *Journal of Marketing*, Vol. 58 (October), pp. 1–15.

Anderson, James C. and James A. Narus (1984), "A Model of the Distributor's Perspective of Distributor-Manufacturer Working Relationships," *Journal of Marketing*, Vol. 48 (Fall), pp. 62–74.

Andrews, John (1987), "Indonesia," *The Economist* (August), pp. 3–18.

Angelmar, Reinhard and Louis W. Stern (1978), "Development of a Content Analytic System for Analysis of Bargaining Communication in Marketing," *Journal of Marketing Research*, Vol. 15 (February), pp. 93–102.

Asian Wall Street Journal Weekly (1993), May 3, p. 19.

Aztel, Roger (1985), Ed., *Do's and Taboos Around the World*. New York: John Wiley.

"Background Notes: Australia" (1986). Washington, D.C.: U.S. Department of State, Bureau of Public Affairs.

Bagozzi, Richard P. (1980), "Performance and Satisfaction in an Industrial Sales Force: An Examination of Their Antecedents and Simultaneity," *Journal of Marketing*, Vol. 44 (Spring), pp. 65–77.

Baker, Anne and Lynne Waymon (1993), "Grooming the Ugly American," *Carlson Voyageur* (February-March-April), pp. 28–30.

Ballon, Robert J. (1977), "Americans, Europeans, and Japanese," in *PHP, Kiyomu Ennokoshi*, Ed., pp. 73–80. Tokyo: PHP Institute, Inc.

218

Ballon, Robert J., S.J. (1994), Interviewed by Camille Schuster at Sophia University, Tokyo, Japan, November 11.

Banthin, Joanna (1991), "Negotiating with the Japanese," *Mid-Atlantic Journal of Business*, Vol. 27 (April), pp. 79–81.

Bass, Bernard M. (1971), "The American Advisor Abroad," *Journal of Applied Behavioral Science*, Vol. 7, No. 3, pp. 285–307.

Bazerman, Max H., Elizabeth A. Mannix, Harris Sondak, and Leigh Thompson (1983), "Negotiator Behavior and Decision Processes in Dyads, Groups, and Markets," Working Paper. Dispute Resolution Center at Northwestern University, Evanston, Illinois.

Bennett, Douglas C. and Kenneth E. Sharpe (1970), "Agenda Setting and Bargaining Power: The Mexican State versus Transnational Corporations," *World Politics*, Vol. 32, No. 1 (October), pp. 57–89.

Biggar, Joanna (1987), "Meeting of the Twain," *Psychology Today* (November), pp. 46–52.

Black, J. Stewart and Lyman W. Porter (1991), "Managerial Behaviors and Job Performance: A Successful Manager in Los Angeles May Not Succeed in Hong Kong," *Journal of International Business Studies* (First Quarter), pp. 99–113.

Bowers, Michael R. and D. Layne Rich (1991), "The Effect of Product and Market Factors on the Communication Styles of Salespeople," *Developments in Marketing Science*, Vol. 14, pp. 323–27.

Brigham Young University (1992), "Culturgrams." Provo, Utah: Brigham Young University.

Brunner, James A. and Wang You (1988), "Chinese Negotiating and the Concept of Face," *Journal of International Consumer Marketing*, Vol. 1, No. 1, pp. 27–43.

Bryan, Robert M. and Peter C. Buck (1989), "The Cultural Pitfalls in Cross-Border Negotiations," *Mergers and Acquisitions*, Vol. 24, No. 2 (September–October), pp. 61–63.

Buller, David B. and Judee K. Burgoon (1986), "The Effects of Vocalics and Nonverbal Sensitivity on Compliance: A Replication and Extension," *Human Communication Research*, Vol. 13, No. 1 (Fall), pp. 126–44.

Busch, Paul and David T. Wilson (1976), "An Experimental Analysis of a Salesman's Expert and Referent Bases of Social Power in the Buyer-Seller Dyad," *Journal of Marketing Research*, Vol. 13 (February), pp. 3–11.

Campbell, John (1994), "Despite Labor Costs Other Factors Make Pacific Rim Attractive," *Business Record* (August 22–28), p. 14.

Campbell, Nigel C. G., John L. Graham, Alain Jolibert, and Hans Gunther Meissner (1988), "Marketing Negotiations in France, Germany, the

United Kingdom, and the United States," *Journal of Marketing,* Vol. 52 (April), pp. 49–62.

Capon, Noel (1975), "Persuasive Effects of Sales Messages Developed from Interaction Process Analysis," *Journal of Applied Psychology,* Vol. 60, No. 2, pp. 238–44.

Cappella, Joseph N. (1979), "Talk-Silence Sequences in Informal Conversations I," *Human Communication Research,* Vol. 6, No. 1 (Fall), pp. 3–17.

Catoline, James E. (1982), "Bridging Cultures: Strategies for Managing Cultural Transitions," Digital Equipment Corporation (June).

Cavusgil, S. Tamer and Pervez N. Ghauri (1990), *Doing Business in Developing Countries: Entry and Negotiation Strategies.* London: Routledge.

Chorafas, Dimitris N. (1969), "The Communication Barrier in International Management," Report distributed by the American Management Association.

Chu, Priscilla and Wai-sum Siu (1993), "Women Entrepreneurs in Hong Kong," *Journal of Asian Business,* Vol. 9, No. 1 (Winter), pp. 55–68.

Chua, Amy (2003), *World on Fire: How Exporting Free Market Democracy Breeds Ethnic Hatred and Global Instability.* New York: Doubleday.

Churchill, Gilbert A., Jr., Neil M. Ford, Steven W. Hartley, and Orville C. Walker, Jr. (1985), "The Determinants of Salesperson Performance: A Meta-Analysis," *Journal of Marketing Research,* Vol. 22 (May), pp. 103–18.

CIA World Factbook (2005), www.globaledge.msu.edu, updated sites 10-31-05 and 11-1-05.

Clarke, Clifford (2006), Comments on Japanese Business Practices in Notes to Authors. June.

Clopton, Stephen W. (1984), "Seller and Buying Firm Factors Affecting Industrial Buyers' Negotiation Behavior and Outcomes," *Journal of Marketing Research,* Vol. 21 (February), pp. 39–53.

Copeland, Lennie (1985), "Cross-Cultural Training: The Competitive Edge," *Training World,* pp. 49–53.

Copeland, Lennie (1986), "Skills Transfer and Training Overseas," *Personnel Administrator* (June), pp. 107–17.

Copeland, Lennie and Lewis Griggs (1986), "Getting the Best From Foreign Employees," *Management Review* (June), pp. 19–26.

Copeland, Lennie and Lewis Griggs (1983), *Managing the Overseas Assignment.* Videotape. San Francisco: Copeland and Griggs, Inc.

Copeland, Michael J. (1987), "International Training" in *Training and Development Handbook,* 3rd Ed., Robert L. Craig, Ed. New York: McGraw-Hill Book Company.

Copeland, Michael J. (1988), "Cross-Cultural Dynamics in the Workplace," Presentation delivered in Istanbul, Turkey, for Procter & Gamble managers.

Copeland, Michael J. (1993), "Managing in a Multicultural Workplace," Presentation delivered in Hong Kong for Procter & Gamble managers (June).

"Corporate Giving: Who Spends the Most and for What?" (1990), *Across the Board*, Vol. 27, No. 5 (May), pp. 30, 34.

Country Insights (2005), www.globaledge.msu.edu, November.

Covey, Stephen R. (1989), *The 7 Habits of Highly Effective People*. New York: Simon & Schuster.

Cummings, Richard (1979), *Contemporary Selling*. Chicago: Rand McNally Publishing Company.

Davis, Harry L. and Alvin J. Silk (1972), "Interaction and Influence Processes in Personal Selling," *Sloan Management Review*, Vol. 13 (Winter), pp. 59–76.

Davis, Stanley M. (1969), "U.S. versus Latin America: Business and Culture," *Harvard Business Review* (June), pp. 19–26.

Day, George S. and Saul Klein (1987), "Cooperative Behavior in Vertical Markets: The Influence of Transaction Costs and Competitive Strategies," in *Reviewing of Marketing*, Michael J. Houston, Ed., pp. 39–66. Chicago: American Marketing Association.

DeMente, Boye Lafayette (1990), *Japan's Secret Weapon: The Kata Factor*. Phoenix: Phoenix Books.

deTurck, Mark A. (1986), "A Transactional Analysis of Compliance-Gaining Behavior: Effects of Noncompliance, Relational Contexts, and Actors' Gender." *Human Communication Research*, Vol. 12, No. 1 (Fall), pp. 54–78.

Deutsch, Claudia H. (1988), "Losing Innocence, Abroad," *New York Times* (July 10), pp. 1, 26.

Deutsch, Morton and Robert M. Krass (1987), "Studies of Interpersonal Bargaining," *Journal of Conflict Resolution*, Vol. 6, No. 1, pp. 52–59.

"Doing Business in Japan: Negotiating a Contract" (1977), Discussion/User's Guide and Manual. Vision Associates for The Business Council for International Understanding.

Dong, Jie Lin (1994), "In China, an Understanding of Guanxi Can Help Open Doors," *Asian Wall Street Journal Weekly* (May 16), pp. 7A–B.

Donohue, William A. (1981), "Development of a Model of Rule Use in Negotiation Interaction," *Communication Monographs,* Vol. 48 (June), pp. 106–20.

Donohue, William A., Mary E. Diez, and Mark Hamilton (1984), "Cooling Naturalistic Negotiation Interaction," *Human Communication Research*, Vol. 10, No. 3 (Spring), pp. 403–25.

Drabble, Peter (1994), "Selling to Canadians," *Export Today*, Vol. 10, No. 9 (November–December), pp. 54–55.

Duerr, Edwin C. (1980), "Coffee, Tea and Class Distinction in England," *The Bridge* (Fall), pp. 13, 38.

Dunning, John H. (1989), "The Study of International Business: A Plea for a More Interdisciplinary Approach," *Journal of International Business Studies*, Vol. 2, No. 3 (Fall), pp. 411–36.

Edwards, Linda (1978), "Present Shock, and How to Avoid It Abroad," *Across the Board* (February), pp. 36–41.

Eliashberg, Jehoshua, Stephen A. LaTour, Arvind Rangaswamy, and Louis W. Stern (1986), "Assessing the Predictive Accuracy of Two Utility-Based Theories in a Marketing Channel Negotiation Context," *Journal of Marketing Research*, Vol. 23 (May), pp. 101–10.

England, George W. (1978), "Managers and Their Value Systems: A Five-Country Comparative Study," *Columbia Journal of World Business* (Summer), pp. 35–42.

Enis, Ben M. (1976), *Personal Selling: Foundations, Process, and Management.* Santa Monica, California: Goodyear Publishing Company.

"Establishing a Business in Australia" (1986), 3rd Ed. New South Wales, Australia: Westpac Banking Corporation.

Eyuboglu, Nermin and Nicholas M. Didow (1987), "A Preliminary Test of the Applicability of Interdependence Theory in Explaining Power and Conflict in Distribution Channels," *Proceedings*, Vol. 29, American Marketing Association Educators' Conference, Chicago.

Fadiman, Jeffrey A. (1989), "Should Smaller Firms Use Third World Methods to Enter Third World Markets: The Project Head as Point Man Overseas," *Journal of Business and Industrial Marketing*, Vol. 4, No. 1 (Winter–Spring), pp. 17–28.

Farley, John U. and Robert L. Swinth (1967), "Effects of Choice and Sales Message on Customer-Salesman Interaction," *Journal of Applied Psychology*, Vol. 51, No. 2, pp. 107–10.

Fieg, John P. and John J. Blair (1975), *There Is A Difference.* Washington, D.C.: Meridian House International.

Fisher, Glen (1980), *International Negotiation: A Cross-Cultural Perspective,* Chicago: Intercultural Press.

Fisher, Roger and William Ury (1981), *Getting to Yes: Negotiating Agreement Without Giving In.* New York: Penguin Books.

Fisher, Roger, William Ury, and Bruce Patton (1993), *Getting to Yes: Negotiating Agreement Without Giving In.* New York: Houghton Mifflin Company.

Flanigen, James (1985), "'Multinational,' As We Know It, Is Obsolete," *Forbes* (August), p. 26.

Ford, David (1990), *Understanding Business Markets: Interaction, Relationships and Networks.* New York: Academic Press.

Foy, Nancy and Herman Gadon (1976), "Worker Participation: Contrasts in Three Countries," *Harvard Business Review* (May–June), pp. 71–83.

Francis, June N. P. (1991), "When In Rome? The Effects of Cultural Adaptation on Intercultural Business Negotiations," *Journal of International Business Studies* (Third Quarter), pp. 403–28.

Frankenstein, John and Hassan Hosseni (1988), "Advice from the Field: Essential Training for Japanese Duty," *Management Review* (July), pp. 40–43.

Frazier, Gary L., James D. Gill, and Sudhir H. Kale (1989), "Dealer Dependence Levels and Reciprocal Actions in a Channel of Distribution in a Developing Country," *Journal of Marketing*, Vol. 53 (January), pp. 50–69.

Frazier, Gary L. and John O. Summers (1984), "Interfirm Influence Strategies and Their Application Within Distribution Channels," *Journal of Marketing*, Vol. 48 (Summer), pp. 43–55.

Frazier, Gary L. and John O. Summers (1986), "Perceptions of Interfirm Power and Its Use Within a Franchise Channel of Distribution," *Journal of Marketing Research*, Vol. 23 (May), pp. 169–76.

Fung, Vigor (1985), "As Chinese Markets Open, Foreign Businessmen Learn the Special Tricks of Making a Deal There," *Wall Street Journal* (August 1), p. 22.

Futrell, Charles (1988), *Fundamentals of Selling*. Homewood, Illinois: Irwin.

Galante, Steven (1984), "U.S. Firms Aim to Avert Cultural Clashes," *Wall Street Journal* (July 30).

Garten, Jeffrey E. (1992), *A Cold Peace*. New York: Times Books.

Gaski, John F. (1984), "The Theory of Power and Conflict in Channels of Distribution," *Journal of Marketing*, Vol. 48 (Summer), pp. 9–29.

George, William W. (1983), "How Honeywell Takes Advantage of National Cultural Differences," *AMA Forum* (September), pp. 30–31.

Ghauri, Pervez N. (1986), "Guidelines for International Business Negotiations," *International Marketing Review*, Vol. 3, No. 6 (Autumn), pp. 72–82.

Gilbert, Nick (1985), "The China *Guanxi*," *Forbes* (July), p. 104.

Gordon, Raymond (1976), *Living in Latin America*. Skokie, Illinois: National Textbook Company.

Gosling, L. A. Peter (1990), "Your Face is Your Fortune: Fortune Telling and Business in Southeast Asia," *Journal of Southeast Asia Business*, Vol. 6, No. 4, pp. 41–52.

Graburn, Nelson H. H. (1971), "Traditional Economic Institutions and the Acculturation of Canadian Eskimos," in *Studies in Economic Anthropology*, George Walton (Ed.). Washington, D.C.: American Anthropological Association.

Graham, John L. (1981), "A Hidden Cause of America's Trade Deficit with Japan," *Columbia Journal of International Business Studies* (Spring–Summer), pp. 47–61.

Graham, John L. (1983), "Brazilian, Japanese, and American Business Negotiations," *Journal of International Business Studies* (Spring–Summer), pp. 47–61.

Graham, John L. (1984), "A Comparison of Japanese and American Business Negotiations," *International Journal of Research in Marketing*, Vol. 1, pp. 51–68.

Graham, John L. (1985), "Cross-Cultural Marketing Negotiations: A Laboratory Experiment," *Marketing Science*, Vol. 4, No. 21 (Spring), pp. 130–46.

Graham, John L. (1985), "The Influence of Culture on Business Negotiations," *Journal of International Business Studies*, Vol. 16, No. 1 (Spring), pp. 81–96.

Graham, John L. (1987), "Deference Given the Buyer: Variations Across Twelve Cultures," in *Cooperative Strategies in International Business*, P. Lorange and F. Contractor (Eds.). Lexington, MA: Lexington Books.

Graham, John L. and J. Douglas Andrews (1987), "A Holistic Analysis of Cross-Cultural Business Negotiations," *Journal of Business Communications*, Vol. 23, pp. 63–77.

Graham, John. L., Leonid l. Evenko, and Mahesh N. Rajan (1992), "An Empirical Comparison of Soviet and American Business Negotiations," *Journal of International Business Studies* (Third Quarter), pp. 387–418.

Graham, John L. and Roy Herberger, Jr. (1983), "Negotiators Abroad— Don't Shoot From the Hip," *Harvard Business Review* (July–August), pp. 160–68.

Graham, John L. and C. Y. Lin (1986), "A Comparison of Marketing and Negotiations in the Republic of China (Taiwan) and the United States," in *Advances in International Marketing*, S. Tamer Cavusgil, Ed. Greenwich, Connecticut: JAI Press.

Graham, John L. and Yoshihiro Sano (1984), *Smart Bargaining: Doing Business with the Japanese*. Cambridge, Massachusetts: Ballinger.

Grancrose, Cherlyn (1992), "Careers of Asian Managers in U.S. Firms in Thailand, Singapore, and Malaysia," *Journal of Southeast Asia Business*, Vol. 8, No. 2, pp. 58–73.

Grikscheit, Gary M. and William J. E. Crissy (1976), "Communication Correlates of Sales Success," *Industrial Marketing Management*, Vol. 5, pp. 175–77.

Grimaldi, Antonio (1986), "Interpreting Popular Culture: The Missing Link Between Local Labor and International Management," *Columbia Journal of World Business* (Winter), pp. 67–72.

A Guide to Investment in Australia (1986), Melbourne, Australia: Nelson Wheeler Chartered Accountants.

Guittard, Stephen W. (1974), "Negotiating and Administering an International Sales Contract with the Japanese," *International Lawyer*, Vol. 8, pp. 822–31.

Hair, Joseph F., Jr., Francis Notturno, and Federick A. Russ (1991), *Effective Selling*. Cincinnati: South-Western Publishing Company.

Hakansson, Hakan, Jan Johanson, and Bjorn Wootz (1977), "Influence Tactics in Buyer-Seller Processes," *Industrial Marketing Management*, Vol. 5, pp. 319–32.

Hall, Edward T. (1990), *The Hidden Dimension*. New York: Doubleday Publishing Group.

Hall, Edward T. (1976), "How Cultures Collide," *Psychology Today* (July), reprint.

Hall, Edward T. (1980), "Learning the Arabs' Silent Language," *The Bridge* (Spring), pp. 5–6, 31–34.

Hall, Edward T. (1981), *Beyond Culture*. New York: Doubleday Publishing Group.

Harris, D. George (1982), "How National Cultures Shape Management Styles," *Management Review* (July), pp. 58–61.

Harris, Philip R. and Robert T. Moran (1991), *Managing Cultural Differences*. Houston: Gulf Publishing Company.

Hartman, C. R. (1987), "Selling in Japan," *D & B Reports* (May–June), pp. 51–54.

Haske, Barbara G. (1974), "Disparities, Strategies, and Opportunity Costs," *International Studies Quarterly*, Vol. 18, No. 1 (March), pp. 3–30.

Haugland, Sven A. (1990), "The Governance of International Buyer-Seller Relationships," *Proceedings*, American Marketing Association Winter Educators' Conference, Chicago, pp. 205–11.

Hawrysh, Brian Mark and Judith Lynne Zaichkowsky (1983), "Cultural Approaches to Negotiations: Understanding the Japanese," *International Marketing Review*, Vol. 7, No. 2, pp. 28–42.

Hendon, Donald W. and Rebecca Angeles Hendon (1990), *World-Class Negotiating: Dealmaking the Global Marketplace*. New York: John Wiley.

Hesseling, Pjotr (1973), "Studies in Cross-Cultural Organization," *Columbia Journal of World Business* (December), pp. 120–34.

Hill, John S. and Meg Birdseye (1989), "Salesperson Selection in Multinational Corporations: An Empirical Study," *Journal of Personal Selling and Sales Management*, Vol. 9 (Summer), pp. 39–47.

Hixon, Allen L. (1986), "Why Corporations Make Haphazard Overseas Staffing Decisions," *Personnel Administrator* (March), pp. 91–94.

Hoffman, Richard C. (1988), "Nation Versus Other Contingencies Affecting Strategic Management Practices: An Empirical Assessment," Presentation at annual meeting of Eastern Academy of Management.

Hofstede, Geert (1984), *Culture's Consequences*, Vol. 5. London: Sage Publications.

Hofstede, Geert (1980), "Motivation, Leadership, and Organization: Do American Theories Apply Abroad?" *Organizational Dynamics* 9, No. 1 (Summer), pp. 42–63.

Hofstede, Geert (2005), ITIM International, www.geert-hofstede.com.

Hofstede, Geert and Michael Harris Bond (1988), "The Confucius Connection: From Cultural Roots to Economic Growth," *Organizational Dynamics*, Vol. 16, No. 4 (Spring), pp. 4–21.

Holbrook, Morris and John O'Shaughnessy (1975), "Influence Processes in Interpersonal Persuasion," *Advances in Consumer Research*, Vol. 3, pp. 363–69.

Hulbert, James and Noel Capon (1972), "Interpersonal Communication in Marketing: An Overview," *Journal of Marketing Research*, Vol. 9 (February), pp. 27–34.

Huneeus, Pablo (1984), "Finding the Lush Life in Latin America," *Wall Street Journal* (May 11), p. 23.

Hutt, Michael D., Wesley J. Johnston, and John R. Ronchetto, Jr. (1985), "Selling Centers and Buying Centers: Formulating Strategic Exchange Patterns," *Journal of Personal Selling and Sales Management* (May), pp. 33–40.

Jacobs, Deborah L. (1991), "Becoming Multicultural Without Leaving Home," *National Business Employment Weekly* (Fall), pp. 11–12, 30.

Jayachandran, C. (1991), "International Technology Collaborations: Issues in Negotiations," *Management Decision: Quarterly Review of Management Technology*, Vol. 29, No. 6 (November), pp. 80–85.

John, George and Torger Reve (1982), "The Reliability and Validity of Key Informant Data from Dyadic Relationships in Marketing Channels," *Journal of Marketing Research*, Vol. 19 (November), pp. 517–24.

Johnson, Paul R., John C. Kim, and Kyung-il Gymm (1992), "Studying Foreign Import Managers' Purchasing Behavior," in *1992 Conference on U.S. Competitiveness in the Global Marketplace*, David O. Braaten and Gary Anders, Eds., pp. 269–75. Phoenix: Thunderbird Publishing Group.

Jordan, Terry G. and Lester Rowntree (1986), *The Human Mosaic*, 4th Ed. New York: Harper and Row.

Joy, Robert O. (1989), "Cultural and Procedural Differences That Influence Business Strategies and Operations in the People's Republic of China," *SAM Advanced Management Journal*, (Summer), pp. 29–33.

Kale, Sudhir H. (1986), "Dealer Perceptions of Manufacturer Power and Influence Strategies in a Developing Country," *Journal of Marketing Research,*Vol. 23 (November), p. 387–93.

Kale, Sudhir H. and John W. Barnes (1992), "Understanding the Domain of Cross-National Buyer-Seller Interactions," *Journal of International Business Studies* (First Quarter), pp. 101–32.

Kaufman, Doug (1992), "Playing By the Rules," *Link* (June), pp. 17–26.

Kazuo, Ogura (1979), "How the 'Inscrutables' Negotiate with the 'Inscrutables': Chinese Negotiation Tactics Vis-à-vis the Japanese," *China Quarterly*, No. 79, pp. 529–52.

Kellerman, Kathy (1986), "Anticipation of Future Interaction and Information Exchange in Initial Interaction," *Human Communication Research*, Vol. 13, No. 1 (Fall), pp. 41–75.

Kennedy, John J. (1967), "The Management of Negotiation," *Journal of Purchasing* (August), pp. 41–51.

Kotkin, Joel (1993), *Tribes.* New York: Random House.

Krapfel, Robert E., Jr., and Robert Spekman (1987), "Channel Power Sources, Satisfaction and Performance: An Exploration," *Proceedings, American Marketing Association Educators' Conference*, pp. 30–34.

Kras, Eva (1989), *Management in Two Cultures—Bridging the Gap Between U.S. and Mexican Managers.*Yarmouth, Maine: Intercultural Press.

Kumayama, Akihisa (1990), "Workshop on Sales and Negotiation in Japan," Ninth Annual Conference on Languages and Communication for World Business and the Professions, Eastern Michigan University, East Lansing, Michigan.

Lambrechts, Ludo (1994), "Expanding the Horizons of the Global Marketplace," Videotape. Chicago: American Marketing Association.

Langan, Patricia A. (1990), "Trying to Clone U.S. Style MBAs," *Fortune* (October 8), pp. 145–48.

Lanier, Alison R. (1978), "Marketing in Varied Worlds," *Duns World Marketing Management,*Vol. 4, pp. 6–7.

Laurent, Andre (1991), "Managing Across Cultures and National Borders," in *Single Market Europe: Opportunities and Challenges for Business*, Spyros G. Makridakis and Associates, Ed., pp. 195–214. San Francisco: Jossey-Bass.

Lee, Eve (1980), "Saudis as *We*, Americans as *They*," *The Bridge* (Fall), pp. 3–5, 32–34.

Lee, James A. (1966), "Cultural Analysis in Overseas Operations," *Harvard Business Review* (March–April), pp. 106–12.

Lee, James A. (1968), "Developing Managers in Developing Countries," *Harvard Business Review* (November–December), pp. 55–65.

Leigh, Thomas W. and Arno J. Rethans (1984), "A Script-Theoretic Analysis of Industrial Purchasing Behavior," *Journal of Marketing*, Vol. 48 (Fall), pp. 22–32.

Levoy, Gregg (1982), "Eating Your Words," *Cincinnati Enquirer* (December 7), p. D-1.

March, Robert (1985), "East Meets West at the Negotiating Table," *Winds* (April), pp. 55–57.

Margolis, Mac (1989), "Reinventing Brazil," *World Monitor* (November), pp. 31–38.

Masterson, Bob and Bob Murphy (1986), "Internal Cross-Cultural Management," *Training and Development Journal* (April), pp. 56–60.

Mathews, H. Lee, David T. Wilson, and John F. Monoky, Jr. (1972), "Bargaining Behavior in a Buyer-Seller Dyad," *Journal of Marketing Research*, Vol. 9 (February), pp. 103–5.

Mayo, Edward J., Hanjoon Lee, and Robert F. Reck (1991), "Personal Selling and Communication Style: An Exploratory Test of the Communication Style Model," *Developments in Marketing Science*, Vol. 14, pp. 328–32.

McAlister, Leigh, Max H. Bazerman, and Peter Fader (1986), "Power and Goal Setting in Channel Negotiations," *Journal of Marketing Research*, Vol. 23 (August), pp. 228–36.

McCaffrey, James A. and Craig R. Hafner (1985), "When Two Cultures Collide: Doing Business Overseas," *Training and Development Journal* (October), pp. 26–31.

McCooey, Christopher (1984), "Dolly Parton & Lobsters," *Winds* (December), pp. 41–47.

McGregor, James (1993a), "Agency in China Changes Its Priorities," *Asian Wall Street Journal Weekly* (April 21), p. A10.

McGregor, James (1993b), "Deng Seems to Aim at Reforming Chinese Law While Strengthening Hand of Politburo Cadre." *Asian Wall Street Journal Weekly* (March 22), p. 12.

Mendonsa, Eugene L. (1988), "How To Do Business in Latin America," *Purchasing World*, Vol. 32, No. 7 (July), pp. 58–59.

Miller, Stuart (1987), *Painted in Blood: Understanding Europeans.* New York: Atheneum.

Milligan, John W. (1981), "Saudi Risk Management: A Lesson in Irony," *Business Insurance* (August 17), p. 10.

Moncrief, William C. (1993), "A Comparison of Sales Activities in an International Setting," in *The Global Business: Four Key Marketing Strategies*, Erdener Kaynak, Ed., pp. 141-57. New York: Haworth Press.

Montagu-Pollack, Matthew (1991), "All the Right Connections," *Asian Business* (January), pp. 20–24.

Moran, Robert T. (1985), "Getting Everyone To Pull Together in Multicultural Firms," *International Management* (May), p. 41.

Moran, Robert T. and William G. Stripp (1991), *Successful International Business Negotiations*. Houston: Gulf Publishing Company.

Morris, Michael H., Ramon A. Avila, and Joseph D. Chapman (1988), "Balanced Relationships as a Determinant of Industrial Source Loyalty," *Proceedings*, National Conference in Sales Management (April), pp. 36–40.

Mortenson, Eileen A. (1992), "Business Opportunities in the Pacific Rim for Americans in Small Business: The Importance of Cultural Differences in Doing Business," in *1992 Conference on U.S. Competitiveness in the Global Marketplace*, David O. Braaten and Gary Answers, Eds. Phoenix: Thunderbird Publishing Group.

Mudhavan, Ravindranath, Rechina H. Shah, and Rajiv Grover (1994), "Motivations for and Theoretical Foundations of Relationship Marketing," in *Marketing Theory and Applications*, Vol. 5, C. Whan Park and Daniel C. Smith, Eds. Chicago: American Marketing Association.

Murray, F. T. and Alice Haller Murray (1986), "SMR Forum: Global Managers for Global Business, *Sloan Management Review* (Winter), pp. 75–80.

Nach, J. F. (1950), "The Bargaining Problem," *Econometrics*, Vol. 18, pp. 155–62.

Nadler, I. Berl and Samuel W. McScoggins (1993), "A Primer on Canadian Law," *Business Record* (November 29–December 5), p. 10.

Nadler, Leonard (1985), "High Stakes HRD: Working Internationally," *Training and Development Journal* (October).

Neslin, Scott A. and Leonard Greenhalgh (1986), "The Ability of Nash's Theory of Cooperative Games to Predict the Outcomes of Buyer-Seller Negotiations: A Dyad-Level Test," *Management Science,* Vol. 32, No. 4 (April), pp. 480–98.

Nevis, Thomas J. (1980), "Expatriate Manager Can Succeed Only By Respecting Japanese Ways and Systems," *Japan Economic Journal* (June 10), pp. 24–25, 31.

Nye, Daniel A. (1987), "Formation of Contracts: The Law in Norway," *North Carolina Journal of International Law and Commercial Regulation*, Vol. 12 (Spring), pp. 187–248.

Olshavsky, Richard (1973), "Customer-Salesman Interaction in Appliance Retailing," *Journal of Marketing Research*, Vol. 10, No. 4 (May), pp. 208–12.

Organovitch, Serge (1980), "How to Design an International Training Program," *Training and Development Journal* (August), reprint.

O'Shaughnessy, John (1971–72), "Selling as an Interpersonal Influence Process," *Journal of Retailing*, Vol. 47, No. 4 (Winter), pp. 32–46.

Pace, R. Wayne (1962), "Oral Communication and Sales Effectiveness," *Journal of Applied Psychology*, Vol. 46, No. 5, pp. 321–24.

Pacelle, Mitchell (1994), "Our Mother-in-Law Would Pick the Office with a River View, Too," *Wall Street Journal* (March 10).

Parkinson, S. T. (1985), "Factors Influencing Buyer-Seller Relationships in the Market for High-Technology Products," *Journal of Business Research*, Vol. 13, No. 1 (February), pp. 49–60.

PCGlobe (1992), Software. Tempe, Arizona: PCGlobe.

Pederson, Carlton A., Milburn D. Wrights, and Barton A. Weitz (1988), *Selling: Principles and Methods*. Homewood, Illinois: Irwin.

Pennington, Allan L. (1968), "Customer-Salesman Bargaining Behavior in Retail Transactions," *Journal of Marketing Research*, Vol. 5 (August), p. 255–62.

Perdue, Barbara C., Ralph L. Day, and Ronald E. Michaels (1986), "Negotiation Styles of Industrial Buyers," *Industrial Marketing Management*, Vol. 15, No. 3 (August), pp. 171–76.

Perkins, Anne G. (1993), "Diversity," *Harvard Business Review* (September–October), p. 14.

Pfeiffer, Sandra L. (1972), "The Maslow Hierarchy," in *The 1972 Annual Handbook for Group Facilitators*, J. William Pfeiffer and John E. Jones, Eds. San Diego: University Associates.

Piturro, Marlene C. (1988), "Southeast Asia: Doing Business in Paradise?" *Management Review* (July), pp. 30–34.

Planalp, Sally (1985), "Relational Schemata: A Test of Alternative Forms of Relational Knowledge as Guides to Communication," *Human Communication Research*, Vol. 12, No. 1 (Fall), pp. 3–29.

Radway, Robert J. (1978), "Negotiating in the Caribbean Basin: Trade and Investment Contracts," *International Trade Law Journal*, Vol. 4 (Winter), pp. 164–69.

Ralston, David A., David J. Gustafson, Fanny M. Cheung, and Robert H. Terpstra (1993), "Differences in Managerial Values: A Study of U.D., Hong Kong and PRC Managers," *Journal of International Business Studies*, Vol. 24, No. 2 (Second Quarter), pp. 249–75.

Ramsey, Sheila and Judy Birk (1983), "Preparation of North Americans for Interaction with Japanese: Considerations of Language and Communication Style," in *The Handbook of Intercultural Training*, Landis and Brislin, Eds., pp. 227–59. New York: Pergamon Press.

Rand, Edward J. (1976), "Learning to Do Business in the Middle East," *Conference Board Record* (February), pp. 49–51.

Reddy, N. Mohan and Michael P. Marvin (1986), "Developing a Manufacturer-Distributor Information Partnership," *Industrial Marketing Management*, Vol. 15, No. 2 (May), pp. 157–63.

Renwick, George W. (1982), "Malays and Americans: Definite Differences, Unique Opportunities," in *Americans, Malays and Chinese: Intercultural Relations in Malaysia*, George W. Renwick, Ed. Chicago: Intercultural Press.

Rinehart, Lloyd M. and Thomas J. Page, Jr. (1992), "The Development and Test of a Model of Transaction Negotiation," *Journal of Marketing*, Vol. 56 (October), pp. 18–32.

Riordan, Edward A., Richard L. Oliver, and James H. Donnelly, Jr. (1977), "The Unsold Prospect: Dyadic and Attitudinal Determinants," *Journal of Marketing Research*, Vol. 14 (November), pp. 530–37.

Ronchetto, John R., Jr., Michael D. Hutt, and Peter H. Reingen (1989), "Embedded Influence Patterns in Organizational Buying Systems," *Journal of Marketing*, Vol. 53 (October), pp. 51–62.

Ronngang, Yang (1986), "Public Relations: A Chinese Viewpoint." Presentation at ChinAd '86, Chicago Westin Hotel (November 17–18).

Rotzoll, Kim B. (1986), "Advertising in China: Reflection on an Evolving Institution," Advertising Working Papers, Department of Advertising, University of Illinois at Urbana–Champaign.

Rubin, Jeffrey Z. and Bert B. Brown (1975), *The Social Psychology of Bargaining and Negotiation*. New York: Academic Press.

Russell, Frederick A., Frank H. Beach, and Richard H. Buskirk (1988), *Selling: Principles and Practices*. New York: McGraw-Hill Book Company.

Salacuse, Jewald (1991), *Making Global Deals*. Boston: Houghton Mifflin Company.

Saxe, Robert and Barton A. Weitz (1982), "The SOCO Scale: A Measure of the Customer Orientation of Salespeople," *Journal of Marketing Research*, Vol. 19 (August), pp. 343–51.

Schmidt, Robert D. (1987), "Business Negotiations with the Soviet Union," in *Private Diplomacy with the Soviet Union*, Institute for the Study of Diplomacy. Lanham, Maryland: University Press of America.

Schnapper, Mel (1981), "International Sales Skills," *The Bridge* (Summer), pp. 30–31.

Schurr, Paul H. and Greg J. Lessen (1983), "Methods for Laboratory Negotiation Research in Industrial Marketing," in *Research Methods and Causal Modeling in Marketing: Proceedings of the 1983 AMA Winter Educators' Conference*, William R. Darden, Kent B. Monroe, and William R. Dillon, Eds. Chicago: American Marketing Association.

Schurr, Paul H. and Julie L. Ozanne (1985), "Influence on Exchange Processes: Buyers' Preconceptions of a Seller's Trustworthiness and Bargaining Toughness," *Journal of Consumer Research*, Vol. 11 (March), pp. 939–53.

Schurr, Paul H., Louis H. Stone, and Lee Ann Beller (1985), "Effective Selling Approaches to Buyers' Objections," *Industrial Marketing Management*, Vol. 14 (August), pp. 195–202.

Schuster, Camille P. (1987), "Using Depth Interviews to Examine the Organizational Buying Process in International Markets," *Proceedings*, AMA Winter Educator Conference, Chicago, pp. 157–60.

Schuster, Camille P. (1988), "Interact Matrix System: A Method for Analyzing Sales Interaction," *Research in Consumer Behavior*, Vol. 3, pp. 271–323.

Schuster, Camille P. (1993), "Sensitivity to Differences in Cultures Can Smooth Dealings," *The Business Record* (August 22–28), p. 15.

Schuster, Camille P. and Charles D. Bodkin (1992), "Toward Adaptation in Japan: An Expansion of the Contingency Model," *Proceedings*, Vol. 15, Academy of Marketing Science Conference, pp. 159–99.

Schuster, Camille P. and Michael J. Copeland (1996), *Global Business: Planning for Sales and Negotiations*. Ft. Worth: The Dryden Press.

Schuster, Camille P. and Jeffrey E. Danes (1986), "Asking Questions: Some Characteristics of Successful Sales Encounters," *Journal of Personal Selling and Sales Management*, Vol. 6, pp. 17–27.

Schuster, Camille P. and Janet Keith (1993), "Factors That Affect the Sales Force Choice Decision in International Market Entry Strategies," *Journal of Global Marketing*, Vol. 7, No. 2.

Shipp, Ralph D., Jr. (1980), *Practical Selling*. Boston: Houghton Mifflin Company.

Snyder, Julie (1993), "Promoting Consumer Goods and Services in Quebec, Canada's Distinct French-Speaking Market," *Business America* (November), pp. 22–23.

Soldow, Gary F. and Gloria Penn Thomas (1984), "Relational Communication: Form Versus Content in the Sales Interaction," *Journal of Marketing*, Vol. 48 (Winter), pp. 84–93.

Solomon, Michael R., Carol Suprenant, John A. Czepiel, and Evelyn G. Gutman (1985), "A Role Theory Perspective on Dyadic Interactions: The Service Encounter," *Journal of Marketing*, Vol. 49 (Winter), pp. 99–111.

Spiro, Rosann L. and William D. Perreault, Jr. (1979), "Influence Use by Industrial Salesmen: Influence-Strategy Mixes and Situational Determinants," *Journal of Business*, Vol. 52, No. 3, pp. 435–55.

Spiro, Rosann L., William D. Perreault, Jr., and Fred D. Reynolds (1977), "Personal Selling Process: A Critical Review and Model," *Industrial Marketing Management*, Vol. 6, No. 5, pp. 351–64.

Spiro, Rosann L. and Barton A. Weitz (1990), "Adaptive Selling: Conceptualization, Measurement and Nomological Validity," *Journal of Marketing Research*, Vol. 27 (February), pp. 61–79.

Stone, Ray (1989), "Negotiating in Asia," *Practicing Manager,* Vol. 9, No. 2 (Autumn), pp. 36–39.

Sujan, Mita, James R. Bettman, and Harish Sujan (1986), "Effects of Consumer Expectations on Information Processing in Selling Encounters," *Journal of Marketing Research,* Vol. 23 (November), pp. 346–53.

Swan, John E., I. Frederick Trawick, and David W. Silva (1985), "How Industrial Salespeople Gain Customer Trust," *Industrial Marketing Management,* Vol. 14, pp. 203–11.

Templeman, Thane Peterson and Gail E. Shares (1989), "A New Economic Miracle?" *Business Week* (November 27), pp. 58–64.

Terpstra, Vern (1983), *International Dimensions of Marketing.* Boston: PWS-Kent Publishing Company.

Theye, Larry D. and William J. Seiler (1979), "Interaction Analysis in Collective Bargaining: An Alternative Approach to the Prediction of Negotiated Outcomes," Paper presented at annual convention of the International Communication Association, Philadelphia, Pennsylvania.

Thomas, Myrna (1994), Presentation and handouts on behalf of Hill Knowlton at "Doing Business in Asia" course at the York Hotel, Singapore.

Thorelli, Hans B. (1986), "Networks: Between Markets and Hierarchies," *Strategic Management Journal,* Vol. 7, pp. 37–51.

Trompenaars, Fons (1991), "The International Relativity of Human Resource Management," 23rd International Human Resource Management Conference, Brussels, Belgium.

Trompenaars, Fons (1991), *Understanding Cultural Diversity in Business.* London: The Economist Books.

Tucker, Michael (1982), Lecture presented in Cincinnati, Ohio, for Procter & Gamble managers (October).

Tung, Rosalie L. (1981), "Patterns of Motivation in Chinese Industrial Enterprises," *Academy of Management Review,* pp. 481–89.

Turnbull, Peter W. (1987), "Interaction and International Marketing: An Investment Process," *International Marketing Review* (Winter), pp. 7-19.

Tutzauer, Frank (1986), "Bargaining as a Dynamical System," *Behavioral Science,* Vol. 31 (April), pp. 65–81.

Van Zandt, Howard F. (1970), "How to Negotiate in Japan," *Harvard Business Review* (November–December), pp. 45–56.

Walle, Alf H. (1986), "Conceptualizing Personal Selling for International Business: A Continuum of Exchange Perspective," *Journal of Personal Selling and Sales Management,* Vol. 6 (November), pp. 9–17.

Wallin, Theodore O. (1976), "The International Executive's Baggage: Cultural Values of the American Frontier," *MSU Business Topics* (Spring), pp. 13–22.

Wasnak, Lynn (1986), "Knowing When to Bow," *Ohio Business* (March), pp. 31–38.

Watson, Hilbourne A. (1978), "The Caribbean Basin, Its Subregions and Their Internal and International Social and Economic Dynamics," *International Trade Law Journal*, Vol. 4 (Winter), pp. 197–213.

Webb, Michael W. (1983), "Cross-Cultural Awareness: A Framework for Interaction," *Personnel and Guidance Journal*, Vol. 61, No. 8 (April), pp. 498–500.

Webster, Frederick (1978), "Interpersonal Communication and Salesman Effectiveness," *Journal of Marketing*, Vol. 32 (July), pp. 7–13.

Weiss, Stephen E. (1990), "The Long Path to the IBM-Mexico Agreement: An Analysis of the Microcomputer Investment Negotiations 1983–86," *Journal of International Business Studies* (Fourth Quarter), pp. 565–96.

Weiss, Stephen E. and W. G. Stripp (1985), "Negotiating with Foreign Businesspersons: An Introduction with Propositions on Six Cultures," Working Paper Series No. 85–86. New York University, Faculty of Business Administration.

Weitz, Barton A. (1981), "Effectiveness in Sales Interactions: A Contingency Framework," *Journal of Marketing*, Vol. 45, pp. 85–103.

Weitz, Barton A., Harish Sujan, and Mita Sujan (1986), "Knowledge, Motivation, and Adaptive Behavior: A Framework for Improving Selling Effectiveness," *Journal of Marketing*, Vol. 50 (October), pp. 174–91.

Wendell, Richard F. and Walter Gorman (1988), *Selling: Personal Preparation, Persuasion Strategy*. New York: Random House Business Division.

Wiener, Joshua L., Raymond W. LaForge, and Jerry R. Goolsby (1990), "Personal Communication in Marketing: An Examination of Self-Interest Contingency Relationships," *Journal of Marketing Research*, Vol. 27 (May), pp. 227–31.

Willett, Ronald and Allan L. Pennington (1966), "Customer and Salesman: The Anatomy of Choice and Influence in a Retail Setting," *Proceedings*, American Marketing Association Educators' Conference, Chicago, pp. 598–616.

Williams, Kaylene C. and Rosann L. Spiro (1985), "Communication Style in the Salesperson-Customer Dyad," *Journal of Marketing Research*, Vol. 22 (November), pp. 434–42.

Williams, Kaylene C., Rosann L. Spiro, and Leslie M. Fine (1990), "The Customer-Salesperson Dyad: An Interaction/Communication Model and Review," *Journal of Personal Selling and Sales Management* (Summer), pp. 29–43.

Winham, Gilbert R. (1979), "Bureaucratic Politics and Canadian Trade Negotiation," *International Journal*, Vol. 34, No. 1, pp. 64–89.

Wosinski, Mark and Gena Zischke (1992), "Doing Business in Central Europe: Opportunity for the Small and Medium-Size U.S. Companies," in *1992 Conference on U.S. Competitiveness in the Global Marketplace*, David O. Braaten and Gary Anders, Eds., p. 328. Phoenix: Thunderbird Publishing Group.

Wotruba, Thomas R. and Edwin K. Simpson (1989), *Sales Management*. Boston: PWS-Kent Publishing Company.

Yoshimo, M. (1968), *Japan's Managerial System*. Cambridge, Massachusetts: MIT Press.

Young, James R. and R. Wayne Monday (1982), *Personal Selling*, 2nd Ed. Chicago: The Dryden Press.

Zamet, Jonathan M. and Murray E. Bovarnick (1986), "Employee Relations for Multinational Companies in China," *Columbia Journal of World Business*, Vol. 21, No. 1 (Spring), reprint.

Zemke, Ron (1988), "Scandinavian Management—A Look At Our Future," *Management Review* (July), pp. 44–47.

Zhang, Danian and Kenji Kuroda (1989), "Beware of Japanese Negotiation Style: How to Negotiate with Japanese Companies," *Northwestern Journal of Law and Business*, Vol. 10 (Fall), pp. 195–212.

INDEX

About TEXERE

Texere, a progressive and authoritative voice in business publishing, brings to the global business community the expertise and insights of leading thinkers. Our books educate, enlighten, and entertain, and provide an intersection where our authors and our readers share cutting edge ideas, practices, and innovative solutions. Texere seeks to cultivate, enhance, and disseminate information that illuminates the global business landscape.

www.thomson.com/learning/texere

About the typeface

This book was set in 10.5 point Bembo. Bembo was cut by Francesco Griffo for the Venitian printer Aldus Manutius to publish in 1495 *De Aetna* by Cardinal Pietro Bembo. Stanley Morison supervised the design of Bembo for the Monotype Corporation in 1929. The Bembo is a readable and classical typeface because of its well-proportioned letterforms, functional serifs, and lack of peculiarities.

Library of Congress Cataloging-in-Publication Data

Schuster, Camille Passler-
   Global business practices : adapting for success / Camille P. Schuster and Michael J. Copeland.
      p. cm.
   Includes bibliographical references and index.
   ISBN 0-324-23309-4
   1. Corporate culture. 2. Intercultural communication. 3. International business enterprises. I. Copeland, Michael J. II. Title.
   HD58.7.S3477 2006
   658'.049—dc22

                                                          2006014874